# EVALUATING SCIENTIFIC RESEARCH

## Fred Leavitt

*California State University–Hayward*

WAVELAND

PRESS, INC.

Long Grove, Illinois

For information about this book, contact:
    Waveland Press, Inc.
    4180 IL Route 83, Suite 101
    Long Grove, IL  60047-9580
    (847) 634-0081
    info@waveland.com
    www.waveland.com

# Contents

## 4  Finding Interesting Problems and Studying Them Creatively   46

## 5  Selecting and Measuring Variables   57

## 6  Choosing the Best Research Design   75

# Experimenting: Two Groups   90

# Variations on the Simple Experiment   108

# Comparing Existing Groups   118

# Correlational Strategies to Predict and Assess Relationships   126

# Case Studies   135

## Data Analysis   210

## Philosophical Challenges   227

 # Preface

*"Omission and simplification help us to understand—but help us, in many cases, to understand the wrong thing."* Aldous Huxley

*"Most people would rather die sooner than think. In fact, they do so."* George Bernard Shaw

*"What good fortune for those in power that people do not think."* Adolph Hitler

Writing this book has kept me in a state of perpetual anger. While reviewing the literature in preparation for revising my how-to book on research methodology (Leavitt, 1991), I kept coming across books and articles that documented serious misuses of science. They persuaded me to change direction and write a much more critical book than was originally intended. Anger, like misery, loves company, so I'll be disappointed if readers don't come to share my emotion. Only if enough people become angry will changes be made.

I wrote with two groups of readers in mind. The smaller is comprised of college students enrolled in a methodology course who hope to do original research someday. Many texts for such courses present a large technical vocabulary and complex formulas for analyzing data statistically, but knowing such esoterica no more makes people scientists than knowing how to paint by numbers makes them artists. Good scientists think creatively and critically about the literature they read, the questions they ask, the conceptual foundations of various research designs, and proper inferences from those designs. I try to sensitize readers to such issues.

The second group is everybody else. Science plays a profound role in our lives, and decisions with far-reaching consequences are often based on scientific evidence. Yet, the evidence is often controversial or misleading. Medical and social scientists receive years of training in their specialties, but developing the ability to evaluate research is a considerably less formidable undertaking and does not require brilliance.

The fruits of scientific theory and research are most evident in technological developments such as computers and high-resolution television sets, but science has also had a huge impact on social, esthetic, and religious beliefs. Before Galileo, people believed that angels, heavenly bodies, beasts, and elements all had their place in a fixed hierarchy. His proof that the universe is not only much greater than previously supposed, but that it changes continuously, was so threatening that the Catholic Church condemned Galileo to house arrest. For the poet John Milton, Galileo's proof created "a wide gaping void that threatened even the angels with loss of being." Philosophy was changed profoundly, and even the rules of evidence of law were reevaluated.

In the 17th century, the ideas of Galileo, Descartes, Robert Boyle, and Kepler shaped metaphysics, political theory, and theology. Newton's gravitational theory provided a unified explanation of phenomena previously thought unrelated, a triumph that encouraged the belief that humanity's moral and political problems could be similarly solved. Social theorist Saint Simon urged that traditional Christianity be replaced by a Religion of Newton. About 150 years later, Darwin's evolutionary theory repudiated the descent of humans from angels and thus devastated Victorian England. Social Darwinists horribly misused the theory to justify slavery, master race theory, and other tyrannies of the well-placed over the needy. More recently, philosophers invoked quantum theory in debates about free will versus determinism.

The tangible side of biomedical research is most evident in procedures such as organ transplants and cloning, but biomedical research also influences quality of life and, by lengthening life span, changes family dynamics and societal norms. Scientists play a major role in the criminal justice system. They analyze crime scenes for blood, semen, and other physical evidence, and their findings often mean the difference between conviction and acquittal (Neufeld & Colman, 1990). Connors, Lundregan, Miller, and McEwen (1996) documented 28 cases of people convicted of serious crimes who used DNA tests on existing evidence to successfully challenge the jury verdicts. They had been sentenced to long prison terms and served, on average, 7 years in prison.

The outcomes of civil trials, including class action lawsuits involving millions of plaintiffs, often hinge on scientific testimony. Experts testified for and against the claims that silicone gel breast implants cause a variety of medical problems, that exposure to asbestos fibers causes lung disease, that the Dalkon contraceptive shield causes toxic shock syndrome, and that tobacco is both addicting and harmful.

The effects of social science theory, though subtle, are considerable. Freud left a substantial legacy. He introduced terms such as *wish fulfillment, frustration, regression, repression, unconscious impulses, sublimation, anxieties, neuroses,* and *defense mechanisms,* all now widely used in character descriptions. He gave people freedom to express interest in sexuality and question Puritan ethics. Freudian theory influenced modern literature, cinema, art, philosophy, and ideas about male/female differences.

Social science research has implications for allocations of taxes; many other aspects of public policy; decisions about potential candidates for public office; voting behaviors; television programming; teaching methods; the self-esteem of whole classes of people; and attitudes about dating, marriage, sexuality, and child rearing. Social scientists played an important role in formulating and assessing public policies on adolescent pregnancy. Information about the social and economic costs encouraged legislators to fund family planning clinics to prevent unintended teenage pregnancies, and evaluations of services for pregnant adolescents led policymakers to provide programs for reducing the negative consequences (Vinovskis, 1989).

A social scientist's report that previous criminal convictions could be used to accurately predict whether a person would commit future crimes inspired legislation to sentence convicted criminals based partially on predictions of future criminality (Greenwood, 1982). This finding was relevant for "three-strikes-and-you're-out" laws.

Historian of science Bernard Cohen (1927) wrote, "Scientific ideas have exerted a force on our civilization fully as great as the more tangible practical applications of scientific research." And, in the words of psychologist Gustave Le Bon (cited in Seldes, 1977, p. 404):

> The sudden political revolutions which strike the historian most forcibly are often the least important. The great revolutions are those of manners and thought. The true revolutions, those which transform the destinies of people, are most frequently accomplished so slowly that the historians can hardly point to their beginnings. Scientific revolutions are by far the most important.

All that notwithstanding, some artists and musicians proudly proclaim their ignorance of science, and so do many college undergraduates majoring in psychology. They envision careers as psychotherapists, industrial psychologists, testing specialists, and so forth. If they take a course in scientific methodology, it is because their university requires it, not because research intrigues them. Their attitude is not just unfortunate; it is immoral. Literally hundreds of therapeutic techniques are promoted, including ineffective and harmful ones. Many industrial innovations fail to improve morale or increase productivity, and many tests are invalid or biased.

People in the helping professions who do not think critically about research have no way to distinguish the good from the bad. They are likely to harm their clients and bring disrespect to their field.

Studying science is not just for the college crowd. Bauer (1992, p. 147) wrote that it

> is excellent training for the mind, much better than the classically prescribed study of Latin. When you study science in the right way, you learn about reality therapy; and that is worth applying to other things than science. Science can show that some things are quite definitely wrong; that knowledge is a much better guide than ignorance; and it can teach humility in posing endless questions to which we have no good answers.

Science at its best can be as esthetically and intellectually satisfying as the greatest masterworks of music and art. Greek astronomer Ptolemy wrote, "I know that I am a mortal, a creature of the day; but when I search into the multitudinous revolving spirals of the stars, my feet no longer rest on the earth, but, standing by Zeus himself, I take my fill of ambrosia, the food of the gods." Almost 2,000 years later, Nobel laureate Steven Weinberg (1994) wrote, "The effort to understand the universe is one of the very few things that lifts human life a little above the level of farce and gives it some of the grace of tragedy."

Unfortunately, scientific articles for professional audiences are written in a dry, technical language beyond the comprehension of most laypeople. The language intimidates and has done so for centuries. More than 200 years ago, Empress Catherine of Russia invited atheist philosopher Denis Diderot to visit her. Her advisors worried that he might corrupt his listeners but were unwilling to confront him, so they devised a plan. They told him that the famous mathematician Leonhard Euler had constructed a mathematical proof of the existence of God. Diderot was ignorant of mathematics but agreed to listen. Euler confidently said:

$$(a + bn)/n = x. \text{ Therefore, God exists.}$$

Diderot, confused and embarrassed, asked for and was granted permission to return immediately to France.

Like Diderot, many people today may assume that what they cannot understand is correct. By so doing, they cede power to a coterie of scientists and science writers. Yet a substantial proportion of published research, with far-ranging ramifications for health and happiness, is flawed. Bad research (and improper interpretations of good research) has adversely affected many people's lives.* In 1917, prominent psychologist Henry Goddard

---

*On the other hand, the world of research is exciting, intellectually challenging, and of tremendous cultural and practical value. Any decent library contains dozens of positive expositions. I felt no need to cover the same ground.

wrote that a high proportion of Jewish, Italian, and Russian immigrants to the United States were mentally retarded. His report helped inspire the imposition of strict immigration quotas, and a result was that desperate refugees fleeing Nazi Germany or Soviet-dominated territory during World War II were denied entry into the United States.

Evidence, probably misinterpreted, on the high costs of drug abuse provided the rationale for subjecting employees and job applicants to urine tests for illegal drugs (cf. Horgan, 1990). According to spokespeople for the National Cancer Institute, the U.S. Department of Health and Human Services, the National Breast Cancer Coalition, and the American Cancer Society (cf. Melbye, 1997; National Cancer Institute, 1996), frightening reports that abortions increase the risk of breast cancer (cf. Loose, 1996) are at odds with the evidence. Sales of dietary supplements, natural foods, and natural personal care items totaled $65 billion worldwide last year (Nutrition Business Journal, 1998), even though critics argue that many of the health claims for the supplements are unfounded or misleading.

The book is divided into six sections, each dealing with a separate type of problem.

I. Definition and Discussion of Limitations of Science (Chapter 1). Although science transforms society and is the most effective tool ever invented for predicting and controlling events, historians and philosophers do not agree about what it is. Many successful scientists used methods that most of their contemporaries frowned upon. Questions about ethics, the existence of God, and the possibility of an afterlife are not within the realm of science.

Scientists often derive such accurate predictions from their theories that they seem to have penetrated ultimate reality. But modern philosophers assert that theories can never be proven and absolute truth is unattainable.

II. Preparing for Research (Chapters 2 to 4).

A. Reading and Evaluating the Literature. The scientific literature is enormous, rapidly growing, and often overwhelming. Not even the most dedicated expert can keep up with everything published in her field. In addition, many good studies are never published, and many published articles are never cited by reviewers of the literature. Many potentially important connections between published articles are never made. As reports of research make their way from scientific journals to textbooks to popular magazines and newspapers, findings are often distorted to make them appear more significant, glamorous, and indisputable than they really are.

B. Conflicts of Interest. Scientific research is often a high-stakes enterprise, with certain outcomes considered far more desirable than others. But unlike lawyers who insist on the innocence of their clients, or salespeople who proclaim their products the best on the market, scientists may appear to laypeople as impartial seekers after truth.

C. Finding a Good Problem and Asking Good Questions. Good researchers pick solvable problems and ask good questions about them.

III. Measurement Issues (Chapter 5). Many scientific controversies revolve around disagreements or misunderstandings about what should be measured. For example, clinics that treat alcohol abuse often use abstinence from alcohol as the sole criterion for success. But many "recovering" alcoholics develop problems with relationships, health, work, and other drugs.

IV. Research Designs (Chapters 6 to 16). This section, the longest in the book, is divided into subsections describing the rationale behind and appropriate procedures for conducting experiments, comparative and correlational research, case study analysis, descriptive research, survey research, archival research, and research using animal models of human conditions. There are also brief sections on computer simulations and qualitative research. Scientific researchers need specialized knowledge and technical skills, but intelligent nonscientists should have no trouble understanding the conceptual foundations underlying each research design. They should make the effort, because published research is plagued by statistical errors, inappropriate generalizations, and errors in logic. (The discussion of interactions and individual differences will help people evaluate the relevance of research findings to their own lives.)

V. Data Analysis (Chapter 17). Eminent critics have argued for decades that the dominant method for analyzing statistical data, null hypothesis testing, is seriously misguided. The criticisms are presented and alternative methods suggested.

VI. Philosophical Issues (Chapter 18). Unsophisticated laypeople, unaware of the importance of control groups and other refinements, frequently misinterpret observations. For example, they commit the cardinal sin of drawing causal conclusions ($X$ caused $Y$) from correlational data (as $X$ changes, $Y$ also changes). Textbook writers give examples of such errors to emphasize the virtues of the scientific method. Yet the writers generally ignore philosophical challenges to scientific inferences. For example, scientists observe and experiment to determine how one variable changes with another. Then they try to find the equations. But an *infinite* number of equations yielding an *infinite* number of different predictions can be found to fit *any* set of data.

The following reviewers provided useful suggestions: Susan H. Fanzblau, Fayetteville State University; Donna LaVoie, St. Louis University; and Mary McVey, San Jose State University.

Fred Leavitt
fleavitt@bay.csuhayward.edu

# Checklist
# for Evaluating
# Research

I. Measurement Issues
  A. Did the researcher define and measure variables reliably, sensitively, and validly? The answer may depend on the specific project. For example, an animal's rate of bar pressing for food reward is generally a good indicator of its hunger, but not if the animal has received a high dose of amphetamine. The answer to the question "What is your annual income?" may be taken at face value in many situations, but not when given by a suspected tax evader to an agent of the IRS.
  B. Did the researcher switch between definitions of key variables, especially between technical and popular definitions? If so, did the definitions correspond?
  C. Did any extraneous variables have unusual values?
II. Appropriateness of Inferences
  A. Did the researcher conclude that one variable caused a change in another? If so, did she assign subjects randomly to groups or expose them to each value of the independent variable in random order? If not, then the conclusion was premature. The study was not an experiment and, except in rare instances (see pp. 139–140), only experiments justify the assertion that one event caused another. When evaluating experimental evidence, consider the following:
  ■ Experiments are designed to show that changes in a dependent variable are attributable to an independent variable (IV). The logic requires that experimental and control subjects receive identical treatment except for the IV. Possible confounding factors include but are not limited to time and place of testing, expectations raised, and the experimenters themselves. If any of those factors vary between groups, they, rather than the IV, might account for subsequent differences.
  ■ Showing that a treated group outperforms a no-treatment control group may be unimportant if an effective treatment is already available.

■ Make sure that the treatment group improved rather than that the control group got worse (see discussion of active placebos, p. 94).

■ Check whether all subjects who began the study finished it. If not, ask how the authors treated dropout data.

B. Did the researcher draw conclusions about the characteristics of a population? One strategy for learning about population characteristics, such as the number of Californians who plan to buy a computer in the next 6 months, is to do a survey. There are many reasons for treating survey data cautiously. At the least, make sure that everyone in the population had an equal chance of being in the survey and that generalizations were restricted to that population.

C. Did the researcher draw his conclusions from data collected by others? Archival research (or other types of available evidence, such as graffiti or fossils) usually cannot put to rest two key concerns:

■ Are the original data trustworthy?

■ Did the researcher sample properly from the available data?

D. Were the researcher's conclusions based on naturalistic observations (observing subjects in their natural environments with minimal interference on the researcher's part)? If so, did he observe enough subjects and make enough observations on each one? Consider the possibility that certain subjects or behaviors were more easily observed than others.

E. Did the researcher conclude that two groups differ in some way? If so, might the results be explained by differences in how the groups were recruited? How did the researcher equate or account for possible differences between the groups in perception of the stimulus, motivation, experience, and so forth?

F. Did the researcher conclude that the results support a theory? If so, does the theory clearly predict one outcome over another? Can all the steps and assumptions from theory to prediction be clearly stated? Can all the steps and assumptions from data to conclusion be clearly stated?

G. What types of generalizations did the researcher make? Research is done in a specific setting and with specific subjects, levels and operational definitions of variables, and methods of data collection. The results may not generalize to other circumstances.

III. Additional Considerations

A. Who funded the research? Why did the funding organization support it?

B. What were the scientist's nonscientific reasons for doing the research? Was it so she could gain tenure, be promoted, make money, prove a point? Did she have a strong preference for one outcome rather than another?

C. Was the article published in a peer-reviewed journal?

# What Is Science?

*By the time you finish reading this chapter, you should be able to answer the following questions:*

What is the key characteristic of science?

Why did philosopher Thomas Kuhn argue that a large component of irrationality underlies the choice between theories?

Why did philosopher Paul Feyerabend argue that scientists should occasionally deliberately ignore methodological rules?

Should scientists collect data as an end in itself?

What types of questions will scientists never be able to answer?

Do the intellectual backgrounds of scientists influence how they collect and interpret data?

Does it make sense to talk about a feminist methodology for science?

What types of assumptions do we typically make when reading a scientific article?

Can love be studied scientifically?

■  ■  ■  ■  ■

*"The hypotheses and theories advanced in empirical science must be capable of test by reference to evidence obtained by observation or experimentation."* Carl Hempel

## ■ SCIENTIFIC THEORIES ARE TESTABLE

Although science transforms society and is the most effective tool ever invented for predicting and controlling events, historians and philosophers do not agree on its defining characteristics. Many successful researchers used methods that most of their contemporaries frowned upon. One incorrect stereotype is that good scientists are cautious to the point of timidity when interpreting data. The attitude is exemplified in an anecdote about two scientists who see a flock of sheep. One says, "Look, those sheep have just been sheared." The other answers, "Sheared on this side, anyway." Whether amusing or not, the story grossly distorts how scientists think. They willingly risk errors whenever they draw inferences, generalize, or construct a theory.

Philosopher Karl Popper (1963) contrasted the theories of Albert Einstein, Sigmund Freud, and Alfred Adler to support his view that the distinguishing characteristic of science is risk taking. Each theory generated predictions, but with a crucial difference. After Einstein predicted that light from a distant star would remain visible during a solar eclipse because the star's light would be bent by the sun's gravitational field, Einstein's colleagues eagerly awaited an eclipse so the theory could be tested. The risk, not the truth or falsity of the prediction, is what made it scientific. Popper wrote that, by contrast:

> Every conceivable case could be interpreted in the light of Adler's theory, or equally of Freud's. I may illustrate this by two very different examples of human behavior: that of a man who pushes a child into the water with the intention of drowning it, and that of a man who sacrifices his life in an attempt to save the child. Each of these two cases can be explained with equal ease in Freudian and Adlerian terms. According to Freud the first man suffered from repression (say, of some component of his Oedipus complex), while the second man had achieved sublimation. According to Adler the first man suffered from feelings of inferiority (producing perhaps the need to prove to himself that he dared to commit some crime), and so did the second man (whose need was to prove to himself that he dared to rescue the child). I could not think of any human behavior which could not be interpreted in terms of either theory.

The theories of Adler and Freud, while seeming to explain everything, were interpreted so vaguely that no outcome could ever disconfirm them. Thus, they actually explained nothing. The theories did not satisfy Popper's (1968) key criterion for science, because they did not "make assertions which may clash with observations." That is, they were not falsifiable. A theory is falsifiable only if it can in principle be refuted by data. Popper wrote that scientists should construct theories boldly but try ruthlessly to falsify them. The U.S. Supreme Court adopted falsificationism as the criterion by which judges should distinguish scientific from nonscientific statements in the courtroom.

Many people who claim to be scientists attempt to salvage unsatisfactory predictions by any means possible. They are like Stephen Leacock's (1916) fictional detective, who may have been charming and well respected but was no scientist.

Stephen Leacock

*Stories Shorter Still*
*An Irreducible Detective Story*
*Hanged by a Hair or A Murder Mystery Minimized*

The mystery had now reached its climax. First, the man had been undoubtedly murdered. Secondly, it was absolutely certain that no conceivable person had done it. It was therefore time to call in the great detective. He gave one searching glance at the corpse. In a moment he whipped out a microscope. "Ha! Ha!" he said, as he picked a hair off the lapel of the dead man's coat. "The mystery is now solved." He held up the hair. "Listen," he said, "we have only to find the man who lost this hair and the criminal is in our hands." The inexorable chain of logic was complete. The detective set himself to the search. For four days and nights he moved, unobserved, through the streets of New York scanning closely every face he passed, looking for a man who had lost a hair. On the fifth day he discovered a man, disguised as a tourist, his head enveloped in a steamer cap that reached below his ears. The man was about to go on board the Gloritania. The detective followed him on board. "Arrest him!" he said, and then drawing himself to his full height, he brandished aloft the hair. "This is his," said the great detective. "It proves his guilt." "Remove his hat," said the ship's captain sternly. They did so. The man was entirely bald. "Ha!" said the great detective, without a moment of hesitation. "He has committed not one murder but about a million."

For a nonfictional example of the same attitude, consider Sigmund Freud's daughter Anna's (1948) description of a young female patient. (Both Freuds believed that all young girls suffer from penis envy.) The patient "had succeeded in so completely repressing her envy of her little brother's penis—an affect by which her life was entirely dominated—that even in analysis it was exceptionally difficult to detect any traces of it."

Conventional Freudians, such as Anna Freud, refused to modify or discard the theory despite contradictory data. They were not falsificationists, hence, by Popper's criterion, they were not scientists.

Not all philosophers accept falsifiability as an appropriate criterion. Duhem (1954) and Quine (1953) independently argued that theories are never tested in isolation, so falsifications can never be conclusive. Hempel (1966) gave an example. During the years 1844 to 1848, many women contracted a serious and often fatal illness during childbirth. Physician Ignaz Semmelweiss noticed that medical students frequently performed dissections, then washed superficially and went straight to the maternity ward to examine the women. He hypothesized that the students were transmitting infectious material and thus causing the childbed fever. So Semmelweiss ordered students to wash their hands in a chlorinated lime solution before making an examination, and the mortality rate fell dramatically. But what if it hadn't fallen?

Semmelweiss had assumed that washing of hands would prevent transmission of infectious material and that chlorinated lime solution was an effective way to wash. If one or both of those assumptions had been incorrect, or if errors had been made in analyzing the mortality data, the theory would have appeared falsified.*

Feyerabend (1975) claimed that not a single interesting theory agrees with all the known facts in its domain, and Chalmers (1976) noted that several theories currently held in high esteem would have been rejected in their infancy if scientists were strict falsificationists. Newton's gravitational theory was falsified by observations of the moon's orbit, Bohr's theory of the atom by the observation that some atomic particles are stable for longer periods than predicted, and the kinetic theory of gases by measurements on the specific heats of gases. A direct experiment that seemed incompatible with the theory of evolution did not persuade Darwin to revise it. When Einstein was told that certain facts refuted his theory of relativity, he said, "The facts are wrong."

Eminent physicist Michael Faraday blatantly ignored apparent falsifications until he was fairly certain he had a strongly supported hypothesis. Then, sometimes abruptly, Faraday investigated possible artifacts and designed experiments pitting his hypothesis against potential alternatives (Tweney, 1985). Mynatt et al. (1978) asked both college students and active scientists to infer laws from computer-generated shapes. The most successful subjects behaved like Faraday by trying first to confirm and only later seeking disconfirmation. Subjects who tried early on to falsify their hypotheses did very badly—as did subjects who tried only to confirm.

Psychological and biomedical theories often predict that subjects treated in a particular way will differ from subjects treated differently. A

---

* Scientific findings do not always translate into changes in behavior. Several studies (cf. Lohr, Ingram, Dudley et al., 1991; Meengs, Giles, Chisholm et al., 1994) have shown that an unacceptably high proportion of physicians still fail to take hand-washing breaks between patient contacts.

finding of no differences represents a falsification of the theory. But many editors discourage authors from submitting papers reporting a finding of no differences. So, despite proclamations to the contrary, in practice the editors reject falsificationism.

## ■ SCIENTISTS ORGANIZE FACTS TO SOLVE MEANINGFUL PROBLEMS

Anything that varies can be a variable in a research project. An independent variable (IV) is a variable manipulated by an experimenter. A dependent variable (DV) is a behavior recorded and measured at the end of a study to see whether the IV has affected it. For example, a researcher interested in the effects of alcohol on stress might give subjects alcohol—the IV—and measure changes in epinephrine, a hormone secreted during times of stress. Epinephrine secretion would be the DV. To study the effects of stress on drinking, she might tell subjects to expect a painful electric shock—the IV—and then offer them alcohol. The amount drunk would be the DV. Because the number of potential variables is infinite, so is the number of possible combinations of IV and DV. An experimenter restricted to just 100 IVs and 100 DVs could pair them in 10,000 distinct ways. But most pairings would not satisfy a second criterion discussed by Popper. He wrote that scientists should study variables not for the purpose of accumulating facts, but to help them construct laws and theories that organize the facts, unify diverse phenomena, and make sense of the world: "Only if it is an answer to a problem—a difficult, a fertile problem, a problem of some depth—does a truth, or a conjecture about the truth, become relevant to science."

Unfortunately, because career success is tied to volume of publication, many researchers take the safe path of collecting data rather than trying to solve difficult problems. Their occasional surprising and even counterintuitive findings are cited as proof that even deeply held beliefs must be tested. But the benefits of such research should be weighed against the negative consequences: Money is siphoned off from scientists trying to solve genuine, pertinent problems; the workloads of editors and reviewers are increased; and readers must wade through pages of journal chaff to find scientific grains of wheat. The fact accumulators trivialize rather than advance science.

Some years ago, the psychology department of a first-rank university evaluated candidates for a staff vacancy. When the hiring committee made a recommendation, the chairman greeted it unenthusiastically. He said he had never heard of the person. A shocked committee member told the chairman that the candidate had published more than 200 papers. The chairman, so the story goes, said: "Two hundred publications and I never heard of him. That's all the more reason not to hire him."

## ■ ADDITIONAL VIEWS ON PHILOSOPHY OF SCIENCE

Thomas Kuhn (1970) argued that a large component of irrationality underlies the choice between theories. In mature sciences, virtually all scientists at a given time use the same key concepts and methods and agree on the significant problems. That is, they share a common paradigm. They solve problems and fill in details within the paradigm while ignoring the occasional anomalies (falsifications) that inevitably arise. So the anomalies accumulate until a revolutionary scientist insists that they must be dealt with and produces a new paradigm. The new paradigm demands methodological rules that seem illogical to adherents of the old one. Thus, the choice between paradigms is irrational.

Bauer (1992) asserted that the only thing that separates science from nonscience is the approval of scientific institutions: "If it were only application of scientific method that made something scientific, then nothing should be labeled pseudoscience if that method is followed. But if reported results seriously contradict established knowledge, the results will be rejected" (p. 147).

Social relativists argue that the results of science have no validity beyond the culture in which they emerge. In particular, they say, 20th-century Western science has no special claim to truth. Brown (1988) responded that the argument for social relativity depends on accepting the results of one Western science, anthropology. Those who cite anthropological data to support social relativism assume that anthropology has validity beyond the culture in which it was developed.

Paul Feyerabend's (1975) *Against Method* is a nightmare for methodologists. He gave many historical examples to support his position that for every methodological rule, circumstances will arise that make it advisable not only to ignore the rule but to adopt its opposite. Every rule is associated with assumptions that may be wrong. Hypotheses should be developed inconsistent with highly confirmed theories, because the evidence that might refute a theory can often be unearthed only with the help of an incompatible alternative.

Whatever their stance on falsificationism, virtually all philosophers of science agree that no sharp line demarcates scientific from nonscientific fields. The criteria, epitomized in Casti's (1994) epigram that science is more a verb than a noun, involve attitudes and methods rather than subject matter. Historical research as conducted by some historians is similar in important respects to paleontological research (observe, guess at relationships, collect data, make predictions, collect new data against which to test the predictions). The German word for science, *Wissenschaft*, includes all the branches of scholarship, including literary and historical studies (Ziman, 1968). Certain areas of psychology, such as those involving questions about love, peace, and happiness, have been stigmatized as "unscientific." They are certainly difficult to study, posing definitional, ethical, and other problems—but creative researchers have studied them in ways that satisfy both of Popper's criteria. Here are three findings from the research on love:

- College students in Japan placed less value on romantic love than did students in Germany and the United .States. In fact, romantic love was viewed negatively in Japan. It was associated with confusion, jealousy, and probable disillusionment (Simmons, Von Kolker, & Shimizu, 1986).
- Hazan and Shaver (1987) defined three types of love relationships: (a) Secure adults develop trusting relationships. (b) Anxious-ambivalent adults are preoccupied with the possibility that they will be rejected. (c) Avoidant adults have trouble getting close to others and form relationships that lack intimacy. The types of love relationship parallel, and appear to be influenced by, the types of infant-mother attachments.
- Couples of mixed religious background reported stronger feelings of romantic love, possibly because conflicts with family members increased arousal (Rubin, 1973).

## ■ A FEW NONCRITICAL FEATURES

Experimentation, control groups, replicability, and statistical analysis of data help scientists predict, explain, and keep errors to a minimum, but they are not among Popper's criteria for science. They are not essential. Darwin and Einstein did not conduct double-blind experiments or use computers, microscopes, or inferential statistics. Even today, some of those are luxuries rarely available to naturalists, astronomers, and paleontologists.

## ■ LIMITATIONS OF SCIENCE

### Scientists Can Answer Only Certain Kinds of Questions

Questions about ethics, the existence of God, and the possibility of an afterlife are not within the realm of science. Despite their importance, they cannot be expressed in the form of falsifiable hypotheses. The same is true for definitional questions such as, What is truth? and What is beauty?

## Scientists Cannot Establish Absolute Truth

Scientific predictions are often so accurate that they seem to have penetrated ultimate reality. But philosophers assert that theories can never be proven and absolute truth is unattainable. New theories constantly replace old ones and inviolable laws are superseded. Although modern physics and chemistry owe much to their 17th-century predecessors, they are vastly different conceptions, not merely updated versions. The chemist Arrhenius received a Nobel Prize for developing the electrolytic theory of dissociation. The chemist Debye received a Nobel Prize for showing that Arrhenius's theory is deficient. Nietzsche anticipated the modern view called social constructionism when he wrote, "There are no facts, only interpretations." Disagreements arise between scientists because every important phase of their professional lives is influenced by their intellectual histories and values.

**Intellectual Values Influence Choice of Discipline.** Each scientific discipline focuses on different aspects of phenomena and creates unique perspectives for attacking problems. Consider research on depression. Personality theorists seek causes in early childhood experiences, disturbed interpersonal relationships, and loss of self-esteem. Developmental psychologists study incidence of depression throughout the life span. Environmental psychologists investigate whether interventions such as exposure to artificial lights relieve depression. Epidemiologists document patterns of incidence throughout the world. Anthropologists and cross-cultural psychologists compare symptoms of depressed people in different cultures. Physiologists study factors such as the role of sex hormones in contributing to a higher incidence of depression in women than men. Neuroanatomists and pharmacologists study anatomical and neurochemical correlates. Geneticists study patterns of inheritance. Each discipline has its own training requirements, specialized equipment, preferred types of research designs, and typical subjects. Results are presented in journals or at conferences for audiences comprised primarily of scientists from the same discipline. Exchange of ideas between disciplines is limited.

**Intellectual Values Influence the Questions Scientists Ask.** Even within a single discipline, intellectual values affect the questioning process. Just as men and women differ in many of the problems they face, so also do they differ in the phenomena they would like science to explain. Harding (1987) wondered why most men find child care and housework distasteful, why men's sexuality is defined in terms of power, and why risking death is considered a distinctively human act but giving birth is regarded as merely natural. Nurturing, considered a feminine trait, has been largely ignored.

Although glial cells are much more numerous than nerve cells, they were thought to merely nurture (feed nerve cells and clean up afterward) and so attracted little scientific interest. Yet they may be vitally important to complex thinking (Diamond, Schrebel, Murphy, & Harvey, 1985).

Tiefer (1978) noted that sex researchers (mostly men) define sex in terms of genital responses, yet "some women contend that...looking at the beloved or anticipating a reunion or recalling an emotionally intense interaction can be erotically, though not genitally, ecstatic." Tiefer added that the genital intercourse bias of sex research has precluded study of the psychological and physiological role of foreplay.

**Intellectual History Influences Observational Data.** Hanson (1958) argued that two observers with normal eyesight who are gazing at the same object might see different things. For example, Figure 1.1 can be seen as either an old or a young woman and Figure 1.2 as either opposing faces or a goblet. Figure 1.3 is seen as meaningful by some people but not all. Two viewers asked to draw what they saw might produce identical results, but if one saw an old woman and the other a young one in Figure 1.1, they would in an important sense be observing differently. In Hanson's words, "There is more to seeing than meets the eye." Physicist Sir Arthur Eddington wrote,

**FIGURE 1.1**
This classic drawing can be viewed as either a young woman or an old woman.

**FIGURE 1.2** Do you see opposing faces or a goblet? Both images are possible.

> It is a good rule not to put overmuch confidence in a theory until it has been confirmed by observation. I hope I shall not shock the experimental physicists too much if I add that it is also a good rule not to put overmuch confidence in the observational results that are put forward until they have been confirmed by theory.

In 1903, French physicist Andre Blondlot announced his discovery of a new kind of ray, which he called an N-ray, that intensified reflected light and was bent by aluminum. By 1906, at least 40 people, including several eminent scientists, had reported observing N-rays, and more than 300 scien-

**FIGURE 1.3** Can you make sense of this figure? It includes a dog.

tific papers had described their properties. Then Blondlot gave a public demonstration. He placed an aluminum prism in the middle of several lenses and, with the room darkened (because N-rays are affected by light), he manipulated an apparatus to turn the prism. As the apparatus was moved, Blondlot's assistant reported changes in the intensity of the readings. But when the lights came back on, the audience saw physicist R. W. Wood in the front row with the prism in his hand. He had secretly removed it early in the demonstration. Yet the observers' preconceptions had helped them "see" the nonexistent N-rays.

**Intellectual Values Influence What Scientists Read.** Most British doctors could not name a single French medical journal, and the French named an average of slightly more than one British journal (Payer, 1988). Between 1950 and 1990, more than 99% of editors and board members and 95% of authors of major American psychology journals were affiliated with institutions in North America; and more than 90% of their references were to North American authors (Gielen, 1994). Commercial indexing services ignore most of the world's journals, and U.S. libraries do not subscribe to them. So even though 24.1% of the world's scientists are in developing countries, they are largely invisible to U.S. scientists.

**Intellectual Values Influence How Scientists Interpret Data.** Koehler (1993) paid advanced graduate students in the sciences to read short summaries about two fictitious controversies. Some summaries had arguments strongly favoring a particular research hypothesis and others had weak arguments. Readers of the strong arguments developed stronger beliefs in the hypotheses. Next, Koehler asked them to evaluate detailed research reports related to the issues. The subjects tended to judge a report to be of higher quality when its results agreed rather than disagreed with the induced beliefs. Yet subjects stated that prior beliefs did not and should not influence their judgments of the quality of the new reports.

Then Koehler identified 195 scientists who believed in extrasensory perception and 131 skeptics. He mailed each a description of one of several versions of a fictitious parapsychological research report. The scientists judged studies that supported their beliefs as stronger methodologically than otherwise identical studies that opposed their beliefs. The scientists stated that prior beliefs did not, nor should not have, influenced their judgments of the quality of the new reports.

**Intellectual Values Influence Theoretical Models.** There is a saying, "Scratch a theory and find a biography." Cell biologists of the 1930s viewed the relationship between nucleus and cytoplasm as similar to that between husband and wife, and Beldecos et al. (1988) described competing views of eminent scientists on the exact nature of the relationship. From autocratic

Germany came a model in which the nucleus contained all the executive functions and the cytoplasm acted on its commands. The leading American geneticist, T. H. Morgan, modeled the cell after his family—nucleus and cytoplasm exchanged information although the nucleus made the final decision. British socialist C. H. Waddington, who viewed his marriage as a partnership, theorized that nucleus and cytoplasm were equals. And in the model of African American embryologist E. E. Just, the cytoplasm dominated.

**Intellectual Values Influence the Methodologies That Scientists Consider Valid.** Prominent scientists and philosophers support each of the following positions: (a) A theory is useful only if it makes surprising predictions that turn out correct. (b) A theory that explains a broad range of phenomena is acceptable even if it has not made startling predictions. (c) A theory must be tested against a wide variety of supporting instances. (d) A large number of confirming instances is sufficient even if they have little variety. (e) Both direct and indirect evidence must demonstrate the existence of entities postulated by the theory (Laudan, 1984).

## Feminist Methodology

The founders of modern science imbued it with a masculine bias. Francis Bacon (cited in Shepherd, 1993, p. 20) wrote that the goal of science is to "bind her [nature] to your service and make her your slave." Chemist Robert Boyle (quoted in Shepherd, 1993) wrote that there can be no greater male triumph than "to know the ways of captivating Nature, and making her subserve our purposes." Descriptions of the proper scientific attitude typically include adjectives such as independent, analytic, logical, objective, quantitative, unemotional, and reductionistic. Several feminist scholars (cf. Keller, 1985; Riger, 1992; Tiefer, 1978) called attention to the close match between these values and the Western values for masculinity. Feminists (some of whom are men) acknowledge that methods and goals derived from a masculine worldview produce much of importance, but they contend that any science that relies almost exclusively on such methods cannot be comprehensive. Feminist philosophers of science do not speak with a single voice. Harding (1987) described three distinct positions. Some feminists emphasize gender biases in the teaching of science and the methods of defining, selecting, and funding research problems. Others believe that because they have relatively little social power, women become more sensitive to the nature of social relationships and the meanings of a broad range of phenomena. Feminist postmodernists challenge the notion of an objective reality.

Each masculine value has a feminine counterpart, and attention to them can enrich science. For example, feminist researchers prefer studying behaviors in their natural contexts rather than isolating the behaviors from supposedly extraneous contaminants. Rather than designing research solely to test the predictive value of hypotheses, feminists try to be receptive to what nature offers. Shepherd (1993) cited many successful scientists on the value of being receptive to nature. Similarly, she discussed with examples the values of feeling, subjectivity, cooperation, intuition, and relatedness.

Barbara McClintock, who won the Nobel Prize in 1983 for her genetic research on corn plants, did not distance herself. She believed that each plant was unique and took pleasure in watching and knowing each plant as it grew from a seedling (Keller, 1985).

Feminist scientists question assumptions about gender that affect data interpretation. For example, early accounts of the fertilization process portrayed sperm as active and eggs as passive. The male semen awakened the slumbering egg as the prince in the fairy tale awoke Sleeping Beauty. Beldecos et al. (1988, p. 177) argued that this interpretation (a) follows from the stereotyped conceptions of men and women and (b) is wrong:

> Freshly ejaculated mammalian sperm are not normally able to fertilize the eggs in many species. They have to become capacitated, which is mediated through secretions of the female genital tract. Furthermore, upon reaching the egg, mammalian sperm release enzymes that digest some of the extracellular vestments surrounding the egg. But the enzymes become activated only by interacting with another secretion of the female reproductive tract. Thus, neither the egg nor the female reproductive tract is a passive element in fertilization.

## ■ SCIENTIFIC INFERENCE

There is a paradox: Scientists are widely portrayed as impartial seekers of truth and the scientific method as the most powerful tool ever invented for establishing it. Yet research findings often fail to create consensus about what the truth is. Despite thousands of published studies, experts still disagree about the effectiveness of psychotherapy, the dangers of marijuana, the reasons for gender differences in mathematical and verbal abilities, the existence of ESP, and a great many others. Why should this be?

No less than beauty, the meaning of data is in the beholder's eye. Mathematician Henri Poincare wrote, "Science is built up with facts as a house is with stones. But a collection of facts is no more a science than a heap of stones is a house." Yet even the barest of facts must be inferred from data, and research conclusions rely on chains of inferences that, like all chains, are no stronger than their weakest links. Readers of research articles face at least seven levels of assumptions and inferences.

*Assumption 1.* There was no bias in the types of data collected or made public.

Negative results (no difference between groups) are less likely than positive ones to be submitted for publication and, if submitted, to be accepted. Thus, the published literature may give a distorted picture of the relationship between variables.

Research requires financing, and granting agencies award money to applicants with goals compatible with their own. Pharmaceutical companies support research designed to show the beneficial effects of their drugs, whereas the National Institute on Drug Abuse and other federal agencies grant money for studying adverse effects of illicit drugs. Woodford (1996) quoted Walter Willett, an outspoken critic of fast foods and processed foods, about the attempt of some food manufacturers to control the presentations at research conferences. Companies have told conference organizers that they will refuse to provide financial support if Willett participates in the conference.

*Assumption 2.* The data are accurate.

Readers typically see only summaries, not original data, and assume that the data are accurate. In considering the possibility of inaccurate data, a researcher's motives and competency, the journal in which she published, and whether there have been successful replications are all relevant factors. Data may be inaccurate because anybody involved with a project entered or tabulated incorrectly or cheated, or because the equipment was faulty.

*Assumption 3.* The data have been analyzed properly.

This assumption is not always justified (cf. Anderson, 1985; Halperin, 1989; Humphreys, 1982; Kalat, 1980; Keren & Lewis, 1993; Robins, 1987; Rosnow & Rosenthal, 1989; Sedlmeier & Gigerenzer, 1989; Thompson, 1988; Wilcox, 1998). Each of the cited references deals with a different type of statistical procedure and errors in using the procedure that appeared in published articles.

*Assumption 4.* There are no unstated assumptions.

Journal space is expensive, so editors put a premium on brevity. Thus, methods sections of articles sometimes lack crucial details. The details that readers fill in—possibly without realizing it—may differ from what actually occurred. For example, many psychotherapists ask clients to list all their complaints and rate the severity of each one during the initial session, then to rerate on completion of therapy. But summing the severity scores to get one total confounds the number of complaints with their severity. On the other hand, averaging severity scores ignores the fact that the primary complaint is typically rated as much more severe than the others. The two measures are not necessarily equally sensitive to therapeutic manipulations. Yet Deane, Spicer, and Todd (1997) noted that many studies do not report the number of complaints elicited, nor do they make clear whether complaints have been summed or averaged. Deane et al. recommended assessing each separate complaint independently to maximize information and avoid the problems noted with the other procedures.

Millard (1976) wrote that 46.1% of articles published in *The Journal of the Experimental Analysis of Behavior* from 1958 to 1975 reported on pigeons pecking at a lighted key for access to food. The reinforcement, according to Ferster and Skinner (1957), "consists of free access to grain for 3.5 to 4 seconds" and "is approximately 0.25 gram." Subsequent researchers apparently assumed that Ferster and Skinner's figures were correct. However, Steinhauer (1994) showed that the amount pigeons eat during each access to food varies depending on the schedule of reinforcement. They eat more rapidly when required to make more key pecks per reinforcer (higher fixed ratio schedules), and the rate of eating is highly correlated with the rate of key pecking.

*Assumption 5.* The reported relationships are trustworthy.

Either because of flaws in the research design or faulty data analysis, inferences from data to conclusions about relationships between variables may be incorrect. With rare exceptions, statements to the effect that one variable has caused another require support from experimental evidence (see chapter 6). Yet newspaper reporters and other commentators often make causal assertions based on nonexperimental research.

*Assumption 6.* Observed relationships have meanings beyond the specific circumstances of the study.

Scientists infer that relationships found between variables under a particular set of test conditions and with specific subjects will hold more generally. Some generalizations seem reasonable and others do not, but the only way to be certain about the correctness of a generalization is to test it. Generalizations are made along many dimensions:

■ To other subjects—from men to women, volunteers to nonvolunteers, healthy subjects to sick ones, and so forth.

Generalizations from rats to people have led to important medical discoveries, but some results do not generalize even to other animals of the same species. Thompson and Olian (1961) injected a drug into pregnant females of three different mouse strains, then compared offspring with offspring of undrugged mothers of the same strains. Activity was elevated above control levels in one strain, depressed in the second, and unchanged in the third.

Some generalizations are implied. Goldman et al. (1988) concluded that all survivors of heart attacks at high or medium risk should be treated with long-term beta-adrenergic-antagonist therapy. Their conclusions about "all survivors" were based on research involving 13,385 men and no women.

■ To different methods of measuring the IVs and DVs.

Suppose a researcher has one group of subjects listen to Bach concertos while trying to associate names with pictures of faces, and a control group performs the same task while listening to white noise. Suppose a second researcher plays hard rock or nothing as her subjects memorize a poem. The researchers may draw different conclusions about the effects of music on learning, purely because they measured the IVs and DVs differently (see pp. 62–63 on operational definitions).

■ To different levels of other variables.

The effects of an IV tested with subjects at a certain level of hunger and alertness and with room temperature and lighting at specific values may differ from the effects of the same dose of the same IV tested under different circumstances. Chapter 8 gives examples of variables that interact in many ways.

College students read three vignettes, each describing a murder or rape, then answered questions about their reactions to the crimes. The vignettes were identical for all students, but the questionnaires were printed on pink, blue, or white paper. Several differences were found in anger aroused by the crimes and judgments about probable guilt and appropriate punishments, depending on the color of the paper used (Weller & Livingston, 1988).

■ To other settings. Experimenters generally administer and measure their variables in one particular context, the laboratory. But people's perceptions of the experimenter's purpose affect their behaviors in laboratory settings (Orne, 1962).

Staessen et al. (1997) gave portable blood pressure monitoring devices to 419 patients who had hypertension while at their doctor's office. The devices constantly measured blood pressure levels outside the office. Twenty-six percent of the patients were hypertensive only while visiting their doctor, and they suffered no ill effects when medication was stopped. The results suggest that many patients are taking antihypertensive drugs unnecessarily.

■ To other methods of data collection. Chapter 5 shows that method of measurement affects results. Researchers are part of the data collection process and may affect it significantly. See pp. 115–116 about experimenters and p. 176 about surveyors.

Laboratory subjects viewed either violent or neutral television programs, then had an opportunity to push a button that delivered shocks (they thought) to another person. Viewers of violent programs typically delivered stronger shocks and also punched a Bobo doll more. Freedman (1984) acknowledged the findings but questioned their relevance for understanding the relationship between television violence and aggression. He pointed out that pushing a shock button and punching a doll are not measures of aggression as usually defined: "Indeed, they are all acceptable behaviors that are allowed or even encouraged by the experimenter and, unlike usual aggression, there is no possibility of retaliation or even punishment" (Freedman, 1984, p. 228).

Many personality research articles involve multiple self-report measures administered in a single session. But Council (1993) showed that the experience of completing one measure may influence responses to subsequent ones. When he measured volunteers within a single session for both hypnotizability and absorption (ability to become highly involved in imaginative activities), the two were positively correlated. But when he measured hypnotizability and absorption in separate sessions, they were not. He gave several similar examples.

*Assumption 7.* The findings have theoretical relevance.

Inferences from data to theory are always problematic. Sapolsky (1964) theorized that some women believe in a "cloacal theory of birth," which involves oral impregnation. According to him, they become compulsive eaters if they wish to get pregnant and anorexic if they wish not to. He reasoned that they should be more likely than others to interpret ambiguous inkblots (the Rorschach test) as cloacal animals such as frogs. So Sapolsky predicted that a higher proportion of Rorschach frog responders than nonresponders would have eating disorders. He tested 31 frog responders and 31 controls and found a significant difference: 19 in the first group, and only five in the second, had eating disorders. Lykken (1968) did not accept that the experiment had justified the conclusion, so he asked 20 of his colleagues to estimate the extent to which they believed Sapolsky's theory prior to reading the experiment. Then they were given a summary of the findings and asked to reassess their beliefs. Lykken reported that they did not believe it beforehand and remained unchanged in disbelief afterward. Sapolsky's data may be accurate. The problem was in going from data to theory. Lykken suggested more plausible explanations for the data, such as that identifying frogs in the inkblots and eating disorders are both symptoms of immaturity, or that squeamish people might tend to both see frogs and have eating problems.

# Reading and Reviewing the Scientific Literature

*By the time you finish reading this chapter, you should be able to answer the following questions:*

How much of the scientific literature in their fields should prospective researchers read?

Why is critical thinking necessary when doing computer searches of the literature?

The published literature almost certainly overestimates many treatment effects. Why?

Where can you read reviews of psychology books?

Why should original sources be read whenever possible?

What is the difference between peer-reviewed and nonpeer-reviewed journals?

What are meta-analyses?

How do biases of readers affect their interpretations of articles?

What are some strategies for reading creatively?

What is meant by the statement that a substantial amount of public knowledge is undiscovered?

■　■　■　■　■

*"Knowledge is of two kinds. We know a subject ourselves, or we know where we can find information upon it."* Samuel Johnson

Active researchers spend much of their professional time reading scientific journals. Reading helps them keep abreast of the most sophisticated techniques while diminishing the likelihood that they will repeat previous work or make mistakes. Different viewpoints on how much reading is necessary reduce to matters of temperament. Philosopher Carl Hempel (1966) quoted economist A. B. Wolfe on what an ideal scientist would do:

> If we try to imagine how a mind of superhuman power and reach, but normal so far as the logical processes of its thought are concerned, would use the scientific method, the process would be as follows: First, all facts would be observed and recorded, without selection or a priori guess as to their relative importance. Secondly, the observed and recorded facts would be analyzed, compared, and classified, without hypothesis or postulates other than those necessarily involved in the logic of thought. Third, from this analysis of the facts generalizations would be inductively drawn as to the relations, classificatory or causal, between them. Fourth, further research would be deductive as well as inductive, employing inferences from previously established generalizations.

Hempel did not quote Wolfe to praise him. He argued that a scientist who followed Wolfe's prescription would soon be paralyzed. Nobody can collect all the facts relevant to a problem, let alone "all facts." Facts that are irrelevant for one scientist may be crucial to another. Hempel gave the example of Ignaz Semmelweiss (see p. 4), who practiced medicine in a maternity ward where about 10% of the women died in childbirth. A priest preceded by an attendant ringing a bell periodically walked through the ward to administer the last sacrament to dying women. This ritual was assumed to scare and debilitate the women and make them susceptible to childbed fever, so Semmelweiss had the priest change his routine. But the deaths continued. Then he hypothesized that the disease was spread by medical students carrying infectious microorganisms—the students frequently examined the women right after dissecting cadavers and without first disinfecting their hands. So he ordered them to wash before examining their patients, and deaths from childbed fever immediately declined. Wolfe's ideal scientist, with no hypothesis to guide him, would still be collecting data.

## ■ IMMENSITY OF THE LITERATURE

The scientific literature doubled from 1960 to 1975 and continues to expand (Ziman, 1980). More than 500,000 articles are published annually, plus books, monographs, symposiums, reports, and newsletters. A scientist who kept up with 75% of the relevant literature in 1985 and continued reading about the same amount each year would be able to keep up with only about 35% in the year 2000. Chemist R. Huffman (1996) reported that in 1995, *Chemical Abstracts* identified 687,789 articles relevant to his interests. He glanced at 346 per day, or 126,244 (18.36%) for the year.

To show the enormity of the literature, I did several computer searches of the PsycINFO database on September 2, 1998 for books and articles published in English within the previous 32 months and got the following results:

| | |
|---|---|
| psychotherapy | 5,540 books and articles |
| drugs | 5,135 |
| IQ tests | 43 |
| measurement | 4,812 |
| measurement error | 98 |

The mass of literature is physically impossible to read, let alone assimilate. Furthermore, oversaturation may reduce the possibility of developing new perspectives. Claude Bernard wrote, "It is that which we do know which is the great hindrance to learning, not that which we do not know." Two types of evidence support his view. First, established experts have greeted many great revolutionary ideas with skepticism, and second, many outstanding scientists, Pasteur, Metchnikoff, and Galvani among them, were not trained in the fields in which they made their most important discoveries.

Garfield (1996) encouraged readers not to be overwhelmed by the voluminous literature, because the total numbers of journals and articles are irrelevant. The bulk of significant scientific results appears in a small number of journals. Five hundred journals publish about half of all scientific articles and more than 70% of the literature cited worldwide.

## ■ HOW TO FIND THE APPROPRIATE MATERIALS

### Computer Searches

Several pages of my 1991 book *Research Methods for Behavioral Scientists* describe printed reference sources useful for searching the scientific literature. In the decade since, computers have made the 1991 discussion obsolete. Most university and many public libraries give patrons the opportunity to do free or low-cost computer searches, and subscribers to an Internet service provider can search from a personal computer and modem in their homes. Searches can be done by subject, title, author, or journal; they can be done for both popular and scientific articles; and key terms can be combined. Many databases are available, such as Medline for the world's biomedical literature, ERIC for education, and PsycINFO for psychology.

Instructions for computer searches are usually found near the computer terminal, and hands-on practice is probably the quickest way to become proficient. The output of a search is a list, which can be printed out, of all relevant articles plus information about where to find the unabridged articles. If an abstract (a 100- to 200-word summary of the key points of the article) is available, it is included. Practiced readers can usually tell from an abstract if an article is appropriate for their needs.

Although computers make literature searches easy, critical thinking and creativity are required because slight differences in search terms may yield strikingly different results. For example, I searched Medline on September 2, 1998, for books and articles published in English within the previous two years and got the following results:

| | |
|---|---|
| genetics and sexuality | 7 books and articles |
| genetics and sex | 1,320 |
| heredity and sexuality | 1 |
| inheritance and sexuality | 0 |
| genes and sexuality | 6 |
| genotype and sexuality | 3 |
| genes and sex | 995 |
| genotype and sex | 516 |
| twin studies and sex | 94 |
| twin studies and sexuality | 1 |
| genes and sexual behavior | 51 |
| genetics and sexual behavior | 49 |
| inheritance and sexual behavior | 2 |
| genotype and sexual behavior | 11 |

## ■ PUBLICATION BIAS

Reviewers may not know about unpublished though methodologically sound studies. Scientists often "file away" negative findings—those that haven't yielded statistically significant results—even though the results are real. Reviewers and editors share the bias against negative studies. Dickersin (1997) contacted the principal investigators of five groups of projects at major research institutes to determine the results and publication status of each completed study from each project. Between 5% and 41% of completed studies were never reported anywhere, and another 4% to 24% were published only as brief abstracts. The unpublished studies were much more likely to have yielded negative results. Dickersin and Yuan (1993) cited research indicating that 95% of articles in major psychology journals and 85% in medical journals that relied on statistical hypothesis testing reported statistically significant results. It is extremely unlikely that the vast majority of all studies undertaken were statistically significant, so we can infer that a higher proportion of studies with negative than positive results go unpublished. Therefore, reviews that exclude unpublished studies will overestimate treatment effects. More generally, if unpublished studies differ systematically from published ones in any important way, a literature review that excludes them will lead to erroneous conclusions.

The widespread use of pilot studies amplifies the file-drawer problem (Meehl, 1990). Scientists do pilot studies to see if a particular line of research is worth pursuing and, if an appreciable effect is detected, to get a rough idea of the number of subjects needed for achieving statistical significance in the main study. But dropping unpromising lines has the same effect as filing away negative studies, and picking the number of subjects to achieve statistical significance ensures that many findings will be trivial.

The language in which an article is written leads to other types of publication bias. Of 36 meta-analyses published in leading English-language medical journals from 1991 to 1993, 26 had restricted their search to studies reported in English (Gregoire, Derderian, & LeLorier, 1995). Scientists from countries in which English is not the dominant language often publish some of their work in local journals. They are likely to report positive findings in English language (international) journals and negative findings in local journals (Dickersin, Scherer, & Lefebure, 1994; Moher et al., 1996). Egger, Zellweger, and Antes (1996) and Egger et al. (1997) compared articles published in five German, Swiss, and Austrian medical journals from 1985 to 1994 with articles by the same first author published in English during the same period. Sixty-three percent of the articles published in English and only 35% of those published in German had produced significant results. Some countries publish unusually high proportions of positive results (Vickers, Goyal, Harland, & Rees, 1998).

Publication bias has serious consequences. Although 16 published studies indicated that combination chemotherapy increased survival time of cancer patients, the advantage disappeared when several unpublished studies were located and combined with the first group (Simes, 1986). Similarly, publication bias in reviews of studies on the treatment of obesity resulted in overestimates of the effectiveness of the treatments (Allison, Faith, & Gorman, 1996).

## Reviews of Research

Many disciplines publish annual reviews (*Annual Review of Psychology, Annual Review of Sociology, Annual Review of Biology*, etc.) written by eminent scientists. These discuss recent developments, primarily empirical rather than theoretical, and include extensive reference lists. However, the strong opinions of the reviewers sometimes interfere with their objectivity (cf. Antman, Kupelnick, Masteller, & Chalmers, 1992; Mulrow, 1987; Oxman & Guyatt, 1993). Joyce, Rabe, and Wessely (1998) searched several databases for review articles on chronic fatigue syndrome that claimed to be comprehensive. Of the 89 reviews considered suitable for further analysis, only three reported on the databases used. The authors of the other 86 listed no objective criteria for including or excluding articles, and they chose articles selectively according to both their disciplines and the country in which they lived.

## Other Strategies

Scientific journals specialize, so a journal that has published a relevant article is likely to have others as well. Many journals have letters sections in which correspondents comment, usually critically, on recently published articles. The original authors are given an opportunity to reply. Readers can learn a great deal about both the substantive topic and methodological issues.

*Contemporary Psychology* is a monthly journal of book reviews, and the *Mental Health Book Review Index* tells where reviews of psychology books can be found. References to reviews of books on psychological measurement and testing are found in the *Mental Measurements Yearbook*.

## ■ READ EFFICIENTLY, CRITICALLY, AND CREATIVELY

## Read Efficiently

An abstract is a brief (usually 100- to 200-word) summary of the key points of an article. The abstract provides an overview and indicates whether the entire article is appropriate for the reader's interests. Read abstracts first, then skim articles of only peripheral interest and make a card index of important ones. At the top of each 5 × 8 card, put location information (author, title, journal, year, volume, pages). Summarize the article on the rest of the card. Card indexes can be easily rearranged to accommodate different organizational schemes.

## Read Critically

**Read the Original Sources.** Readers cannot realistically be expected to locate and read through every article from which they want to learn. On the other hand, review articles and other secondary sources may be inaccurate. Most introductory and many advanced psychology texts refer to Watson and Rayner's (1920) conditioning of the infant Albert B., and most contain inaccuracies. Minor errors involve Albert's name, age, and whether he was initially conditioned to fear a rat or rabbit. Other errors are more serious, including erroneous lists of stimuli to which Albert's fear had generalized and false reports (sometimes in detail) that Watson eventually removed Albert's fears (Harris, 1979).

Hansen and McIntire (1994) compared information in 97 articles with citations of those articles in medical journals. There were three major and 32 minor errors in citation accuracy, and seven major errors and two minor errors in citation appropriateness. George and Robbins (1994) checked 240 randomly picked citations and reported a 41% error rate in information identifying the source and a 35% inconsistency rate between the statement referenced and the original source. Only 36% of references were error-free.

**Distinguish Between Peer-Reviewed and Nonpeer-Reviewed Journals.** Journals indicate their publishing policies within each issue. Although peer review is considerably less than perfect (see pp. 39–42), articles submitted to journals that are not peer reviewed are subjected to much less scrutiny. There have been abuses:

> In 1995, Professor Jean Boddewyn sent a letter to the *New York Times* criticizing them for continuing to cite 1991 studies of the impact of Joe Camel advertising on youth. Professor Boddewyn argued that the 1991 studies had been debunked by at least three other researchers. He did not disclose, however, that at least two of the researchers received funding from the tobacco industry, and that all of the studies were published in marketing journals that are not peer-reviewed and do not require disclosure of conflicts of interest. In contrast, the 1991 studies were published in the *Journal of the American Medical Association*, which is peer-reviewed and does require disclosure of conflicts. Professor Boddewyn also did not disclose that he himself has been paid by, and has frequently appeared as an "expert witness" for the tobacco industry. (Americans for Nonsmokers' Rights, 1996, p. 19)

**Consider the Pros and Cons of Meta-Analyses.** One reason for reading the literature is to assess the effectiveness of an intervention. Does the new drug work? Is teaching method $X$ better than method $Y$? One of the enduring myths about science is that a single study usually settles such questions conclusively, but different studies on the same problem frequently yield dissimilar and even conflicting results. In such cases, a literature review that evaluates and organizes previous work can have a major impact on a field of inquiry. However, until about 25 years ago, reviewers interpreted results unsystematically and with idiosyncratic strategies, and they often disagreed strongly about the collective meaning of a body of evidence (Kamin, 1978; Munsinger, 1974, 1978). Since then meta-analysis, a group of statistical methods for combining results, has been developed to improve the quality of reviews. Chapter 15 discusses benefits and criticisms. Books such as those by Rosenthal (1991) and Hunter and Schmidt (1990) give step-by-step details. However, meta-analysts face many of the same problems that other reviewers face. For example, one group of meta-analysts included all studies on a particular topic, whereas a second group focused on studies of high methodological quality on the same topic, and they reached strikingly different conclusions (Leizorovicz, Haugh, Chapuis et al., 1992; Nurmohamed et al., 1992).

**Be Aware of Your Biases as a Reader.** Lord, Ross, and Lepper (1979) showed two supposedly new studies to people with opposing views on capital punishment. One study supported and one refuted the idea that capital punishment deters crime. The studies had different methodologies. Subjects were more impressed with the study that supported their initial beliefs and more critical of the other study. At the end, their original beliefs had become more firmly entrenched. Similarly, Pyszczynski, Greenberg, and Holt (1985) told subjects that they had done well or poorly on a test and then showed them two studies, one offering a positive and one a negative assessment of the test. Subjects told they had done well reported that the positive study was methodologically sounder; the other subjects favored the negative study.

Kunda (1987) asked four groups of subjects—men and women, half of whom were heavy caffeine consumers and half light consumers—to read an article claiming that caffeine poses serious health dangers for women. The women heavy consumers, the only ones threatened by the article, were less convinced than any of the other groups. In another study, Sherman and Kunda (1989) asked heavy and light caffeine consumers to read an article. Half in each group read that caffeine hastens the progress of a serious disease, and half read that caffeine retards the disease's progress. Subjects threatened by the article (heavy consumers who read that caffeine hastens the disease's progress, light consumers who read that caffeine retards it) rated various methodological aspects of the study as less sound than did nonthreatened subjects.

## Read Creatively

■ Search for flaws in published papers. Even data gathered with insufficient rigor may be provocative. If the topic interests you, do a similar study without the flaws.

■ If two studies conflict in data or interpretations, resolve the conflict by designing a new study that pits alternative predictions against each other.

■ Pay attention to results that do not seem to make sense. Scrutinize individual research reports for data points that are unusually extreme (outliers) and entire fields for aberrant individual findings. These may suggest new directions for investigation. W. Humphreys (1968) wrote that "both the logical structure of scientific theories and their historical evolution are organized around the identification, clarification, and explanation of anomalies."

■ Theories have testable consequences. Deduce a consequence and test it.

■ Discussion sections of research articles often suggest still unanswered questions and possible follow-up studies. Many journals have comments sections in which researchers and their critics debate the legitimacy of procedures and interpretations. Read them for ideas.

■ Consider testing the generalizability of a study. Would additional work with different kinds of subjects, settings, or ways of measuring variables be profitable?

Library research can be creative and important. Swanson (1991) noted that scientific specialties tend to develop independently of one another with little interdisciplinary communication. Possible interconnections between them, which increase exponentially in number with each new scientific finding, go undiscovered as the specialties become mutually isolated. For example, journal 1 may publish several articles documenting irrefutably that treatment A leads to result B, and journal 2 may publish equally convincing articles showing that B is associated with an improvement in disease syndrome C. But because nobody reads both journals, nobody draws the obvious inference that treatment A would help disease syndrome C.

Swanson (1990, 1991) called such information undiscovered public knowledge and suggested heuristics for uncovering it. Library, not laboratory, research led him to propose treating Raynaud's syndrome with dietary fish oils and migraine headaches with magnesium supplements. Subsequent clinical and laboratory tests supported him. More recently, Swanson and Smalheiser (1997) developed an interactive software program that can be accessed from the Internet (http://kiwi.uchicago.edu/index.html). The program, based on the premise that information developed in one area of research can be of value in another area without anyone being aware of the fact, extends (although it does not replace) conventional database searching.

# Conflicts of Interest and Bias

*By the time you finish reading this chapter, you should be able to answer the following questions:*

What are the three safeguards that are supposed to protect against misinformation in science?

Almost all scientific research requires funding. What types of biases do funding sources have?

Peer reviewers read scientific proposals to decide which get funded. Other peer reviewers read submissions to scientific journals to decide which get published. Why are critics unhappy with the peer-review process?

What incentives do some scientists have to distort the truth?

When fraud is discovered, how does the scientific community deal with it?

What are replications, and are they encouraged?

What types of pressures exist on the media to distort scientific findings?

■  ■  ■  ■  ■

*"Most of the major figures in drug research serve as consultants to drug firms and, at the same time, to NIMH and the Food and Drug Administration, which licenses the drugs. They review each other's grant proposals, sit on the same committees, work on the same studies, write for each other's journals. NIMH employees collaborate with drug-company consultants in mental health research; NIMH consultants appear before FDA review committees on behalf of drug companies; editors of journals heavily supported by drug-company advertising serve on "impartial" FDA committees reviewing the safety and efficacy of medication produced by their advertisers."* P. Schrag (1978)

Imagine a headline in tomorrow's newspaper: MIRACLE DRUG DOUBLES LEARNING ABILITY IN RATS. Suppose the story told of an experiment in which drugged rats learned a complex task twice as quickly as untreated controls. Impulsive readers might bombard their physicians or pharmacists with prescription requests. Cautious ones would note that people are not rats, while sophisticates might track down the original article to check for flaws. But only the most cynical would question the integrity of the study's authors and suggest that the results might have been achieved dishonestly. Unless an ulterior motive is obvious, as when a scientist testifies as an expert witness in a courtroom and favors the side paying him, scientists are largely exempt from accusations of playing loose with the truth. By contrast, when salespeople expound on the virtues of their products or lawyers proclaim the innocence of their clients or politicians tell us that all hope of global peace and prosperity will vanish unless they are elected, we recognize that their arguments may be colored by self-interest.

According to the model presented in textbooks, three safeguards protect against the persistence of false, inaccurate, or misleading data and interpretations. First, to secure funding for their projects, scientists must submit proposals that are evaluated by experts. Competition for funds is stiff, so only the most well-designed studies receive support. Second, completed work is written up and sent off to journals, where reviewers decide whether the work is worthy of publication. Third, other scientists try to replicate interesting results, and failed replications lead to the correction of misleading information.

Yet while in graduate school I learned that textbook discussions of proper methodology omit a great deal. I occasionally sat in with the research group of James Olds, a brilliant scientist whose weekly meetings with his graduate students often included free-ranging discussions of re-

---

Author's Note: The trust accorded to scientists is partially justified. Science attracts people who enjoy trying to unravel the mysteries of nature, and this requires devotion to truth. Almost certainly (though we cannot know for sure), the vast majority of scientists are honest people dedicated to their work. They will be unfairly tarnished by this chapter, and for that I apologize.

cently published research. During one session I brashly and inadvisably criticized the methodology of a study that Olds had praised. He called me aside afterward, put a paternal hand on my shoulder, and said that he knew all the researchers personally (the field was much smaller then). He trusted some, distrusted others, and judged their research accordingly. Their scientific writing, other than conclusions and a broad description of methods, was in his view largely irrelevant.

Though disconcerting, Olds's remarks should be taken seriously. A substantial literature exists on ESP, astrology, dowsing, recording of emotions in plants, telekinesis, homeopathic medicine, color therapy, and so on, including many articles with methodology sections that are paragons of scientific virtue. Yet mainstream scientists ignore or discount them.

Bias is not all bad. When Mitroff (1974) interviewed scientists working on the Apollo moon project, one man, representative of most in the group, commented: "I wouldn't like scientists to be without bias since a lot of the sides of the argument would never be presented. We must be emotionally committed to the things we do energetically. No one is able to do anything with liberal energy if there is no emotion connected with it" (p. 65).

But bias is often bad. The safeguards of science are not inviolable, and "facts" are influenced by many variables that do not show up in research reports. Potential conflicts arise even prior to conception of a research project and continue through every step of the way, up to and including presentation of the final results in the media.

## ■ FUNDING SOURCES

Almost all scientific research requires financial support, so funding sources control what gets studied. Federal government agencies are the major source of funding for U.S. science, but corporate support has increased from less than $5 million in 1974 to hundreds of millions in the early 1990s (Haber, 1996). With the goal of improving sales, drug companies sponsor research to explore new uses for company products rather than to identify potential adverse effects. About three fourths of their research money goes toward developing insignificant variants of existing drugs. Dozens of virtually identical decongestants are already on the market (and dozens of penicillins, beta-blockers, cephalosporins, etc.), but companies would rather develop their own versions of these products than fund research on new possibly life-saving drugs with limited sales potential. Companies rarely sponsor research on unpatentable substances such as vitamins and herbs.

In comparisons of new drugs with traditional therapies, 43% of studies funded by a drug company, and only 13% of studies funded from other sources, favored the new drug (Davidson, 1986). New drugs are protected by patent, so the drug companies prefer having them turn out to be superior.

Furthermore, no drug manufactured by the sponsoring company was found to be inferior to an alternative product manufactured by another company.

Federal government agencies also have well-defined objectives. Organizations such as the National Institute on Drug Abuse grant far more money for studying adverse rather than beneficial effects of drugs. Because research money for studying gases came primarily from the military, scientists learned more about nerve gases than about safer ones. As a result, when electronics companies needed a special atmosphere for clean manufacturing, the deadly nerve gases were used because they were the only ones for which appropriate information existed.

The Center for Indoor Air Research (CIAR) is financed by the tobacco industry. CIAR funds peer-reviewed projects that are evaluated on their merits by independent scientists. CIAR also funds projects that are awarded directly by tobacco industry executives. These special-reviewed projects are more likely to be related to secondhand smoke, to support the tobacco industry position, and to be used to argue that smoking should not be regulated in public places. Barnes and Bero (1996) speculated that CIAR finances peer-reviewed projects only to enhance its credibility so that readers will regard the special-reviewed projects more favorably.

Some corporations award funds on the condition that research results cannot be published without their approval. Then they suppress unsatisfactory results. The British pharmaceutical company Boots manufactures Synthroid™, the first synthetic thyroid drug. Introduced in 1958, Synthroid™ had by the 1990s captured 84% of the U.S. market for drugs to control hypothyroidism. Then three much cheaper generics began making inroads into Boots's sales, so Boots awarded a $250,000 grant to a team of researchers to compare Synthroid™ with the rivals, fully expecting Synthroid™ to come out on top. But when the researchers found that all four drugs were essentially interchangeable and submitted a paper for publication, Boots cited the contract forbidding publication of the findings without Boots's approval, and Boots refused to approve. Fortunately for the many people who need hypothyroid medication, the researchers reported their findings to the *Wall Street Journal*.

Funding sources may suppress both original research and reviews of research that support unpopular positions. The February 21, 1998, edition of *New Scientist* featured an article entitled "What the WHO doesn't want you to know about marijuana." The authors claimed that a World Health Organization panel of experts concluded that marijuana is much more benign than alcohol, and the comparison was due to be published in December 1997. But, according to a document leaked to *New Scientist*, advisers from the National Institute on Drug Abuse and the UN International Drug Control Programme pressured the WHO into withdrawing the document.

Epstein (1998) documented how priorities of the National Cancer Institute and American Cancer Society (ACS) have impeded efforts to prevent various cancers. The ACS receives substantial financial support from large corporations that discharge known and potential pollutants into the environment. A consequence is that the ACS largely ignores those pollutants while focusing on research on new (patentable) drugs to fight cancer and on lifestyles that increase cancer risk.

In the 1990s, several juries awarded multimillion-dollar settlements to women who had received breast implants and then suffered a variety of painful ailments. In 1994, to forestall further suits, seven manufacturers offered a class-action settlement to women who had undergone breast implantation. On June 16, 1994, one day before the deadline for plaintiffs to accept the offer, *The New England Journal of Medicine* published a Mayo Clinic study that found no link between breast implants and connective tissue diseases. A second study done at the University of Michigan found no link between implants and sclerodoma, a potentially fatal illness. In addition to criticizing both studies on methodological grounds, the plaintiffs' attorneys raised conflict-of-interest issues. They expressed suspicion about the timing of the Mayo Clinic study and claimed that it was secretly funded by implant manufacturers. Dow Corning, a onetime implant manufacturer, funded the Michigan study.

Easterbrook et al. (1991) and Dickersin et al. (1992) did follow-ups on approved research proposals. Of 285 studies approved by one research ethics committee between 1984 and 1987 that had been completed and analyzed, 138 had been published by 1990. A smaller proportion of drug-company–sponsored studies were published than those supported by government or voluntary organizations. Easterbrook and Dickersin and their colleagues cited data management by these companies as a reason for nonpublication, inferring that drug companies discourage publication of studies they have funded that have negative results.

Because funding is their lifeblood, scientists learn to slant proposals to suit the donor agencies. A scientist interested in studying the mating habits of butterflies might include in her proposal an experiment on the effects of nerve gas on butterfly mating. To get money to study cognitive differences in spatial perception, she might add a section on how hypothyroidism affects spatial perception. Scientists who do not play along are likely to find their money cut off.

## ■ PEER REVIEW OF PROPOSALS FOR FUNDING

Whether corporate or government, funding agencies want their money to yield dividends, so they choose expert scientists (peer reviewers) to evaluate and rank applications according to merit. Critics have claimed that the peer review process is biased toward familiar authors, theories, methods, and topics (cf. Broad & Wade, 1982; Chubin & Hackett, 1990; Harcum & Rosen, 1993). When there is a range of opinions about a topic, grants are most often given to people holding a position in the middle (the position most of the referees hold). So experienced applicants try to propose safe research—continuations of work for which they have previously received grants or even work they have already completed but not yet published.

Kraus (1994) cited a report that applications from researchers under 36 years of age for National Institutes of Health funding declined about 55% between 1985 and 1993. Young applicants have a relatively low rate of success in obtaining funds, which she attributed to their greater likelihood of presenting new and original viewpoints. Their high failure rate sends a message that existing views should not be challenged. Because dissent and innovation are discouraged, progress in science is retarded.

Chubin and Hackett (1990, p. 80) noted that

> the pool of appropriate reviewers may shrink to include only those likely to have a conflict of interest because they are so close to the proposer (as collaborators or colleagues). Selecting reviewers from outside this pool would invite an incompetent, incomplete, or inappropriate review, yet within the circle friendships, rivalries, and professional relations jeopardize the character and quality of reviews.

Reviewers may be reluctant to offer constructive criticism, because that would strengthen the proposals of their rivals.

Peer reviewers have stolen the ideas of applicants. Two chemists plagiarized grant applications they had reviewed (Zurer, 1993a); one reviewer received a proposal plagiarized from an earlier proposal of his (Zurer, 1993b); and a Nobel Prize–winning chemist no longer puts his most original ideas in his proposals: "I hold back anything that another investigator might hop on and carry out. When I was starting out, people respected each other's research more than they do today, and there was less stealing of ideas" (quoted in Browne, 1989, pp. C1, 14).

Krimsky, Ennis, and Weissman (1991) developed a database of scientists on biology faculties in U.S. universities who also had a formal tie, such as a managerial position, with a biotechnology firm. Then they obtained a list of potential and actual peer reviewers for the National Science Foundation. Of the 832 scientists in the database, 343 reviewed at least one proposal during the 2-year period covered by the study. Krimsky et al. noted that unethical reviewers can channel innovative proposal ideas to commercial enterprises with which they have ties; this compromises the whole process.

# ■ INDIVIDUAL SCIENTISTS

## Examples

Conflicts of interest often lead to misrepresentation and even complete fabrication of results—in short, fraud. Broad and Wade (1982) documented many cases of fraud and then suggested that three factors influence its frequency of occurrence: the potential rewards, the perceived chances of getting caught, and the personal ethics of scientists. Scientists' ethics, they argued, are no different from those of other members of society. Because access to laboratories and data is restricted, the only people close enough to suspect misconduct are likely to be friends of or collaborators with the perpetrator, with no power or inclination to investigate. So the chance of getting caught is minuscule. Most frauds have been uncovered by accident. The other factor is rewards, which are in many cases both direct and substantial. Several people who conduct clinical tests of drugs are paid by the drug manufacturers and gross more than $1 million a year (Kohn, 1986).

Drugs called calcium channel blockers are used to treat spasms in the heart. In the mid-1990s, following the publication of three studies suggesting that the drugs increase the risk of death from heart attack, a vigorous debate erupted within the medical literature between critics and defenders of calcium channel blockers. Stelfox, Chua, O'Rourke, and Detsky (1998) identified 70 articles and letters related to the controversy and sent surveys to the 89 authors asking them about their financial relationships with manufacturers of calcium channel blockers. Ninety-six percent of the authors who had written in support of the drugs, 60% of neutral authors, and 37% of critics reported financial relationships. Only two of the articles mentioned the author's financial relationships.

Barnes and Bero (1998) identified 106 reviews of the health effects of passive smoking published from 1980 to 1995. Of the 39 reviews that concluded that passive smoking is not harmful to health, 31 were written by authors who had affiliations with the tobacco industry. Three quarters of the articles failed to disclose the sources of funding for the research. The authors inferred that "the tobacco industry may be attempting to influence scientific opinion by flooding the scientific literature with large numbers of review articles supporting its position that passive smoking is not harmful to health."

Of nearly 800 articles in major medical and biomedical journals analyzed by Krimsky, Rothenberg, Stott, and Kyle (1996), 34% listed at least one author affiliated with a nonprofit academic or research institution who also had a financial interest in the research. The relationships with industry were almost never mentioned, so unsuspecting readers were likely to assume that the authors were unbiased. Krimsky et al. gave several reasons for suspecting that their data underestimate the problem.

Reasons other than immediate financial gain may lead a scientist to hope that results will turn out one way rather than another. The cliché "publish or perish" accurately describes hiring and promotion policies at many institutions around the world. Scientists are expected to be productive, and the primary criterion is publication in respected journals. At some universities, five or six young faculty are hired for each tenure-track position, and at the end of a few years only the most productive is offered a permanent job. Recognition, prestige, and prizes also go to prolific publishers.

One unintended consequence is that few scientists, especially untenured ones, do longitudinal research (studying the same subjects over many years). Although longitudinal studies may offer unique insights, the payoff is too far in the future to meet the publication needs of most scientists.

Personal biases influence experimental outcomes, as can be inferred from inspecting the collected works of scientists. In areas of controversy, unbiased researchers might be expected to find both confirmatory and dis-confirmatory evidence for a particular position. More typically, the most productive scientists report results exclusively on one side of the contro-versy. Pastore (1949) reported an almost perfect relationship between scien-tists' advocacy of conservative philosophies and research that emphasized hereditary influences on behavior, and between liberal philosophies and emphasis on environmental factors. He wrote, "This inner relationship sug-gests that it would be as reasonable to classify the nature-nurture contro-versy as sociological in nature as to classify it as scientific in nature." Similarly, biographical data of psychologists accurately predicted how the psychologists had interpreted studies on racial differences in IQ scores (Sherwood & Nataupsky, 1968). Gould (1981) documented many instances of both (possibly) unintentional and clearly intentional bias perpetrated by leading psychologists in the intelligence testing field. The bias, which had and continues to have profound effects on educational practices and the self-esteem of many people, "proved" that white men are superior to men of other races and to women.

Two men with towering reputations, a British psychologist and a Vi-ennese emigrant to the United States who practiced psychiatry, were ex-posed as frauds after their deaths. Cyril Burt became famous in the 1920s for his research on the inheritance of intelligence. He gained considerable influ-ence on educational matters and helped set up a system for segregating British students based on their IQ scores. After Burt's death in 1971, psy-chologist Leon Kamin scrutinized his data and became suspicious. Burt had calculated the average correlation between IQ scores of pairs of twins who had been separated shortly after birth. He subsequently located two addi-tional sets of pairs and calculated new correlations. The three correlation co-efficients were identical to the third decimal point, as were his reported correlations of twins reared together in three separate studies. Such results are extremely implausible. A reporter for London's *Sunday Times* failed to locate two people named in Burt's articles as his collaborators and who had signed several reviews praising him (in the *British Journal of Statistical Psychology*, which Burt edited). Burt's housekeeper acknowledged that he frequently used pseudonyms, and the reporter concluded that the "collabo-rators" had never existed.

Bruno Bettelheim developed an international reputation for restoring severely disturbed children, especially autistic ones, to normal lives. He blamed autism on bad mothering. In his best-selling 1967 book *The Empty*

*Fortress,* Bettelheim wrote that "the precipitating factor in infantile autism is the parent's wish that his child should not exist." He compared parents of autistic children to devouring witches, infanticidal kings, and SS guards in concentration camps. The accusations, which caused thousands of parents tremendous guilt and anguish, had no evidentiary support.

Pollak (1997), on the basis of documents and interviews with people who had known, worked with, and been patients of Bettelheim, wrote a damning biography. He revealed Bettelheim's lies about the extent of his university training, awards, and authorship of books. Bettelheim claimed to have cared for an autistic girl in his Vienna home, so Pollak interviewed her. She had lived in his house but was not autistic and had received care exclusively from his wife. Bettelheim claimed an 85% cure rate for his autistic children. That too was false, even though most of the children had been neither severely disturbed nor autistic. Moreover, many of them reported that they had been subjected to physical brutality and sexual abuse.

For more than three decades, Rosenthal (1963, 1977, 1994) has studied experimenter bias. He found an error rate in published data of about 1%, with more than 70% of the errors favoring the researcher's hypothesis. Rosenthal told some students that they would be training rats bred for brightness and others that their rats had been bred for dullness. Although the rats did not differ genetically, those labeled bright learned faster. The relevance of his work to humans was shown in a second study, when he gave the names (chosen at random) of 20% of the children at an elementary school to their teachers. He said they had scored exceptionally well on a test for intellectual blooming and were anticipated to show remarkable gains in intellectual competence during the next eight school months. They did. By the school year's end, the selected children showed a significantly greater IQ gain than did controls. Moreover, teachers rated them as more interesting, curious, happy, adjusted, affectionate, and appealing. Some of the control children also gained in IQ, but the more an individual undesignated child gained, the more she or he was regarded as less well adjusted, interesting, and affectionate.

So how serious is the problem of scientific misconduct? In my view, there is no justification for attaching the word "educated" to "guesses." How can we estimate the total number of cheaters when our primary information is the number of cheaters who have been caught? Nevertheless, several people have given estimates. Daniel Koshland (1987), editor of *Science,* acknowledged that scientists occasionally cheat but added that the vast majority of reports are accurate and truthful. At the other end of the estimation spectrum, Broad and Wade (1982) guessed that for each case of major fraud uncovered (more than one per year for the last 30 years), about 100,000 major and minor ones go undetected.

The little relevant information is not reassuring. Swazey et al. (1993) surveyed 4,000 graduate students and faculty members at 99 large graduate departments. Forty-four percent of student and 50% of faculty respondents reported having direct evidence of two or more types of misconduct and questionable research practices by their teachers or colleagues. In June 1992, the Office of Research Integrity (ORI) was established to investigate misconduct findings. ORI deals only with cases involving research supported by U.S. Public Health Services funds or applications for such funds. By September 1994, ORI had found 27 people guilty of scientific misconduct. The 14 misconduct findings in 1997 equaled the annual average since 1992. During the first 6 months of 1998, ORI opened 21 new cases (ORI, 1994, 1999a, 1999b).

The problem is international. The editors of several British journals set up a Committee on Publication Ethics (COPE) after one of them encountered four cases of misconduct in his first year as editor (*eBMJ*, 1998). Frank Wells set up a private agency to investigate possible cases of research misconduct and said that his agency is constantly busy. Since 1989, Wells has reported 17 cases to the General Medical Council; all resulted in findings of serious professional misconduct. The agency has another 12 cases pending. Philip Fulford (1998), the editor of *Journal of Bone and Joint Surgery*, said, "Fraud now seems to be endemic in many scientific disciplines and in most countries. Recent cases have attracted media attention, but these are probably only the tip of an unpleasant iceberg."

Even after documented fraud, the self-correcting mechanisms of science work slowly. Between May 1997 and May 1998, several committees concluded that two scientists had invented data for 47 scientific articles published in 19 journals. By late 1998, only two of the journals had retracted the articles. Most journals do not retract articles unless the relevant author agrees to do so, and some journals require the consent of every coauthor. The journal *Blood* asked one of the authors, the only person authorized to annul his publications, to retract seven articles. He did not respond to the request (*BMJ*, 1998).

Retracted articles should be regarded as invalid but may nevertheless be favorably cited. Budd, Slevert, and Schultz (1998) located 235 retracted articles from 1966 to 1997 in the MEDLINE database. Ninety-one had been retracted because of error, 86 because of scientific misconduct, 38 because the author(s) could not replicate the results, and 20 for unclassifiable reasons. Budd et al. then used *Science Citation Index* to count the number of citations to the retracted articles that appeared in journals indexed in the *Abridged Index Medicus* after the retraction had been in print for at least a year. They found 299 citations to the retracted articles, and the vast majority either explicitly or implicitly treated the retracted article as valid.

Wrongdoers who are caught, prosecuted, and convicted generally face fairly mild punishments. A typical punishment is forfeiture of the right to participate in any federal contracts for 3 years. Whistleblowers, by contrast, often suffer severe consequences. Many have been transferred, fired, or subjected to such intense verbal abuse and isolation that they have resigned. Many have suffered severe financial loss and deterioration of health (Lennane, 1995).

Goodstein (1991) wrote with a more optimistic perspective than mine. He noted that scientific papers omit many details, including false steps, blind alleys, and outright mistakes, because the researcher's goal is to put results in proper perspective. Such behavior is not fraud, which occurs only if the procedures needed to replicate the results or the results themselves are knowingly misrepresented. Real fraud is almost always found in the biomedical sciences, never in fields such as physics or astronomy or geology. The reason is that biological organisms are variable, so identical procedures may not give identical results. This provides some cover for a biologist tempted to cheat. Woolf (1988) found that 21 of 26 cases made public between 1980 and 1986 came from biomedical science, two from chemistry and biochemistry, one from physiology, and the other two from psychology. Many of the cases involved physicians who regarded the welfare of their patients as more important than scientific truth.

Goodstein was unimpressed by the *American Scientist* study. Although the important measure of scientific misconduct is how often scientists falsify data, the authors used the term to encompass the relatively minor misdeeds of keeping poor research records and violating government regulations. Few respondents reported directly witnessing more serious misbehaviors even once or twice. Furthermore, respondents are probably not representative of the whole group. Goodstein added that science, always (until recently) a purely intellectual competition, has become an intense competition for scarce research funds resources, and he made an ominous prediction: This competition will continue and will negatively affect scientists' ethical behavior, leading to more instances of scientific fraud.

## ■ ARTICLES PUBLISHED WITHOUT PEER REVIEW

To become part of public knowledge, findings must be published. As the Internet grows, people have increasing access to reports of questionable value. Some, written in the format of scientific papers, are presented with the intent of persuading readers to buy products. Misrepresentations are deliberate and commonplace. Other contributors have more benign motives, but the Internet provides no mechanism for checking the accuracy of their data or inferences.

Researchers sometimes present preliminary, nonrefereed results at meetings. They hope to get feedback from other scientists or lay the groundwork for continuing financial support. Media reports of such research rarely indicate their incompleteness.

Several journals publish mostly peer-reviewed articles, but they also publish special supplementary issues under the aegis of corporate sponsors. Unwary readers may not distinguish between the two. Furthermore, nonpeer-reviewed articles may be listed in bibliographic databanks.

## ■ PEER REVIEW OF ARTICLES SUBMITTED FOR PUBLICATION

The only journals that most scientists take seriously are peer reviewed. Authors who wish to publish in peer-reviewed journals submit manuscripts to editors, who send them to experts for review. The reviewers evaluate the research and recommend for or against publication. Although peer review ensures that the work meets certain minimal standards, many criticisms of the grant evaluation process apply with equal force to reviews of articles submitted for publication. Leading scientists are aware of the problems and have held several international conferences to find ways to improve the process. The July 15, 1998, issue of the *Journal of the American Medical Association (JAMA)* includes 33 articles from the most recent conference.

### Editors

Journal editors are the first people to read submissions and can reject them summarily or forward them to reviewers with pronounced favorable or unfavorable biases. Bernard (1982, p. 202) quoted the editor of the *American Anthropologist*: "It is really quite simple for me as an editor to guarantee that an article will be killed by referees. All I need to do is to select referees I know can be trusted to clobber a particular manuscript."

Because many journals are subsidized by industry, research critical of an industry product may create editorial discomfort. Seymour Fisher (7/23/1995; 9/7/1995; 9/20/1995) posted a series of articles on the Internet describing what he believes was a clear case of editorial misfeasance. Fisher submitted a manuscript indicating that the drug sertraline (Zoloft™) induces many adverse reactions. Although the three reviews were favorable, the journal's editor raised (what Fisher claims were inappropriate) barriers that delayed publication until 14 months after acceptance. Fisher reviewed 119 articles published in the journal from July 1993 through April 1995 and reported a mean lag time from acceptance to publication of 8 months. No other article had a lag time of as much as 12 months. Fisher thought it no coincidence that Pfizer Incorporated, which heavily subsidizes the journal to which he submitted the paper, manufactures Zoloft™. Fisher claimed that his experience is not unique and that he can document pharmaceutical company influences on National Institute of Health funding.

Industry money can corrupt editorials about research. A pharmaceutical manufacturer representative asked Troyen Brennan (1994, p. 673) to write an editorial for a medical journal: "The caller said that I would not really have to do much work on this project. I would discuss the matter with them, and they would then have a professional writer compose the editorial, which I could modify as I saw fit. I would earn $2,500 for what was estimated to be several hours of work." Brennan reviewed copies of other editorials the firm had commissioned. The few that acknowledged industry support did so in such a way that readers were likely to misconstrue the true nature of the support. Brennan wrote:

> Reading that editorial at the time of its publication, I had assumed the acknowledgment meant that at one time or another the author had received support from the drug company for a clinical trial. With this new information, the editorial seemed part of a deliberate strategy to change the opinion of readers, a goal that was also suggested by the memorandum [from the public relations firm] that accompanied the articles. The memorandum stated, "We are providing these materials to you in confidence, as we do not generally divulge the specific nature of projects conducted on behalf of our clients."

Editors of journals that publish book reviews choose the reviewers. In her book *Living Downstream: An Ecologist Looks at Cancer and the Environment*, Steingraber (1997) asserted that cancer rates are on the rise because of industrial and environmental pollutants. Berke (1997) blasted the book in the *New England Journal of Medicine* as "an environmental polemic and an unapologetic call to arms" (p. 1562). Berke is medical director of W. R. Grace, a chemical company accused of polluting drinking water in Boston and contaminating soils in Maryland. The review does not mention his affiliation. *NEJM*'s editor in chief called publication of Berke's review an oversight. In an earlier oversight in the August 29, 1996, issue, the same journal published an editorial that maintained that the risk of obesity outweighs the dangers of appetite suppressant drugs. Only after publication did the editors learn that the experts they had solicited to write the editorial had been paid consultants for companies that manufacture appetite suppressant drugs. In the February 24, 2000 issue of the *New England Journal of Medicine*, the editors reported that they had reviewed their files on drug therapy articles published since January 1, 2000. They found 18 instances in which one or more authors of the articles received major research support from relevant companies or served as consultants for those companies at the time they were invited to prepare their articles.

## Reviewers

Reviewers are unpaid, and many are either unqualified or do not take their work sufficiently seriously. Cicchetti (1982, 1991) and Marsh and Ball (1989) reported that referee agreement in judgments about manuscripts is not much better than chance. Bornstein (1991, p. 139) wrote, "Peer review fails miserably with respect to every technical criterion for establishing the reliability and validity of an assessment instrument."

Mahoney (1977) sent manuscripts describing a fictitious experiment to 75 reviewers for one scientific journal. Their judgments about its quality were strongly influenced by whether or not the study supported their own theoretical perspectives. Similarly, Ernst and Resch (1994) identified 33 authors of research papers that had reported data either clearly favorable or clearly unfavorable to the effectiveness of transcutaneous electrical nerve stimulation (TENS). Without telling the authors they were being tested, Ernst and Resch asked them to review a fictitious, flawed scientific paper showing a TENS-induced reduction of pain in certain patients. The 16 who sent back reviews showed low interrater reliability. Furthermore, pro-TENS referees judged the paper significantly more favorably than anti-TENS referees.

Godlee et al. (cited by Smith, 1997) inserted eight deliberate errors into a paper about to be published in the *British Medical Journal* and sent the paper to 420 potential reviewers. The 221 respondents spotted a median of two errors, nobody spotted more than five, and 16% did not spot any. Callaham, Baxt, Waeckerle, and Wears (1998) sent a fictitious manuscript containing 10 major and 13 minor flaws to reviewers who, during the same period, also reviewed 2,143 genuine manuscripts. They detected a mean of 3.4 of the major flaws and 3.1 of the minor ones. (For their prior work, the reviewers had received a mean rating from editors of 3.65 on a scale ranging from 1 [poor] to 5 [excellent]).

Nylenna et al. (1994) sent two fictitious manuscripts, one in English and the other in the national language, to 180 Scandinavian referees. Each manuscript had several methodological flaws. Judgments about manuscript quality were influenced by the age and experience of the referees and the language of the manuscript. Link (1998) reported that both U.S. and non-U.S. reviewers evaluated papers submitted by U.S. authors more favorably.

Wilson, DePaulo, Mook, and Klaaren (1993) wrote brief descriptions of six pairs of seriously flawed fictitious research studies. Each pair of studies was identical except that one version dealt with an important topic, for example, the relationship between moderate alcohol drinking and cardiovascular disease, and the other with an unimportant topic, for example, the relationship between moderate alcohol drinking and heartburn. Packets containing the important versions of three studies and unimportant versions of the other three were sent to medical school faculty and research scientists. Many had served as editors of scientific journals. Asked to judge the publishability of each study in their packet, they recommended significantly more of the important versions. Asked to judge methodological rigor, they detected fewer flaws in the important versions.

Harvard physician John Darsee committed fraud on a colossal scale. He published nearly 100 papers in 2 years, most based on forged data.

Stewart and Feder (1987) examined 18 of his articles and found errors in all but two. One paper had 28 errors, one had 39, and 12 had at least 10 errors detectable from the text alone. Yet the papers had passed the scrutiny of reviewers and editors.

# ■ REPLICATION

Hersen and Barlow (1976) called replication "the heart of any science." But the assumption that fraud and error are inevitably followed by publication of failed replications is false. Exact replications are difficult and, in the social and medical sciences, impossible: Researchers must either use different subjects or the same subjects, now older and more experienced. The experimenter, date, place, and other potentially significant factors are rarely identical from one study to the next. Amir and Shamon (1991) reported that in the majority of 35 randomly selected studies from psychology journals, the methodology sections were not detailed enough to permit replication. The editors of *Science* (1992) wrote that, to be accepted for publication, research articles must present original data that point to a new breakthrough in the field. In short, replication studies are unwelcome in *Science* and many other scientific journals.

Neuliep and Crandall (1990, 1993) surveyed journal editors and reviewers. Nearly 94% of editors discouraged replication studies, and 42% reported that no replication study had ever been submitted to their journal. One editor commented that replication studies represent the worst of the publish or perish mentality. Ninety-two percent of reviewers had never reviewed a direct replication and only one had recommended a direct replication for publication.

The problem is not quite as bad as it seems, because good research stimulates further research and the offshoots usually require similar apparatus and procedures. Thus, a continuing line of research is essentially a series of partial replications. Conversely, exciting research with no published follow-ups suggests the possibility that replications have failed.

# ■ THE MEDIA

Prominent astronomer Carl Sagan noted shortly before his death that "almost every newspaper in America has a daily astrology column. Most do not even have a weekly science column." Yet despite their limited coverage, the media have a huge impact on laypeople's views of science. For example, surveyors found that 64% of people get their information about cancer prevention from magazines, 60% from newspapers, and 58% from television

(Nelkin, 1987). Most probably assume that science stories are bias-free. But scientific discoveries and controversies often have political or economic ramifications, and media outlets with leftist, rightist, business, or environmental leanings slant their coverage accordingly. Lowe (1998) cited Brian Trench, who concluded, after comparing reports of the same story in major Irish, French, German, Spanish, and British newspapers, that readers of different papers might not realize they were reading about the same research. Dowie (1998) argued that influential *New York Times* science reporter Gina Kolata (and by extension, the *Times*) is anti-environment and pro-corporate in her approach to scientific inquiry. He supported his position by analyzing her articles on AIDS research, silicone breast implants, breast cancer, food irradiation, and environmental hormones.

Articles published in scientific journals are read primarily by trained professionals, whereas newspaper, magazine, and television accounts of the articles reach a much greater audience. Conventional wisdom is not newsworthy, so the media play on public fears while emphasizing the frontiers and fringes of science. Reporters with limited scientific training and under severe time constraints sometimes use just one source and thus present just one point of view (Simons, 1987). They fail to distinguish between preliminary findings, conference reports, small pilot studies, and more substantial works. They compress lengthy, complex articles into brief stories or 60-second time slots, omitting important details in the process. They prefer definitive answers, which leads to speculations beyond what the data warrant (Nelkin, 1987). Not surprisingly, the overwhelming majority of 670 scientists who responded to a survey said that few in the media understand the nature of science and technology (Hartz & Chappell, 1997). Only 11% said they had a great deal of confidence in the press, and 22% said they had hardly any confidence at all.

Editors issue press releases in advance of publication to alert reporters to potentially interesting stories. De Semir, Ribas, and Revuelta (1998) found that 84% of news stories that mentioned journal articles cited articles mentioned in press releases. But whereas scientists regard results cautiously, reporters often accept them uncritically. Deary, Whiteman, and Fowkes (1998) described the media's handling of one study. The authors of the study concluded that a submissive personality may protect against nonfatal heart attacks, especially in women. But the study cautioned that the effects of personality on the development of coronary heart disease needed further study. *The Lancet*'s press release was similarly restrained: "The finding indicates, the researchers conclude, that it is important for scientists studying heart disease to look at a wide variety of psychological risk factors." But the headline in the *Daily Telegraph* ran, "Put down that rolling pin, darling, it's bad for your heart."

Vendors of scientific products capitalize on reporters' quotas and deadlines. The vendors' public relations departments produce and distribute press kits, including entire scripts, for television science reporters. Their slick video news releases, essentially lengthy commercials, are more compelling than most reporters' best efforts and are often shown in their entirety, masquerading as news. Schwitzer (1992) cited a survey of 2,500 editors and reporters that found that 90% of ideas for health articles had originated with a public relations person.

The media are answerable to their sponsors and to various external pressures. Richard Horton (1998), editor of *The Lancet*, wrote that Piers Morgan, editor of England's *Daily Mirror*, acknowledged that he bases his decisions on what to print on whether or not an article will sell. Health scares and breakthroughs sell; discussions of methodological flaws, qualifications, and uncertainties do not.

In 1996, Fox television station WTVT hired two award-winning reporters to produce a series on milk from cows treated with bovine growth hormone (rBGH). Evidence suggests that humans who drink such milk increase their risk of getting cancer. Three days before the series was scheduled to air, Monsanto lawyers sent a letter to Fox TV executives saying that Monsanto would suffer "enormous damage" if the series ran. After receiving a second letter warning of "dire consequences" for Fox if the series aired as it stood, WTVT canceled the series. Fox lawyers offered to edit the series and pay the two reporters if they would leave the station and keep silent. The reporters refused and were fired. In April 1998, they filed a lawsuit charging that WTVT violated its license from the Federal Communications Commission by demanding that they include known falsehoods in their rBGH series (*Rachel's Environment & Health Weekly*, 1998).

Gorman (1994) presented an interesting case study on both popular and professional reporting bias. He contrasted the receptions accorded to two studies published within 8 months of each other, both in respected journals on a similar topic. Swaab and Hofman (1990) reported that the suprachiasmatic nucleus of the hypothalamus is larger in homosexual than in heterosexual men, and LeVay (1991) that the third interstitial nucleus of the anterior hypothalamus is smaller in homosexual than in heterosexual men. In newspapers and nonspecialist magazines during the time period between December 1990 and March 1993, the three stories that mentioned Swaab's work were primarily about LeVay's. During the same period, LeVay was mentioned more than 100 times. A similar discrepancy occurred in citations in scientific journals.

The interstitial nucleus is larger in heterosexual men than in heterosexual women or homosexual men. The suprachiasmatic nucleus is equal in heterosexual men and women. Thus, LeVay's results appear to sustain the view, popular among scientists and laypeople alike, that homosexual men resemble heterosexual women more than they do heterosexual men. Swaab's work, supplemented by additional evidence from Gorman, disconfirms the popular view. Gorman's explanation for the unequal reception of the two articles is that scientists preferred support for their preconceived ideas and disregarded nonconfirmatory evidence.

## ■ OTHER TACTICS

Spiro (1999, p. 41) described the results of a study on a potential treatment for peptic ulcers:

> At the end of two weeks, the ulcer crater had healed in more than half the patients given the active drug and in only a third of patients taking placebos; that one observation point provided the desired statistical significance to permit the claim that the active drug, in this case cimetidine, "speeded the healing" of peptic ulcer....But at every other period of assessment, cimetidine and the placebo proved equally effective....Statisticians often select the best answers to magnify the claims for the agent.

It is safe to assume that drug research is not unique in that respect.

The Clearinghouse on Environmental Advocacy and Research (1997) described tactics used by corporate interests to resist passage of strong environmental protections. The corporations, which profit from lax regulations, have enlisted (and pay handsomely) a small group of scientists to denounce the scientific basis of environmental policy. They repeatedly condemn the work of environmentalists as "junk science," then argue that, as long as scientists disagree, the public interest is best served by holding off on costly regulations.

# Finding Interesting Problems and Studying Them Creatively

*By the time you finish reading this chapter, you should be able to answer the following questions:*

How do scientists get their ideas for research projects?

Should scientists read popular science magazines?

What strategies other than reading should people use to get ideas?

What are the features of good scientific questions?

What is meant by the statement that good scientific questions must be answerable empirically?

The question "What are the effects of stress on personality?" is not a good one. Why not?

What are the benefits of basic research?

What is a descriptive question?

What is a correlational question?

Which types of questions lead to deep analysis of phenomena?

What is meant by a ruthless test of a theory?

Why should scientists ask questions from multiple perspectives?

Why should psychologists pay attention to the evolutionary perspective?

■ ■ ■ ■ ■

*"If any student comes to me and says he wants to be useful to mankind and go into research to alleviate human suffering, I advise him to go into charity instead. Research wants real egotists who seek their own pleasure and satisfaction, but find it in solving the puzzles of nature."* Albert Szent-Györgi, Nobel Prize–winning biochemist

A former colleague of mine related his despair over the state of research in psychology. Having gone to the annual meeting of the American Psychological Association and being bored through an entire day of presentations, he conducted his own study by informally polling the 30 or so speakers about their reasons for doing research. Only one person mentioned fascination with a problem. The rest talked of status, requirements for doctoral dissertations, or publication pressures from their universities. He believed that his results illustrated a principle: Uninterested researchers tend to produce uninteresting research.

Interest starts with the problem. Merton (1973), summarizing his work with Nobel Prize winners, concluded:

> Almost invariably they (Nobel Laureates) lay great emphasis on the importance of problem-*finding*, not only problem-solving. They uniformly express the strong conviction that what matters most in their work is a developing sense of taste, of judgment, in seizing upon problems that are of fundamental importance.

Unlike solvers of crossword puzzles, who find problems printed daily in newspapers, and detectives who are handed theirs, practicing scientists must find their own. Much of a scientist's skill involves the ability to pick important, solvable problems, and much of his professional joy comes from intense involvement. Personal experiences may create involvement, as when a victim of chronic illness reads the medical literature for possible insights into cures or a marathoner speculates about runner's high.

## ■ BE ATTENTIVE TO BOTH ROUTINE AND UNUSUAL OCCURRENCES

Several research areas began with observations of people with unusual problems. Perhaps someone you know reacts strongly to a particular food or color or piece of music, and you want to find out why. Get in the habit of asking questions:

- ■ Why is my cat neurotic?
- ■ How can I help my friend stop gambling?
- ■ How can I conduct a fair test of astrology?

## ■ READ POPULAR MATERIALS

Reading stimulates ideas. Science columns of newspapers and magazines such as *Scientific American, Psychology Today, Science News,* and *Discover* offer articles about topical research. *Readers Guide to Periodical Literature* provides references to relevant articles. Textbooks introduce technical jargon and give a perspective from which to read more detailed material. This type of reading whets the appetite. Keep in mind that popular magazines may slant their coverage to avoid antagonizing advertisers. For example, magazines carrying cigarette ads were less likely than other magazines to publish articles on the risks of smoking (Warner, Goldenhar, & McLaughlin, 1992).

## ■ DON'T JUST READ

Kasperson (1978) reported that creative scientists place great store in information gathered at conventions and conferences. Unlike journal articles, convention presentations are interactive. Members of the audience can ask questions and make critical comments.

## ■ QUESTION

Asking meaningful and answerable questions is often the most important phase of research. Albert Einstein said, "The formulation of a problem is far more often essential than its solution, which may be merely a matter of mathematical or experimental skill. To raise new questions, new possibilities, to regard old problems from a new angle, requires creative imagination and marks real advance in science." When asked how his parents had contributed to his scientific abilities, Nobel Prize winner Harold Urey answered that his father never asked him "What did you learn in school today?" but always asked "Did you ask a good question today?"

Kurman (1977) noted that

> Any research question limits and defines the range of possible answers. If one asks a "why" question one is likely to come up with explanatory and not descriptive material as the major result. Questions contain directions for their answers.

On the same theme, Nobelist Werner Heisenberg wrote, "What we observe is not nature itself but nature subject to our questions."

## Features of Good Questions

Medawar (1967) advised scientists to practice the "art of the soluble," seeking nontrivial problems that they have the competence and resources to solve. Their questions should be limited in scope. Good scientific questions share three characteristics: They can be answered by empirical means, they indicate the nature of acceptable answers, and they are worth answering.

**Good Scientific Questions Must Be Answerable Empirically.** The following are not scientific questions:

- ■ Is it ethical to experiment with animals? (Questions of value cannot be answered empirically.)
- ■ Is there an afterlife? (This is also unanswerable empirically. If methods are developed for testing for the existence of an afterlife, the question would become scientific.)
- ■ What is science? (Definitions are agreed upon by convention, not by empiricism.)

**Good Scientific Questions Indicate the Nature of Acceptable Answers.** A question such as "What are the effects of stress on personality?" is too broad and vague. One scientist might translate it to mean, "How do loud noises affect exploratory activity in hamsters?" Another might ask, "What are the mechanisms of voodoo death?"

**Good Questions Are Worth Answering.** Selye (1964) told of a man who developed a technique for accurately measuring the iron content of rat feces, then asked colleagues to do research that would require the technique. Although the man was uniquely qualified to answer questions about rat fecal iron content, the value of the information was not apparent. Still, scientific research should not be judged by its perceived likelihood of generating solutions to practical problems. As Selye noted, applied projects stick close to what is already known; they rarely lead to new heights of discovery. On the other hand, questions about the fundamental nature of the universe—basic science, as exemplified in the work of Newton, Pasteur, Mendel, and Einstein—may yield answers that significantly advance technology. G. H. Hardy was a pure mathematician and proud of it. He asserted that the beauty of mathematical topics was directly related to their uselessness and that applied mathematics was repulsively ugly and intolerably dull. Yet, half a century after his death, as he rotates furiously in his grave, Hardy's work has many practical applications. Among other things, he laid the foundation for population genetics by showing how changes in gene frequencies can be analyzed, and he worked on a mathematical function that has been used to investigate the temperature of furnaces.

Lederman (1984) claimed that bright young people are more likely to be attracted by the opportunity to do basic science than by the lure of making practical contributions. Basic science sets standards and provides a shared body of knowledge that simplifies interactions between workers in different disciplines. Instruments and techniques developed to solve questions in basic science often lead to the creation of goods and services. Theoretical work is often used in other fields, as when solutions to certain kinds of equations that occur in elementary particle interactions were applied to the study of polymers. But the major benefit of asking fundamental questions, in Lederman's view, is cultural. Through science, we can construct a coherent account of the world and our place in it.

With the help of more than 100 consultants, Comroe and Dripps (1976) selected 10 major clinical advances in the fields of cardiovascular and pulmonary medicine. Then they identified 529 articles that had contributed crucial steps toward those advances. They defined an article as clinically oriented if the author mentioned even briefly an interest in diagnosis, treatment, or prevention of a clinical disorder or in explaining the mechanisms of a sign or symptom of the disease; they defined it as not clinically oriented if the author neither stated nor suggested any bearing the article might have on a clinical disorder of humans. Basic research was defined as research to determine mechanisms by which living organisms function or drugs act. Comroe and Dripps reported that 41% of the 529 key articles were not clinically oriented and 61.7% involved basic research.

## ■ TYPES OF QUESTIONS

### Questions That Lead Directly to Research Projects

**Descriptive Questions.** Descriptive questions lead to answers about the frequency, duration, and intensity of the behaviors of interest or about the frequency, duration, intensity, and range of behaviors performed by the subjects of interest. Like newspaper reporters, descriptive researchers ask who? what? where? and when? They sometimes ask about behavior sequences, that is, how various behaviors go together.

**Correlational Questions.** Correlations indicate the degree of relationship between variables. Although correlational studies never conclusively prove that one variable causes the other, they may generate ideas about causes.

If variables $X$ and $Y$ are correlated, then $X$ causes $Y$ or $Y$ causes $X$ or some other factor(s) causes both. Thus, a causal link exists between $X$ and $Y$. A researcher interested in relating two seemingly separate areas might analyze several measures for reliable correlations. Then he would seek testable explanations. This scattershot approach is suggested as an exploratory method. Playing with data can be both enjoyable and a great spur to meaningful research questions (Polya, 1954).

**Questions with the Behavior of Interest as Dependent Variable (DV).** The DV is a behavior measured to see if it changes as another variable—the independent variable (IV)—is changed. See p. 5 for further discussion. For example, with a particular biological rhythm as DV, scientists have asked, "Does X modify the rhythm?" In various studies, X has been drugs, lighting conditions, diet, stress, group living, solitary living, and removal of various endocrine glands and brain structures.

**Questions with the Behavior of Interest as Independent Variable.** Any variable can be dependent or independent. Questions with biological rhythms as the IV are of the general form, "How does time of testing affect X?" In various studies, X has been physical strength, endurance, resistance to disease and other forms of stress, mental performance, pulse rate, sensory acuity, job skills, susceptibility to drugs, mood, and episodes of abnormal behavior.

If an IV affects a DV, an important follow-up question is, "Which component(s) of the IV are responsible?" A drug may increase the activity of rats not because of its pharmacological properties, but because injecting it induces stress. A psychotherapist may help a client work through a problem not because of his many years of training, but because he listens sympathetically. Plausible alternatives can be tested by fractionating the IV into its component parts and analyzing them separately (administer the drug by putting it in the rat's food; inject the rat with saline solution instead of the drug; place clients with untrained sympathetic listeners).

Many published studies do little to advance science. A high proportion of them involve testing the effects of whatever is available on a popular DV or testing the effects of an IV on whichever behaviors are easily measured. But creativity of a high order is possible, as illustrated in the work of Zucker and his students (1976) described later.

## Questions That Organize Research Programs

Although many questions can be answered by a single well-designed study, some researchers proceed differently. They too ask descriptive and correlational questions and questions with the procedure or behavior of interest as either IV or DV, but not in isolation. Instead, they plan comprehensive research programs for penetrating deeper aspects of phenomena.

**What Are the Boundaries of a Phenomenon?** Falk (1969) fed food-deprived rats at approximately 1-minute intervals for a few hours per day and observed that they drank enormous quantities of water. During 3-hour test sessions, they drank 10 times their normal 24-hour totals. From this starting point, Falk asked several questions about the boundary conditions:

- How crucial is the 1-minute interval? (Very. If the animals are fed more frequently than 20-second intervals or less frequently than 2-minute intervals, they don't drink excessively.)
- Does excessive drinking occur in animals other than rats? (Yes—with mice, pigeons, monkeys, and apes.)
- Will animals drink excessively if they are deprived of something besides food and that something is given at 1-minute intervals? (Yes, deprivation of a variety of commodities, including sawdust and running wheels, is effective.)
- If water is unavailable, will an animal show a different excessive behavior? (Yes—wheel running, pecking, and attacks against a second animal. Humans, too, show various excessive behaviors if given intermittent rewards.)

Falk kept testing the boundaries and showed that intermittent reinforcement schedules are relevant to drug addiction, overeating, excessive gambling, and many social rituals (Falk, 1984, 1986).

**How Does a Mechanism Work?** Zucker and his students (1976) sought the physiological mechanism that maintains biological rhythms. Rats have millions of brain cells, so randomly stimulating or lesioning various areas of their brains might have taken decades. Instead, Zucker and coworkers asked what features an animal must have if it is to maintain a rhythm. Since all known mammalian rhythms are synchronized by the light-dark cycle, the animal must detect light. But Zucker's rats maintained rhythms even after he eliminated their known visual pathways and they could no longer make simple visual discriminations. Light penetrates directly through the skulls of nonmammalian vertebrates to affect circadian rhythms, but the literature showed that it has no such effect on rats. So Zucker searched the anatomical literature and found a report describing a pathway, function unknown, between the retina and a brain area called the suprachiasmatic nucleus of the hypothalamus. He promptly designed a study in which he lesioned the suprachiasmatic nuclei of several rats; rhythms were disrupted and the main circadian clock thereby localized. His research exemplifies the attitude of most good scientists. Not content to merely demonstrate interesting phenomena, they organize comprehensive programs to get at the underlying mechanisms.

**How Can a Theory Be Tested?** Philosopher of science Karl Popper encouraged scientists to theorize boldly, test the theories ruthlessly, and discard those that fail. (By "ruthless tests" he meant those likely to be failed if the theory is false. Ruthless tests are widely used in the physical but not the social sciences. See p. 217.) Creative researchers deduce interesting theoretical implications and subject them to ruthless, unambiguous, and economical tests. Platt (1964) advised researchers to construct competing explanations for a phenomenon, design and carry out studies so that each possible outcome eliminates at least one explanation, and then refine the remaining possibilities and start again.

**Can Diverse Areas Be Unified?** Bronowski (1956) said:

> The progress of science is the discovery at each step of a new order which gives unity to what had long seemed unlike. Faraday did this when he closed the link between electricity and magnetism. Clerk Maxwell did it when he linked both with light. Einstein linked time with space, mass with energy, and the path of light past the sun with the flight of a bullet; and spent his dying years in trying to add to these likenesses another, which would find a single imaginative order between the equations of Clerk Maxwell and his own geometry of gravitation.

**Can a Paradox or Conflicting Findings Be Explained?** Great scientists welcome unusual or puzzling events. If a theory predicted that people would respond in a certain way to an experimental situation, and 99 of 100 did so, most researchers would probably be delighted and move on. The exceptional researcher, however, might ask questions about the exceptional subject. How did that 1 out of 100 differ from the others?

According to psychology texts of 30 years ago, learning occurs most efficiently if (a) rewards or punishments follow responses by less than a second, and (b) responses and reinforcements are paired many times. But rats are hard to poison, which presented a paradox that John Garcia determined to resolve. The paradox is this: Rats sample novel foods cautiously, and even if they do not get sick until hours later, and despite having tasted the food just once, they do not eat it again.

Garcia, Hawkins, and Rusiniak (1994) fed rats while exposing them to a nausea-inducing dose of radiation. After just one dose, and although they did not get sick until hours later, the rats refused to eat again in the same room. Yet when allowed to run between areas that were and were not exposed to radiation, the rats entered the exposed area repeatedly and accumulated high, often fatal, doses. In another study, Garcia played a clicking sound while rats drank water sweetened with saccharine. Then he punished some rats with radiation and others with electric shocks. Subsequently, the irradiated rats avoided sweetened water but not clicks, whereas the shocked rats retreated from the clicks yet drank sweetened water. Garcia et al. reasoned that behavioral strategies necessary to cope with the external environment are different from those needed to discriminate between nutritious and harmful foods. Clicks and shocks, both part of the external environment, are readily connected; clicks and the gastrointestinal upset caused by radiation are not. Similarly, distinctive tastes are easily associated with feelings of nausea but not with electric shock. Garcia's findings were not immediately accepted. But many replications later, they forced psychologists to revise strongly held beliefs. Psychologists now recognize that animals learn some tasks rapidly and others (from a human standpoint just as easy) with much more difficulty.

**What Is the Cause of a Condition?** Establishing linkages between causes and effects is important and difficult. Causes may be immediate or remote. The immediate cause of syphilis is a spirochete, *Treponema pallidum*, transmitted by sexual intercourse. But the spirochete is transmitted only by people who harbor it, so the sexual partner is also a cause. The partner must have previously been exposed to a carrier, a more remote cause. The analysis can continue back to Adam and Eve, each blaming the other. Causes can always be pushed back a step, and this may be a productive strategy. Having found that $X$ is the cause of $Y$, seek the cause of $X$.

Causes may be necessary but not sufficient. An adequate supply of oxygen is needed for good health, but oxygen by itself is insufficient. Causes may be sufficient but not necessary. Having a giant tortoise fall on one's head may be fatal, but deaths occur in other ways. A cause may contribute only a small part to the effect. Exposure to violent television programs may increase children's levels of aggression, but television violence is not the only cause of aggression and is not necessary for it. There are no spirochetes in psychology, no single, unequivocal causes. Even in relatively advanced sciences like physiology, multiple causes are common.

## ■ ASKING QUESTIONS FROM MULTIPLE PERSPECTIVES

When they are about 2 months old, juvenile male Belding's ground squirrels leave the burrow where they were born and never return. Holekamp and Sherman (1989) asked why. They conducted several experiments and observational studies and showed that there is no single correct answer. Behaviors can be understood from at least four complementary perspectives:

1. *Physiological.* Juvenile ground squirrels do not disperse unless they have been prenatally or neonatally exposed to high concentrations of testosterone. Males are normally exposed; females are not.
2. *Developmental.* Ground squirrels do not disperse until they reach a threshold body weight.
3. *Effects on fitness.* Nondispersing males might mate with relatives. Dispersal reduces the chance of inbreeding, which generally has harmful consequences.

4. *Evolutionary origins.* Male dispersal is the rule in ground squirrels and mammals in general. This suggests that it is an ancient evolutionary trait.

## Asking Questions From an Evolutionary Perspective

Most introductory psychology texts acknowledge our animal heritage but ignore the implications. "Nonbiological" chapters present explanatory models that fail to be informed by, or actively conflict with, current evolutionary thought. Relatively few social scientists use evolutionary concepts in their research programs. Questions about fitness and evolutionary origins are about evolution. Many biologists and biologically oriented psychologists have urged that all students of behavior consider the evolutionary perspective. Cosmides and Tooby (1994) introduced their valuable article with a quote:

> Theodosius Dobzhansky: Nothing in biology makes sense except in light of evolution.

Nobelist Niko Tinbergen (1963) stressed the importance of asking how the frequency, intensity, and exact form of a behavior help an individual in its natural environment. Crawford (1989) showed how evolutionary thinking could enrich psychological research:

■ It would broaden understanding of the causes of behavior. Most psychologists ask about immediate physiological and environmental causes. Evolutionary biologists ask why particular behaviors rather than alternatives have evolved. "Why?" questions help researchers recognize meaningful independent variables, identify environmental factors most likely to alter a behavior, determine which variables should be considered causes and which should be effects, and develop explanations of great generality.

■ It would provide a critical perspective for viewing psychological constructs. A popular theory about why people show empathy conflicts with evolutionary thinking. The evidence supporting evolutionary thinking is much stronger. Either the theory on empathy should be discarded or proponents should devise research to resolve the conflict.

■ It would enrich our repertoire of explanatory constructs. Certain evolutionary concepts, such as genetic relatedness, ability to recognize kin, and altruism, help explain many behaviors.

■ It would help us understand sex differences. Evolutionary theorists believe that the production and rearing of offspring created specialized roles for ancestral males and females. These are reflected in current sex differences in body size, anatomy, and behavior.

■ It would focus attention on ecology. Evolutionary theory can clarify the role played by the social environment in producing a behavior disorder. This may give insights into environmental interventions to alter the behavior.

■ It would help scientists figure out how the mind works. Some neuroscientists believe that once we know enough about neurons, neurotransmitters, and cellular development, figuring out how the human mind works will be trivial. Cosmides and Tooby (1994) disagree, pointing out that the same basic neural tissue is found in millions of animal species, each with its own distinctive cognitive programs. Natural selection designed the human mind to solve problems faced by many generations of our ancestors.

Psychology textbooks are organized according to mechanisms such as attention, memory, reasoning, and learning. By contrast, evolutionary biology and behavioral ecology texts are organized according to adaptive problems: hunting and gathering, kinship recognition, predator defense, resource competition, cooperation, aggression, parental care, dominance and status, courtship, sexual conflict, and so on. Cosmides and Tooby (1994, p. 13) argue for the latter approach, because adaptive problems are the only ones that selection can build mechanisms to solve: "Circuits that are functionally specialized for solving these problems have been found in species after species. No less should be true of humans."

The view that the human brain is a general purpose problem solver—that the same mechanisms "govern how one acquires a language and a gender identity, an aversion to incest and an appreciation of vistas, a desire for friends and a fear of spiders"—has dominated research in cognitive psychology. However, this view conflicts with evolutionary principles. Natural selection tends to replace less efficient designs with ones that perform better.

A general engineering principle is that the same machine is rarely capable of solving two different problems equally well. We have both corkscrews and cups because each solves a particular problem better than the other. It would be extremely difficult to open a bottle of wine with a cup or drink from a corkscrew....The more important the adaptive problem, the more intensely natural selection tends to specialize and improve the performance of the mechanism for solving it....The cognitive programs that govern how you choose a mate should differ from those that govern how you choose your dinner.

Cosmides and Tooby conduct a highly productive research program organized around questions about adaptive functions. See, for example, their chapters in Barkow, Cosmides, and Tooby (1992).

# 5

# Selecting
and
Measuring
Variables

*By the time you finish reading this chapter, you should be able to answer the following questions:*

Why is scientific measurement so important?

What is an operational definition, and why are operational definitions an essential part of scientific work?

Should scientists try to develop new measures whenever they start a new project?

What are the properties of good measures?

What is meant by reliability, sensitivity, and validity?

Can a test be valid if it is constructed without any regard for theory?

What rules should be followed when setting up a system of classification?

Why should independent variables be tested at more than one level?

What is the advantage of measuring variables in more than one way?

What is the advantage of nonreactive measurement?

What are surrogate measures?

■ ■ ■ ■ ■

*"The beginning of wisdom is the definition of terms."* Socrates

The ultimate aim of all scientific research is to discover relationships between variables, and this requires that the variables be properly measured. Investigators often disagree about how to define psychological terms such as self-esteem, creativity, aggressiveness, and paranoid tendencies. Schmidt and Hunter (1996) wrote that of the many bad methodological practices that have retarded progress in the social sciences, measurement error is probably second in importance. (They awarded first place to statistical significance testing—see chapter 17.)

## ■ THE DIFFICULTY OF MEASURING WELL

Even trivial measurements may be deceptively difficult. I ask students in my research methods class to break up into groups of five or six and collectively define a countable set of objects. These can be chairs in the room, doors in the hallway, bathrooms, light fixtures, and so forth. Each group is told to define carefully so that all members are certain about what is to be counted. Then they count individually, with no further talking. In my experience, in only about 5% of the groups does everybody give identical answers. Miscounting errors, say 47 chairs instead of 48, point to the importance of double checking data and calculations. A more frequent type of error is caused by failure to define with enough specificity. While others in a group count only classroom doors, one maverick lumps them with bathroom and hallway doors.

The exercise shows how easy it is to measure incorrectly. Scientific measurements are more intricate than counting exercises, and scientists do not typically meet in groups before their studies to clarify definitions or afterward to find reasons for discrepancies. So measurement errors occur. Box 5.1 could have been greatly expanded in both number and variety.

## ■ SHOULD A NEW MEASURE BE CONSTRUCTED OR A PREVIOUSLY USED ONE RECYCLED?

Bonjean, Hill, and McLemore (1967) examined four sociological journals over a 12-year period and found 3,609 attempts to measure various phenomena by the use of scales and indexes. There were 2,080 different measures, and only 589 were used more than once. At least 15 scales (which correlate poorly with each other) were used to measure hostility in dream reports (Winget & Kramer, 1979), and at least 23 scales measured social

**BOX**

## 5.1

## Examples of Measurement Problems

■ Psychiatric diagnosis, which is a form of measurement, has been used as a tool for controlling and stigmatizing. Behaviors that have been classified as mental disorders include "drapetomania" (the "disorder" that caused slaves to run away from their masters), "childhood masturbation disorder," "lack of vaginal orgasm," "premenstrual syndrome," and "homosexuality." Wakefield (1992) wrote that the concept of mental disorder is fundamental to theory and practice in the mental health field, but no agreed-upon definition exists.

■ Measurement problems have plagued psychotherapists for decades. Eysenck (1952) reported that about two thirds of neurotics improve substantially within 2 years whether or not they enter therapy. His conclusion, based on data from the German Psychoanalytic Association, was that psychotherapy is useless. Bergin (1971) challenged Eysenck on many grounds, especially on the definition of "improved." Eysenck had included only the "cured" and "very much improved" in his calculations of percent improved, and Bergin objected that the decision was misleading.

■ Lambert's (1991) examination of 348 studies published in 20 journals from 1983 to 1989 found 1,430 outcome measures. Of these, 840 measures were used only once. In a further review, 106 studies of agoraphobia outcome published during the 1980s used at least 98 unique outcome measures. (Outcome measures are the dependent variables used to assess treatment effects.)

■ The acute, short-term, and chronic effects of treatments often differ, yet authors do not always acknowledge the differences. Most studies on the effectiveness of antipsychotic drugs cover time periods of a year or less, even though patients treated with drug and placebo become increasingly similar with time (Karon, 1989). Straus and Cavanaugh (1996) asserted that physicians and patients often see immediately positive effects of treatments and incorrectly extrapolate from these. They cited a study on patients who had had heart attacks followed by ventricular arrhythmia; although various drugs were successful in suppressing the arrhythmias, patients maintained on the drugs had a substantially higher mortality rate than patients given placebos. Analogous patterns emerged in tests of quinidine for atrial fibrillation.

■ The measure of success for treatment programs for alcohol abuse has been the ability to get clients to stop abusing alcohol. But many people withdrawing from one drug begin abusing another (Kolb, 1962; Simpson & Sells, 1982) or become extremely irritable (Schachter, Silverstein, & Perlick, 1977) or develop marriage, work, and health problems.

■ Koss (1993) reported large differences in estimates of the percentage of women who have been raped. She attributed these differences to variation among studies in the definitions of the measured phenomenon.

■ Heart rate, respiratory rate, and electrical conductivity of the skin typically increase when a person tells a lie. Polygraphs are devices for measuring these physiological states, and they became popular tools for lie detection. In 1988, about 2 million lie detector tests were administered for police departments, other government agencies, employers, and spouses. But many scientists believe that the physiological measures do not assess lying or truth telling accurately enough to justify the decisions based upon them (Gale, 1988; Lykken, 1981).

■ When certain brain areas are destroyed, vicious laboratory animals become docile (Fulton & Jacobsen, 1935; Mark & Ervin, 1970). The changes appeared desirable to neurosurgeons in the 1930s and stimulated them to make similar lesions with highly aggressive people. By 1950, they had performed prefrontal lobotomies on more than 40,000 patients in the United States. The surgeons measured success by the extent to which their patients became manageable. But other measures indicated impaired intellectual capacity, emotional unresponsiveness, epileptic seizures, and loss of bladder control (Valenstein, 1980).

■ Kohlberg (1984) gave people moral dilemmas such as "A man's wife is dying and needs a special drug. He can't afford the drug and the druggist won't lower his price. Should the man steal the drug?" Kohlberg's findings seemed to indicate that morality develops in stages, with most people becoming more moral as they grow older. But he measured only verbal responses to his dilemmas, not how people behaved when confronted with ethical decisions that had real consequences. Several critics (cf. Schulman & Mekler, 1985) have noted that educated people give "higher-level" explanations of their moral decisions, but that does not mean they are more moral.

■ Measuring auditory acuity might seem easy—present sounds and ask subjects whether they heard them. But the subjects will be uncertain about sounds near their threshold of audibility. Some will tend to say "Yes" if unsure and some will tend to say "No." Signal detection is an alternative method for measuring sensory acuity. Stimuli are presented on some but not all trials, so each trial has one of four possible outcomes: stimulus present and subject responds "Yes"; stimulus present and subject responds "No"; stimulus absent and subject responds "Yes"; stimulus absent and subject responds "No." Signal detection studies show that outcomes are determined by many factors besides acuity, such as the rewards and punishments for correct and incorrect answers. The signal detection approach has been extended to other fields when choices must be made under conditions of uncertainty.

■ Stone (1939) studied the effects of castration (removal of the testes) on the sexual behavior of male rats. He measured the number of times per test session that males mounted females, both prior to and after castration. His surprising finding, that castration had little effect, was due to a measurement artifact.

When a sexually active male and a receptive female rat are placed together, they copulate in a stereotyped way. The male mounts from the rear, and if he has an erection and achieves vaginal penetration, he thrusts. This is called an intromission. He typically has 5 to 10 intromissions and 5 to 15 mounts without penetration before ejaculating. Immediately after he ejaculates both animals lie down, light up cigarettes, turn on the TV, and relax. (Actually, they only pause to rest.) A few minutes later they start over again and repeat for as many as 10 ejaculations, with the pause following ejaculations getting progressively longer.

Stone did not distinguish between mounts, intromissions, and ejaculations. He called all of them copulations. Though the castrated rats were unable to achieve intromissions or ejaculations, they continued to mount. Since they did not ejaculate, there were no long post-ejaculatory pauses and their total number of copulatory responses was equivalent to that of intact animals.

■ Trained actors in the Netherlands entered rooms fitted out like consulting rooms and presented one of eight common medical complaints to Dutch physician volunteers. The interactions between physicians and the pretend patients were videotaped. Then a panel of medical experts analyzed history taking, physical and laboratory examinations, instructions to and treatment of the patients, and follow-up according to published Dutch primary care standards. They gave each physician a score for competence.

Similar actors visited the physicians in their regular offices within 3 years of the competency evaluation and took detailed notes. (Actors made 156 office visits, and none of them were detected.) From these, the physicians' normal performance was assessed. Two important findings emerged. First, normal performance scores were much lower than competence scores—even though the physicians were volunteers and probably had higher standards than unselected physicians. Second, the correlation between competence and performance, on the most significant measure, was .00 (Rethans, 1991).

■ The U.S. Census Bureau measures population inaccurately. Millions of people are missed—blacks more than whites, inner-city residents more than the general population, and many undocumented immigrants. The biases affect congressional representation and allocation of government funds (Choldin, 1994). The incidences of death and serious diseases are probably measured accurately, so a census undercount leads to an overestimate of incidence of mortality and morbidity. (See Choldin for a discussion of methods for estimating the undercounts.)

■ Measurement problems occur throughout science. When physicists measure fundamental constants such as the speed of light, the gravitational constant, and the magnetic moment of protons, they typically include a probable error range. Later estimates have consistently fallen outside the error ranges of earlier ones. Recent estimates of five fundamental constants were outside previously published error ranges in 57% of cases (Henrion & Fischhoff, 1986).

support (Heitzmann & Kaplan, 1988). Before trying to develop their own measures, researchers should search the literature to see what is available. For one thing, good measures are refined and standardized over time, while less satisfactory ones are winnowed out. Also, comparisons between studies are complicated when different measures are involved.

## ■ OPERATIONAL DEFINITIONS

Suppose two researchers independently undertake to study the effects of stress on alcohol consumption. Both consult the *American Heritage Dictionary* and find "stress" defined as a mentally or emotionally disruptive or disquieting influence. Armed with the definition, they both conduct flawless studies. Still, one might observe that stressed college students outdrink unstressed ones, and the other that stressed students drink less. The reason for the difference might be purely definitional.

Dictionaries are legitimate starting points, but researchers must then convert the dictionary definition to a measurement procedure. The method by which a concept is produced or measured becomes its scientific definition. I dislike loud music, so I might create stress by arranging for subjects to sit through a heavy metal concert. You, more conventionally, might give electric shocks. Some researchers consider positive events such as winning a lottery or getting a promotion as stressors. Some future Chicken Little might define stress as the reactions of subjects to an announcement that the sky is falling. (Or we might agree about how to induce stress but measure drinking differently.) The result might be several distinct descriptions of the effects of "stress" on "drinking." We might then increase our own stress levels by debating the merits of our definitions, but such debates are rarely productive. On the other hand, careful description of procedures often is. Readers of a scientific study should never be in doubt about how the concepts were produced or measured. As Francis Bacon wrote, "Truth is more likely to come from error than from confusion."

Stress can be defined as the reaction to 60 minutes in the front row at a heavy metal concert or to 10 one-half-second shocks of 45 volts delivered to the right forearm. Both definitions describe the exact operations used and are called *operational definitions*. Like recipes in cookbooks, operational definitions give exact and explicit directions and are essential for scientific communication. But like recipes, they can be good or bad. Intelligence could be defined as the circumference of a person's head measured by a standard tape measure. The definition would be operational but not useful. Test your understanding of operational definitions with Box 5.2.

If two operational definitions have different consequences, they do not produce or measure the same thing. Operational definitions can measure

**BOX**

## Which Are Operational Definitions of Stress?

1. Resting heart rate in beats per minute.
2. A look of annoyance.
3. Answer to the question, "On a scale of 1 to 10, how stressed are you?"
4. A feeling of tenseness and anxiety.
5. The number of anti-anxiety pills a person swallows per week.
6. The number of times during a week that a person wants to cry from frustration.
7. Change in the number of times a rat presses a bar for food reward after a tone comes on signalling that the rat will soon be shocked.
8. Speaking in a wavering voice.
9. The sensation of having one's stomach tied up in knots.
10. The number of Graduate Record Exam mathematics problems completed correctly in one hour while a 20 decibel siren is sounding.

Answer: 1, 3, 5, 7, and 10 are operational definitions, because they describe the exact procedures used. They are not all good definitions.

---

verbal, behavioral other than verbal, or physiological variables; and the three types do not always correspond. (Nor do two measures of the same type always correspond.) A person may say he is unafraid of snakes but refuse to step into a room with one, or say he is terrified but be willing to handle a snake; his heart may or may not start racing at the sight of a snake. So researchers should try to measure their variables in more than one way. The extra work is worth it, even if conflicts arise. Instead of being discouraged, a scientist might gain valuable insights and launch a new project to discover the reasons.

## ■ CONSTRUCTS

Science requires abstractions in addition to operational definitions, or else it would consist of nothing but descriptions of specific events—the effects of receiving 45 volts of shock, of being in the front row at a heavy metal concert, of hearing that the sky is falling—and no connections between them.

So scientists create high-order abstractions, called constructs. Constructs such as "stress," "authoritarianism," and "aggressiveness" cannot be seen but help make sense out of otherwise unconnected data. Operational definitions tell how to measure the constructs used in laws and theories. As theories are tested and modified, the constructs become clarified and the operational definitions may be revised.

## ■ PROPERTIES OF GOOD MEASURES

Variables should have certain other qualities in addition to being operationally defined:

■ A good measure is affected only minimally by fluctuations in anything other than the characteristic being measured. It is reliable.
■ A good measure is affected by even small changes in the characteristic being measured. It is sensitive.
■ A good measure measures the right thing. It is valid.

Several hypothetical methods for measuring thirst are described on the following pages. Each uses an operational definition, though no decent scientist would ever consider any of them. Each has a serious flaw, noted in parentheses. The discussions following expand on the meanings of reliability, sensitivity, and validity.

### Measures Must Be Reliable

1. Subjects are given a wide, shallow bowl full of beer and told to pour the beer into a shot glass and drink from the glass. The bowl is weighed before and after a 10-minute drinking period, and the difference is the measure of thirst. (More beer would end up on the floor than in anybody's mouth, and the spillage would be largely random. So people with the same degree of thirst might earn very different scores. The measure would be unreliable—unstable when repeated.)

Reliability is the degree to which test scores are free of errors of measurement. It is a composite term, and in addition to stability it may refer to agreement among scorers or consistency among component items of a single test. A good measure is reliable in all respects and has specific requirements appropriate to the research project (a scale reliable enough for a butcher shop would probably be useless for a perfumery). To find a test's stability over time, administer it twice to a group of individuals and measure changes in their scores and relative rankings. As long as whatever is being measured does not change, scores should be consistent. Be aware, however, that although a test may be stable, the subjects may not be. People who quickly drink an enormous quantity of liquid, and thus score high on a thirst scale, may score low if tested 5 minutes later.

Unless interscorer agreement is high, investigators cannot rule out the possibility that differences between subjects' scores are due to differences between scorers. High interscorer agreement also reduces the possibility that scores have been measured reliably but incorrectly (e.g., by using a metric ruler but recording in inches). Two or more scorers are unlikely to make the same mistake.

The reliability of a test may change with subjects and circumstances. Measuring the heights of 30-year-old men and women would yield highly reliable scores 5 years later. Measuring the heights of 1-year-old boys and girls would not.

An assistant of Ivan Pavlov trained mice to run to a feeding place when he rang a bell. Then, to test the belief that acquired characteristics are inherited, he trained their offspring, then their offspring, continuing for several generations. His results seemed to offer strong support—the number of trials before the mice reached the criterion for learning averaged 300 for the first generation, then 100, 30, 10, and 5 for generations two through five. But the assistant's interpretation that each generation had gotten better was in error, because his measure was unreliable. Pavlov later showed that the mice had not changed, but that the assistant had become a more efficient trainer (Razran, 1958; Zirkle, 1958).

Identifying the cause of a problem is often the most significant step toward its solution. The many causes of unreliability are discussed next.

**The Measurement Situation.** Measuring the same property under different conditions may yield dissimilar results. Conditions differ in infinite variety, so the possibilities cannot be enumerated. Besides, variations that affect one type of measurement may be irrelevant to another. Some factors that have affected responsiveness to drugs, which is not a uniquely sensitive behavioral measure, include the route of administration; quantity of food in the stomach; intestinal contents; presence of other drugs; time of day; acidity of urine; temperature of the room; temperature of the drug; temperature of the subject; amount of light; noise level; what the subjects were doing at the time; in rats, whether their cages had been cleaned daily or once a week; in mice, whether their bedding was of ground corn cobs or red cedar chips; and in people, who administered the drug and whether or not the administrator was enthusiastic (Leavitt, 1995). If not held constant, these factors reduce reliability.

**The Task.** Ambiguous test questions yield lower reliabilities than do lucid ones. More generally, ambiguous tasks are less reliable than clearly defined ones. Tests comprised of many items are more reliable than shorter tests.

**The Data Recorder.** Compared to electronic devices, people are poor data recorders. We have fallible memories and slow reflexes, and we make inconsistent judgments. Automation, in the form of timers, counters, and related devices, is preferable. If people must be used, make scoring categories unequivocal and practice until inter-observer agreement is high. Check periodically to ensure that scoring criteria do not shift over time.

## Measures Must Be Sensitive

2. The subjects, all heavy drinkers, have three shot glasses of light beer placed in front of them on a hot day. The researcher calls those subjects thirstiest who empty the most glasses. (All the subjects would probably drink all three glasses. The measure would not permit a sufficient range of responses to allow for discriminations between them.)

3. The subjects have glasses placed in front of them, and the measure is amount drunk, but the drink this time is urine-flavored vodka. (The problem is the same as in the previous example, but from the other side. Nobody would take more than a sip, so the measure would not discriminate.)

4. The subjects are asked to choose between a bottle of beer and a $5.00 bill. (With only two alternatives, no gradations in thirst can be detected. It is generally useful to be able to detect subtle as well as gross differences, but do not go beyond the level of precision needed to answer your research question. Do not invest in a scale sensitive to milligrams if you intend to weigh elephants.)

Sensitivity, like reliability, may vary with the testees and conditions of testing. Having normal adults try to bench press weights up to 200 pounds would discriminate well for weight-lifting ability, but the test would be unsuitable for identifying potential Olympic medalists.

**Indexes and Multiple-Item Scales.** Tests with many items allow a wide range of scores, which increases both reliability and sensitivity, but only if the items are properly combined. Meehl (1954) and Faust (1984) showed that combining should be done by statistical formulas rather than clinical judgments. One of their many examples involved three highly trained pathologists who predicted the survival times of patients diagnosed with Hodgkin's disease. The three identified nine characteristics of cells that had diagnostic significance, but they could not integrate the information to get an aggregate score and so did not predict accurately. Computers can integrate information from large numbers of variables. When a computer was fed data from the first 100 cases about the nine characteristics and subsequent survival times, it assigned weights to each characteristic; formulas were developed and applied independently to the next 93 cases, and predictive accuracy was high.

## Measures Must Be Valid

5. Subjects pour from a large, heavy keg into a glass. The measure is the weight difference in the keg from beginning to end of the drinking period. (The researcher might find that heavy subjects "drink" less than petite ones. The petite subjects would not handle the keg easily, so would spill more beer. The measure would not be valid, since it would be tied more closely to strength than thirst. Valid measures measure what they are supposed to.)

Sledge hammers may be the perfect tool for splitting logs, but they are no good for repairing computers. Measuring devices are also tools, and their usefulness (validity) likewise depends on their purpose. So the question "Is measure X valid?" is not a good one. The inferences made from measures are valid or invalid, not the measures themselves.

**Criterion Validity.** One reason for measuring is to predict, and *criterion validity* is the term used for expressing predictive accuracy. A test may have high criterion validity even if its connection to the criterion is obscure. Suppose, for example, that 10,000 people are asked to name their favorite color and 50 say lavender. Suppose further that, within a year, each of the 50 and few of the others suffer a fatal heart attack. The test would have high criterion validity for heart attacks. In fact, a similar strategy was used in developing the most widely used psychological test in the world, the Minnesota Multiphasic Personality Inventory (MMPI). Both normal people and psychiatric patients were asked to respond to a large number of statements with a "yes," "no," or "neither." The statements that normals and people with various disorders tended to answer differently were compiled into a final version. Many of the statements have no obvious relevance to psychopathology, but the MMPI nevertheless has high criterion validity (actually, validities, since a separate validity coefficient must be calculated for each diagnostic category).

Note three points. First, criterion validity, like reliability and sensitivity, varies with circumstances. Even if item 10 of Box 5.2 accurately predicted anxiety attacks in most people, it might fail with poor readers and people who lacked computational skills or were deaf. Second, both the test and the criterion must be reliable, because unreliable measures do not correlate well with anything else. Many personnel tests do not predict well because the criteria for job success (supervisor's rating, grades in training courses, quality of output, etc.) are subjective and unreliable. Some criteria—grade point average in the first year of college, making the football team, reporting hallucinations—can be measured with high reliability. But the criteria are disputed and unreliable for evaluating creativity, neurotic tendencies, motivation, and so forth. Third, although unreliable measures cannot be valid, invalid measures can be reliable. Intelligence defined as the circumference of a person's head would be a reliable but invalid measure.

**Classification.** A second reason for measuring is to classify, which is actually a type of prediction. Classifications place subjects in categories and stimulate predictions of the form "people in group X will respond better than people in group Y to treatment Z."

Every item to be classified should fit into a category. Classifying television programs into comedies, dramas, musical specials, movies, and children's shows would be unsatisfactory, because it would omit programs such as documentaries and sporting events. The categories should be mutually exclusive, that is, every item should fit into only one category. The television classification fails here, too, because some programs are both comedies and children's shows, both movies and dramas, and so forth. Categories should be created according to whatever principle best suits the research question, and that single principle should be applied consistently. A different principle may be used at each division into subcategories. A scientist who makes several broad categories, each broken down into detailed subclasses, can preserve fine distinctions and analyze data at whatever level is most appropriate. Lazarsfeld and Barton (1951) suggested observing, organizing the observations into a preliminary scheme, applying the scheme systematically to the data, refining the scheme, reapplying it to the data, and so on.

**Construct Validity.** A third reason for measuring is to discover relationships between constructs. To do so, scientists must measure the constructs appropriately. Construct validity assesses the extent to which a measure captures the appropriate meaning of a construct, and any type of information may be relevant. Whereas reliability and criterion validity are calculated according to formulas, judgments about construct validity have strong subjective elements. (A test may be high in one type of validity and low on other types.)

Assessing a measure's construct validity produces evidence about the usefulness, boundaries, and different facets of the construct. Constructs can be modified, subdivided, or discarded because of validity evidence. Many studies are required. First, describe the construct briefly in writing. Then review the relevant literature to see how others have measured and related the construct to other variables. This will clarify its nature and range, identify problems with existing measures, and indicate whether the proposed measure is needed.

Because constructs are complex, researchers should try to determine which aspect of the construct each item measures. The extent to which each item counts toward a final score should be proportional to the importance of that aspect. Items that are supposed to measure the same construct should correlate well with each other, and if an item is meant to discriminate between two groups, its discriminating power should be analyzed. Find out what proportion of each group answer the item in a particular way.

**Convergent and Discriminant Validity.** Scores on the new test should correspond to scores on other measures of the same construct and be distinct from measures of independent constructs. The correspondence is called *convergent validity,* the distinctiveness is called *discriminant validity.* Campbell and Fiske (1959) suggested a technique for analyzing both convergent and discriminant validity. This involves measuring the construct in at least one way other than with the test being analyzed, and measuring at least one additional construct with the test. Their article gives guidelines.

Assessing construct validity is not always necessary. A researcher who showed pictures of snakes to people with snake phobias, then measured changes in heart rate on the assumption that increased rates reflect anxiety, would have to justify (validate) the inference from heart rate to the construct "anxiety." But a researcher who observed large heart rate changes in rats following administration of an experimental drug might conclude that the drug is dangerous, with no further inference required.

**An Example—Test Anxiety.** Some students blame their poor test scores on test anxiety. Horan (1995) analyzed the construct and concluded that test anxiety comes in at least three forms: adaptive, maladaptive, and reactive. Adaptive anxiety is beneficial. Anyone completely unconcerned about an upcoming performance is unlikely to do well. Students who experience adaptive anxiety should be assured that it is normal and that attempts to reduce it are likely to do more harm than good.

Maladaptive anxiety may impair performance but, according to Horan (1995, p. 5), is rare: "In fact, my former students and I collected a bushel basket full of unpublished data from which we failed to identify a single individual with bonafide maladaptive test anxiety in a large class of graduate students who were approaching a final exam....No one's performance declined as a function of the test having implications for one's actual course grade!"

Horan called reactive anxiety realistic and appropriate to the situation: "Taking a test after a night of partying or with full knowledge that for whatever reason our mastery of the curriculum is deficient, really ought to be cause for trepidation" (1995, p. 5). He suggested that most claims of test anxiety are of this type and should be treated by addressing decision-making skills. The important point is that construct analysis can help both researcher and clinician.

# ■ STRATEGIES FOR WORKING WITH INDEPENDENT VARIABLES

In addition to picking reliable, sensitive, and valid IVs, researchers should test them at several levels. The effect of electric shock on drinking depends on the intensity of the shock: A mild shock may increase drinking; a strong one may decrease it. Low doses of alcohol stimulate behavior; high doses cause sleep. A rat deprived of food for 24 hours will be quite active; a rat deprived for 24 days will not be. So review the literature and, perhaps, do a pilot study to get an idea of the appropriate range of IV levels. Try to verify that your IVs have worked as intended. Not all do. Patients in drug studies often secretly dispose of their pills. Sudden loud noises do not frighten deaf people, and a researcher who shouts that the sky is falling is unlikely to create stress (unless you are locked in a room with him and think he may be armed). Consider doing the following as checks on the effectiveness of your IVs:

■ At the conclusion of a study, ask your human subjects for feedback.
■ If your IV is designed to produce a particular state, look for other indicators of that state. Suppose you use loud noises to induce stress in rats. Even though your interest is in the effects of stress upon drinking, you might monitor heart rate, activity, urination, defecation, and vocalizations to see if they show their normal patterns to stressful stimuli.

Do not generalize from a single IV to an entire class of stimuli. Consider the following fictitious study, similar to many real ones published in excellent journals:

Throughout the Christmas season two researchers, one Hispanic and one Asian, dress in Santa Claus costumes and solicit donations in a shopping mall. They alternate collection days and move randomly between different locations. Suppose that one Santa collects substantially more money than the other. Would the conclusion be justified that shoppers respond differently to Hispanics and Asians?

The conclusion would not be justified. Imagine a short, elderly Hispanic man and a tall, young Asian woman. Height, age, and gender would be confounded with race. More generally, when individuals within a category vary in ways relevant to the research question, one individual cannot properly represent the entire category. There is no consensus on the minimum number needed—see Wells and Windschitl (1999) for further discussion.


## ■ USE MULTIPLE MEASURES

Webb et al. (1966) wrote that all psychological measurements tap multiple processes and are theoretically complex. Thus, all operational definitions provide only one out of a potentially infinite number of ways to measure a construct. Even in physics, Webb et al. noted, "no meter ever perfectly measures a single theoretical parameter." The score on any measure embodies assumptions. Webb et al. (1981) imagined a boy who scored 125 on an intelligence test. One conclusion is that the boy is bright, but there are other possibilities: (a) The boy had been coached, (b) the examiner made a mistake in arithmetic, (c) the examiner liked the boy so was extremely generous in his scoring, (d) the boy had taken the test several times previously, and (e) the examiner was the boy's mother. No measurement eliminates all rival hypotheses, and the greater the plausibility of any rival, the weaker the confidence in the measure. So scientists should measure with the specific aim of reducing both the number and the plausibility of rival hypotheses. One way is to use multiple measures.

When a variable is measured in more than one way, the findings may agree or conflict. Two methods for estimating crime rates conflict: (a) police records of all confirmed crimes, and (b) surveys in which randomly chosen people are asked if they have been crime victims. Police records consistently yield lower figures for crime rates than do surveys of possible victims. Whereas agreement does not ensure correctness (all measures may be in error), conflicting results indicate a problem that should be resolved, and the search for reasons may promote deeper understanding of the phenomenon in question. In this case, an important inference is that police underreport crimes or that survey respondents exaggerate.

When a scientist finds a relationship between, say, attending a heavy metal concert and beer drinking, she should seek other evidence of the proposition that stress affects drinking. She should replicate the study, but not exactly, to see if the relationship holds under somewhat altered conditions of testing and measuring; if not, the relationship is probably weak and trivial.

Miller (1956), an early proponent of multiple measures, induced thirst in rats by administering a saline solution via a stomach tube. Fifteen minutes later, the treated rats and uninjected controls bar pressed equally for water. But treated rats drank more and tolerated stronger dilutions of the water with quinine. Three hours later, the difference between the groups in drinking pure water reached its maximum; but differences in bar pressing and drinking quinine-diluted water reached their maxima at least 3 hours after that. So the influence of saline on thirst depended considerably on how thirst was measured. Different operational definitions, different results.

## ■ USE NONREACTIVE MEASURES

Physicists since Heisenberg have accepted that the act of measuring often changes the object measured. That is, the process is often reactive. For example, the rays of light required for observing the location of an electron change its momentum. Social scientists confront a similar problem, but we have an advantage over physicists, because people are more easily tricked than electrons. Social scientists can use nonreactive measurements, and Webb et al. (1981) urged that we do so whenever possible. Rather than obtrusively assessing the effects of an air disaster on next-day travelers by means of interview or questionnaire, a scientist might unobtrusively and nonreactively analyze flight cancellations and new ticket sales, changes in trip insurance policies, and business at the airport bar. The following examples, all referenced in Webb et al. (1966), are instructive for at least three reasons: (a) They indicate feasible alternatives to surveys and experiments, (b) they indicate feasible methods by which surveyors and experimenters can obtain multiple measures, and (c) they illustrate the ingenuity with which good scientists approach their problems.

**Physical Traces: Erosion and Accretion.** Erosion measures evaluate the degree of selective wear on some material.

- Floor tiles are often coated to resist wear. To help museum personnel measure the relative popularities of exhibits, some contractors deliberately leave the tiles uncoated: the more eroded the floor, the more popular the exhibit.
- Mosteller measured the wear and tear on different sections of an encyclopedia by noting dirty edges of pages, frequency of dirt smudges, finger markings, and underlinings. This provided an estimate of the frequency with which the different sections had been read.

Accretion measures give evidence in the form of a deposit of materials.

- Police techniques include many accretion measures, such as soil analyses from shoes and clothing.
- The murder of Napoleon was uncovered on the basis of arsenic traces in remains of his hair.

■ Liquor consumption has been estimated by counting the number of empty liquor bottles in trash carted away from homes.

**Archives: The Running Record.** Various ongoing continuing records of a society (votes, city budgets, births, marriages, deaths, weather reports, newspaper and magazine articles) can be exploited by social scientists.

**Archives: The Episodic and Private Record.** Scientists can seek out materials that occur periodically and are not part of the public record: insurance sales, suicide notes, diaries, a nurse's record on a bedside clipboard.

**Simple Observation.** Clothing, jewelry, shoe style, tattoos, tribal markings, calluses, and scars are examples of exterior physical signs that give nonreactive clues to people's behavior and status:

■ As Charles Darwin noted, expressive movements such as frowning, baring teeth, and erecting hair convey a great deal of information.
■ Where seating is voluntary (in classrooms, lunch counters, and public transportation), the degree to which people of different types (ages, races, men and women) mix has been used to indicate the significance of those variables for acquaintances and friendships.
■ Snippets of conversations have been used as evidence that men and women think differently. Moore walked the streets of New York every night for several weeks and jotted down every bit of audible conversation. He found that 8% of conversations between two men were about women, whereas 44% of conversations between two women were about men.
■ The amount of time people spend working on, watching, or otherwise attending to objects suggests their level of interest in the objects.

Measures can be nonreactive even though they involve hardware or are contrived. Many episodes of the television show *Candid Camera* were prepared by secretly filming people while they responded to the strange situations created by the show's writers:

■ A woman stopped men on the street and asked if they would help her carry a suitcase on the ground next to her. She said she was tired after having carried it a long way. The suitcase was filled with metal. The study was filmed abroad and provides comparisons of men of different cultures. Frenchmen shrugged; Englishmen kept trying to carry the suitcase.

## ■ USE SURROGATE MEASURES

If a variable cannot be measured easily or in timely fashion, a surrogate end point may substitute. Good surrogate end points are easily measured, correlate strongly with the variable of interest, and reduce the length and cost of research projects. For example, high blood pressure and elevated serum cholesterol are surrogate end points for subsequent heart and blood vessel disease. Medical researchers assume that treatments that lower blood pressure or cholesterol level will help control or prevent the diseases. However, assumptions should always be tested. Some surrogate end points, such as concentration of antibiotics in the blood as a predictor of cure of infection, have been misleading (Hyatt, 1995).

# 6

# Choosing the Best Research Design

*By the time you finish reading this chapter, you should be able to answer the following questions:*

What are the advantages of knowing several ways to conduct research?

What data collection methods do social and medical scientists use?

What research strategies do social and medical scientists use?

Which strategy is best for answering questions about incidence and prevalence of a condition in a population?

Of what value are case studies?

Is it proper for scientists to use data collected by others?

Why are nonexperimental strategies unsatisfactory for establishing causes?

What are the defining characteristics of experiments?

How do qualitative and quantitative strategies differ?

What are the reasons for choosing one strategy over another?

■ ■ ■ ■ ■

*"Life is the art of drawing sufficient conclusions from insufficient premises."*
Samuel Butler, English author

*"Every method is imperfect."* Charles-Jean-Henri Nicolle, physician

# ■ MULTIPLE METHODS

The great detectives of fiction and real life have an advantage over most social scientists. The detectives seek out whatever clues are appropriate under
the circumstances of the case, whereas social scientists typically restrict
themselves to one or at most a few methods. Sherlock Holmes checked for
fingerprints and footprints, cigarette and pipe ashes, and bits of cloth torn
from the murderer's coat that remained embedded in the victim's nails. He
interviewed friends, relatives, and rivals of both victim and suspects. His
genius lay less in applying established methods than in choosing them with
an open mind and inventing new ones when necessary. His modern coun-
terparts rely heavily on recent developments in voice, blood, DNA, and hair
analysis. But many social scientists gather evidence from a narrow base.
They rely exclusively on a single type of apparatus such as a Skinner box or
computer. They always observe, or always interview, or always experiment.
Their subjects, whether rats, baboons, or volunteers from introductory psychology courses, are their sole subjects. Their crucial concepts are tied to a
single type of measurement, be it electric shock to induce stress or standardized IQ tests as a measure of intelligence. Their research is always analyzed
by the same statistics. They handicap themselves, much as if Holmes had restricted himself to studying fingerprints.

The various data collection methods and research strategies differ in
costs, are not always equally feasible, and answer different types of questions.
They all have assumptions and weaknesses built in, so they should be viewed
as complementary rather than competitive. Readers of research should identify the method used and the permissible conclusions from that method, and
researchers should choose a strategy based on the question. Whichever
method they settle on, researchers might benefit from using a procedure that
Cobb (1990) called *top-down design*. He claimed that by focusing the design
effort on the goals of the research, top-down design almost ensures that

- ■ Every variable measured actually has a bearing on at least one research hypothesis.
- ■ Controls are in place for all foreseeable threats to the validity of the results.
- ■ The research design is adequate to confirm or disconfirm each research hypothesis.
- ■ Nothing is included in the design that does not contribute to reaching the
goals of the project.

Cobb listed seven steps in top-down design for experimental research that I modified slightly:

1. Write a single-sentence summary of the main result you hope to observe as it might be stated by somebody citing your research.
2. Write the abstract for your study. Invent plausible statistics as needed—your research will provide the actual numbers later.
3. Draw the figure or table that conclusively establishes the main result claimed in Step 2. Invent plausible numbers.
4. Write down every realistic way in which the validity of the figure or table in Step 3 can be attacked. Use this list to identify the controls and comparisons needed in the research design.
5. Write the research methods section for the paper. Determine the necessary sample sizes.
6. Flesh out the full research design, using Step 5 as a guide and including only what is demanded by Step 5.
7. Design the structure of the data so that the figures or tables of Step 3 are readily derivable.

When the design is complete, the research methods section and abstract have been written, the mode of presentation of the results has been settled, the expected results are known, nothing is in the design that is not demanded by the goals of the project, and there is a known probability that the study will succeed (provided by the calculation in Step 5 of sample size).

## ■ DATA COLLECTION

Several data collection methods are available to social scientists:

- *Observation:* Observers study behavior in the subject's natural environment (naturalistic observation) or in special environments. Subjects may or may not be aware they are being studied. The researcher may or may not manipulate variables. She may join the group being studied (participant observation).
- *Questionnaire:* A printed form containing a set of questions is distributed to subjects.
- *Interview:* A researcher asks subjects a series of questions either face-to-face or by telephone.
- *Objective tests:* Subjects are evaluated on the basis of their answers to unambiguous, objectively scored test items.
- *Projective and other indirect tests:* Subjects are evaluated on the basis of their responses to ambiguous stimuli.
- *Archival research:* Existing data are reanalyzed for a different reason than the one for which they were originally gathered.
- *Physical evidence:* Inferences are drawn about behavior from physical traces, such as the contents in a person's garbage.

## ■ RESEARCH DESIGNS

Data should be collected as part of an overall research strategy. The strategies can be divided into two broad categories—quantitative and qualitative. Quantitative researchers generalize from one or more subjects—their sample—to larger populations. Qualitative researchers analyze how people interpret phenomena. This book focuses on quantitative methods, although various qualitative strategies are discussed briefly.

### Quantitative Strategies

- *Experiment:* A treatment is administered to one group, a different treatment to one or more other groups, and scores are measured on a dependent variable. Subjects are assigned to their groups randomly. An alternative experimental approach is to expose each subject in random order to each independent variable.
- *Descriptive study:* Behavior is described as it occurs naturally.
- *Survey:* Data obtained from a sample of individuals are used to generalize to characteristics of a larger population.
- *Case study:* Individual subjects are investigated in detail.
- *Comparative study:* Members of naturally occurring groups, such as men/ women, young/old, Dutch/Turkish, are compared.
- *Correlational study:* Scores are obtained from a group of subjects (people, animals, vegetables, minerals, institutions) on two different measures. The researcher determines if high scores on one measure tend to be associated with high, low, or unpredictable scores on the other measure. Although experimentation is the gold standard for establishing that one event causes another, alternatives are sometimes necessary. For both ethical and practical reasons, epidemiologists (people who study the causes and control of epidemics) rarely have the luxury to experiment. Instead, they rely primarily on two types of correlation designs:

    *Case control:* Victims of a disease and people without the disease are investigated in detail in an attempt to identify lifestyle, diet, or other differences between them.

    *Cohort study:* Volunteers are asked in detail about their lifestyles and environment. Then their health is monitored, often for the rest of their lives, to see which diseases they get and whether the diseases can be associated with specific factors.
- *Archival research:* A researcher uses data that were previously collected for another purpose.
- *Simulation research:* Simulations involve the creation of models such as computer programs that are meant to abstractly represent key aspects of the system being modeled. One purpose of simulations is to predict, for example, how the status of individuals or populations will change during some specified time period. A second purpose is to develop and refine theories. Theoretical possibilities and thought experiments can be explored by observing the behaviors of models under different conditions. Latane (1996) simulated vari-

ous social situations, observed the results, refined his theories accordingly, and then tested the insights gained with formal experiments. (For additional reading, see Gilbert, 1997, and Hanneman & Patrick, 1997.)

## Qualitative Strategies

- *Phenomenology:* A researcher takes narratives from people who have had a common experience. The goal is to find general elements so others can understand the experience.
- *Hermeneutics:* The researcher interprets experiences in light of the political, historical, and sociocultural contexts in which they occur.
- *Life history:* Interviews and analyses of documents such as diaries help create portraits of individuals' lives, including critical points and core themes.
- *Heuristic research:* Heuristics, according to Moustakas (1990, p. 15), is "a way of self-inquiry and dialogue with others aimed at finding the underlying meanings of important human experiences."
- *Ethnography:* Ethnographers immerse themselves in the daily life of a cultural group and try to identify the meanings and passions of the group.

Certain data collection methods are usually used in conjunction with specific research designs, for example, questionnaires with surveys. But that restricts options unnecessarily. Data, however collected, can be analyzed as part of any research strategy. Suppose an unethical researcher sent people letters saying either that they had won an expensive prize or requesting a donation. If he watched them unobtrusively with binoculars and a listening device, he would be observing naturalistically. If he befriended them and secretly recorded their reactions, he would be a participant observer. He could study their garbage, interview them, or ask them to fill out questionnaires or take psychological tests. Whatever his data collection method, if he randomly assigned them to the two groups, he would be experimenting.

## Qualitative versus Quantitative Methods

Several characteristics distinguish qualitative from quantitative methods:

- Qualitative research designs are much less structured than quantitative designs. Research questions, data collection strategies, and data analysis evolve as the researcher learns more about what is being studied.
- Quantitative researchers use the same subjects for an entire study. Qualitative researchers deliberately pick subjects to help them focus on the relevant issues, and they change subjects to extend, test, and fill in information (Lincoln & Guba, 1985). They may pick extreme or deviant cases, typical cases, confirming and disconfirming cases, or politically important cases. Samples are usually small, and size is not determined beforehand. Patton (1990, p. 185) wrote:

The validity, meaningfulness, and insights generated from qualitative inquiry have more to do with the information-richness of the cases selected
and the observational/analytical capabilities of the researcher than with
sample size.... The researcher or evaluator is absolutely obligated to discuss how the sample affected the findings, the strengths and weaknesses of
the sampling procedures, and any other design decisions that are relevant
for interpreting and understanding the reported results.

■ Although both quantitative and qualitative researchers observe and describe,
the latter emphasize contextual details such as physical setting, nonverbal
communication, pauses, and word choices. They may note their feelings, reactions, prejudices, and emotional states. Their goal is not just to hear the subjects' answers but to see the world through the subjects' eyes.

■ Qualitative researchers regard data analysis as an ongoing process. Miles and
Huberman (1984) suggested that researchers cycle back and forth between
thinking about their existing data and generating strategies for collecting new
data.

■ Unlike quantitative researchers, qualitative investigators typically work in
teams and use several data sources, more than one method for gathering data,
and different perspectives for interpreting it.

But most qualitative researchers do not make falsifiable predictions.
Furthermore, they have no agreed-upon empirical method for resolving
controversies about interpretations. Thus, although qualitative research
may suggest areas for scientific study, most of it as practiced today is outside the realm of science.

## ■ ADVANTAGES OF MULTIPLE METHODS

### The Research Question

Different types of questions require different research designs. Table 6.1
lists a variety of questions and the designs generally most appropriate for
answering them.

Questions about relationships between variables can be answered by
both experimental and nonexperimental designs. Questions of the type,
"What is the effect of $X$ on $Y$?" ask about causes. Certain types of case studies provide strong evidence of cause (see pp. 139–140), and experiments are
designed to do so.

### Measurement

The value of multiple measurements is discussed on pp. 71–72.

**TABLE 6.1**

| QUESTION | EXPERIMENTAL DESIGN | COMMENTS |
| --- | --- | --- |
| If rhesus monkeys are put on a restricted diet, is their longevity affected?<br><br>What is the effect of any *X* on any *Y?* | | Experiments, like correlational studies, answer questions about relationships between variables; but only experiments justify the conclusion that changes in one variable cause changes in the other. |
| Do rats bar press more when on fixed-interval 1-minute or fixed ratio 10 schedules? | | Because experimenters manipulate variables, they do not have to wait for the events of interest to occur. |
| According to Freudian theory, a child frustrated during the oral stage of development is likely to develop an eating disorder later in life. Will rats frustrated during their period of nursing develop eating disorders as adults? | | Experimenters test predictions from theories. |

**NONEXPERIMENTAL DESIGNS**

**Descriptive Study**

| | | |
| --- | --- | --- |
| Do students seat themselves in classrooms according to gender or race?<br><br>Do wild chimpanzees form dominance hierarchies?<br><br>When men and women converse, who interrupts more often? | | Descriptive studies tell about the stream of behavior: how frequently various behaviors occur, which behaviors tend to occur together, which reliably precede and follow each other. |

**Survey**

| | | |
| --- | --- | --- |
| What proportion of women are likely to vote for a pro-choice measure?<br><br>Which actor is most popular with white teenage boys?<br><br>What proportion of wild chimpanzees eat meat? | | Surveys measure attitudes on a large scale and provide quantitative descriptions of the characteristics of a population, such as the mean height of all females. |

**Archival Research**

| | | |
| --- | --- | --- |
| Do left- and right-handers have different average life spans?<br><br>Have U.S. newspapers changed during the past 50 years in the relative space they allot to sports and art news?<br><br>Do students visit campus health centers more frequently during exam periods? | | Archival researchers use existing data to answer their questions. They can do so only if the data exist. |

*(table continues)*

**TABLE 6.1**  (*continued*)

| Comparative Research | |
|---|---|
| Is the divorce rate different between people who live on islands and people who live on mainlands? | Note that all the archival questions listed earlier (but not all archival questions) are also comparative, and the first comparative question requires archival research. |
| Is there a difference between carnivores and herbivores in number of hours slept per day? | |
| Is there a difference between wild rats and rats bought from a commercial supplier in production of adrenal hormones following mild electric shock? | |

| Correlational Study | |
|---|---|
| What is the relationship between birth length and weight? | Correlational studies are designed to measure relationships between variables, that is, how scores on one variable correspond to scores on the other. Descriptive studies, surveys, and archival studies often ask correlational questions. |
| What is the relationship between mothers' anxiety levels during pregnancy and birth weights of their children? | |
| What is the relationship between SAT scores and college grades? | |

| QUALITATIVE RESEARCH | |
|---|---|
| What strategies do skilled physicians use to encourage their patients to stop smoking? | Several different techniques are classified together as qualitative research. They have in common a focus on the feelings and experiences of people. |
| How do young children think about death? | |
| How do people describe their feelings of loneliness? | |

| Case Study | |
|---|---|
| A mysterious virus destroyed a man's amygdala. How did his behavior change? | Case studies describe people, events, or settings, often unusual ones. Although they do not conclusively establish causes (except under special circumstances—see chapter 11), they are valuable for suggesting hypotheses about causes. They can be quantitative or qualitative. |
| How did victims of the earthquake respond? | |
| What caused the bizarre behavior of some of Freud's patients? | |

## Interpretation

Research methods shape views of phenomena and reality. White and Farmer (1992) cited correlational data showing that half of all victims of childhood rape or attempted rape are raped again as adults. The correlational approach seems to put at least part of the onus of sexual aggression on personality characteristics of the victims. The individual, whether victim or assailant, is the focus of study. By contrast, experimental approaches encourage thinking about victim and assailant behavior as modifiable by environmental factors.

## Theory Testing

Theory testing is crucial for the advancement of science. Theories can never be proven (see p. 8, 232–3), but their credibility increases or diminishes as the predictions they generate are upheld or disconfirmed. Diverse predictions tested in multiple ways enhance a theory's credibility the most. Brewer and Hunter (1989, p. 48) wrote:

> A single theory may predict or explain observed patterns of behavior, frequency distributions of attitudes in large populations, particular experimental effects, and events from earlier historical eras. To assess fully the validity of the theory, these different kinds of predictions, explanations, and variables should be studied, even though the studies require different types of research methods.

## ■ AN EXAMPLE: CIGARETTE SMOKING AND LUNG CANCER

Debate over the relationship between cigarette smoking and lung cancer illustrates the issues involved in choosing research strategies and selecting evidence. Despite thousands of studies, some scientists and statisticians claim to be unconvinced that smoking causes lung cancer. Their reason is that experiments are lacking on humans. (The collective evidence shows the value of multiple methods—and convinces me.)

1. Statements *a* and *b* below are not equivalent. On the assumption that both are true, which presents a better case for getting smokers to quit? As you read through the chapter, ask yourself which methods justify the more powerful statement. See p. 89 for answers.
   a. Smoking causes lung cancer.
   b. People who smoke are more likely than nonsmokers to get lung cancer.

2. If you were an attorney defending the tobacco industry against the charge that cigarette smoking causes lung cancer, how would you attack the various types of evidence presented later?

## Experiments

Experiments have two defining characteristics: (a) Subjects are either assigned randomly to treatment or control groups or exposed to each IV in random order, and (b) the experimenter manipulates the independent variable. For both legal and moral reasons, experimenters have not randomly assigned human subjects to either a smoking or nonsmoking group and recorded deaths from lung cancer. But they have experimented with animals. They have trained rhesus monkeys, dogs, and baboons to smoke. Rats and Syrian hamsters exposed to air diluted with smoke were more likely than control animals to develop tumors (Dalbey, Nettesheim, Griesemer et al., 1980; Dontenwill & Wiebecke, 1966).

Researchers who wish to analyze the causes of a phenomenon should, if possible, conduct experiments. Because subjects are assigned randomly, the experimental and control groups can be presumed equivalent initially, within tolerable error. Because both groups are treated exactly the same except for the independent variable, any posttreatment differences are assumed to be caused by the IV.

## Surveys

Surveys answer questions about the incidence and prevalence of a phenomenon, as when people are asked how many cigarettes they smoke per day, when they started smoking, how deeply they inhale, whether they use filters, and their favorite brand. Surveys that ask about past events are called *retrospective*, whereas *prospective* studies look to the future: People indicate their current habits and are restudied at a later time. An attempt is made to correlate some current habit with a future condition. In 1951, a prospective study was initiated with a cohort of more than 40,000 British physicians. They responded to a questionnaire about their smoking habits, and mortality data were collected on them for years afterward (Doll, 1995).

Response rates to surveys are often low, and respondents and nonrespondents may differ in important ways. More than 30% of the British physicians did not return their questionnaires, possibly because physician smokers with health problems preferred remaining anonymous. Also, respondents may misunderstand questions, have inaccurate memories, or lie. Widespread publicity on the dangers of cigarette smoking affected self-reports of smoking more than it did actual smoking behavior (Warner, 1977).

## Case Studies

Case studies have a long tradition in clinical medicine and psychology. When an individual with unusual symptoms presents himself to a clinical investigator, the investigator typically hypothesizes about possible causes. The first evidence of a smoking/cancer link might have been a 1761 report by Dr. John Hill that two snuff users had swellings of the nose that he believed to be cancerous. Although case studies stimulate ideas about causes, they should be viewed as starting rather than ending points. Knowing that patients with a particular set of symptoms have been exposed to certain stimuli does not justify the conclusion that the stimuli caused the symptoms. If 999 of 1,000 people were to die within a week of receiving a procedure called LR, that would not prove that LR is deadly. (LR is my abbreviation for last rites.)

Case studies are not only usually incapable of showing a causal relationship (like statement *a* presented earlier), they usually cannot even establish an association (like statement *b*). However, some investigators use varied data collection methods to study individual cases intensively over an extended time period, and their conclusions about causes are as persuasive as those reached by Holmes. See pp. 139–140.

## Archival Research

Archival research is the use of data previously collected for different purposes. Public documents are an excellent source of data and probably underused by social scientists. However, appropriate secondary sources may not be available for specific questions. In addition, archival research is subject to a special source of bias—researchers may be highly selective in their choice of documents. Using records of cigarette sales as an index of amount smoked, researchers found a strong correlation between a country's per capita consumption and its lung cancer deaths (U.S. Department of Health and Human Services, 1982).

## Comparisons

Although the rate of cigarette smoking is high in China, the incidence of heart disease is lower there than in Europe. Cigarette smoking damages the coronary and peripheral vascular systems partly by impairing specialized cells called endothelial cells and thus narrowing blood vessels (Celermajer et al., 1993). Woo et al. (1997) hypothesized that Chinese smokers experience a smaller loss of endothelial function, so they are protected from coronary damage. Woo et al. measured vessel dilatation in smokers and nonsmokers from China, England, and Australia. Nonsmokers had similar values, but the English and Australian smokers had less vessel dilatation than the Chinese smokers. The comparable values for nonsmokers persuaded the authors that the difference in vessel dilatation of smokers is not genetic, though an accompanying editorial disputed the interpretation:

> The difference in vessel dilatation in smokers may be primarily genetic but becomes evident only on exposure to an environmental factor, such as cigarette smoking. Studies of immigrants have been useful for separating the environmental and genetic components of ethnic differences. It would be informative, therefore, to measure vessel dilatation in Chinese smokers and nonsmokers living in Australia, the United Kingdom, or the United States. If the protection seen in Chinese persons living in China is also seen in westernized Chinese persons, the case for involvement of genetic elements would be strengthened. The role of genetic elements would not be proven, however, because immigrants may have brought protective factors, such as diet, with them. (*Annals of Internal Medicine*, 1997, p. 401)

The editorial argues for the value of comparative studies: "Observations of physiologic variation or differences in the prevalence of disease among ethnic groups can be important keys to understanding the causes of complex genetic diseases."

## Correlational Studies

Correlations indicate whether variables are related. They answer questions such as "Do *X* and *Y* occur together?" "Do high scores on *X* correspond with high scores on *Y* and low scores with low scores?" and "Does *X* reliably precede or follow *Y*?" However, correlational studies cannot prove that *X* causes *Y*. Even a strong positive correlation between the number of cigarettes smoked and the likelihood of getting cancer would not by itself be enough to indict smoking as the cause. Whatever factor(s) caused one group of people to smoke and others to refrain from smoking might be the key.

Of the 40,000 physicians who responded in 1951 to the British Medical Association study, more than 11,000 had died by 1973. Mortality rates from cancer were considerably higher among the smokers (U.S. Department of Health and Human Services, 1982). Lung cancer patients were more likely than control subjects to report having been smokers (Doll, 1955; U.S. Public Health Service, 1964). That is, a positive correlation was found between smoking and likelihood of getting cancer (Kunze & Vutuc, 1980; Rimington, 1981) and, in postmortem analyses, between smoking and the incidence of premalignant tumors of the bronchial epithelium (Auerbach et al., 1962). In other prospective studies, smoking cessation was found to reduce the risk of developing cancer (Doll & Hill, 1956).

Several countries publish twin registries, which serve as a data source for both retrospective and prospective correlational studies. Among identical twins discordant for smoking (only one twin smoked), the smokers were more likely to develop lung cancer (Cederlof, Friberg, & Lundman, 1977).

## Computer Simulations

To test tobacco industry claims that tobacco contributes significantly to the economy of every state in the United States, Warner and Fulton (1994) used a computer simulation of the Michigan economy, with and without tobacco product sales, for the years 1992 through 2005. They simulated the economy with tobacco expenditures eliminated or reduced and the equivalent spending redistributed to other goods and services according to consumers' normal spending patterns. Then they compared the results with baseline forecasts of the economy. They concluded that Michigan would have had 5,600 more jobs in 1992 had there been no expenditure on tobacco products; and almost 1,500 more jobs in 2005 than it will have if sales trends for tobacco products continue.

## Qualitative Research

Brown (1996) conducted open-ended interviews with 10 men and 11 women who had permanently quit smoking at age 60 or older. Her goal was to learn about their experiences with quitting. Brown concluded that all her subjects had gone through a process of learning to redefine themselves as nonsmokers. Brown used extensive quotes and many examples to illustrate what the process entailed, and she asserted that both researchers and practitioners can use her findings. For example, subjects reported that the encouragement of family members helped them sustain themselves as nonsmokers. Nagging and policing did not help. Thus, health care providers should recruit family members and teach them to be supportive.

## ■ WHY CHOOSE ONE METHOD OVER ANOTHER?

Researchers should consider three issues when choosing their method. First, for a given question, some methods promise more definitive answers. Only experiments can conclusively establish causes, but experiments in which laboratory animals are forced to smoke may be irrelevant to the smoking of humans. Our metabolic pathways differ, the effects of voluntary and involuntary smoking may differ, and the effects on confined inactive animals may differ from those on free active people. (The belief of most scientists that the animal experiments are conclusive, the denial by some that the experiments are relevant to humans, supports the contention made in chapter 1 that subjective factors play a substantial role in scientific decision making.) Experiments are better than questionnaires for causal analyses. But a researcher who has found that Syrian hamsters that smoke get cancer may learn more from questioning cancer patients about their smoking habits than from a replication with Mongolian gerbils.

The second reason for choosing one method over another is that each requires different resources. Archival research may involve no expenses other than what it costs to surf the Internet or travel to a documents library, whereas a well-equipped biomedical laboratory may contain hundreds of thousands of dollars worth of equipment. A small naturalistic observation study on behavior of students in the college library can be conducted by a single person, but large-scale national surveys require many interviewers and a great deal of money.

The third reason is temperament. Some scientists like running laboratory experiments, some prefer poring over documents in the National Archives, and some would rather observe lions on the Serengeti Plain. Prospective researchers should realize that under the appropriate circumstances, each approach is legitimate.

# ■ ADDITIONAL COMMENTS

Eysenck (1980) dissented from the view that smoking causes cancer. His major argument was that there have been no experiments with human subjects. His book raises certain other methodological issues, two of which are considered briefly:

1. The parallel increases in cigarette smoking and lung cancer during the past 70 years have been used as evidence for a link between them. Eysenck asserted that lung cancer has not increased, but there have been tremendous improvements in its diagnosis. This position shows the importance of proper measurement of the dependent variable.

2. Eysenck argued that no conclusions should be drawn from the study on British doctors because they are not a typical sample. He pointed out that doctors differ from the general population in such variables as education, socioeconomic status, and professional knowledge. But, although scientists should generalize cautiously, generalizations are what make science worthwhile. It would have been inappropriate to generalize from the incomes or the political beliefs of doctors to those of the general population; but as to changes in their lungs due to cigarette smoke, doctors are probably similar to the rest of us.

## ANSWERS

Statement *a* is stronger than statement *b*; *a* implies that smokers are more likely than nonsmokers to get cancer and that the reason they will get cancer is because they smoke. So, if *a* is true, *b* must be true, but the reverse relationship need not hold. For example, the statement that people with gray hair are more likely to get cancer does not imply that gray hair is the cause. The obvious explanation is that older people are more likely than younger ones to be afflicted, and gray hairs are a sign of age. For the same reason, widows and widowers and people receiving Social Security benefits are in the "more likely" category. So are close relatives of cancer victims (to some extent, cancer has a genetic basis), and people who own both a television set and a car (because cancer is more prevalent in industrialized countries).

All of the evidence for a smoking/cancer link, with the exception of the experiments, is of the statement *b* variety. Each type of nonexperiment demonstrates that smokers of a given age and sex die of lung cancer more frequently than nonsmokers, but in no case do they prove conclusively (because nonexperiments cannot prove conclusively) that smoking is the cause.

Attorneys for the tobacco companies emphasized the correlational nature of the case against cigarettes. They sought (and found) evidence that smokers differ statistically from nonsmokers before they start smoking in such traits as blood type, personality characteristics, and morphology. Even before any studies had been done, attorneys could have persuasively argued for a presmoking difference between the groups. To deny such a difference is to claim that smoking behavior is uncaused. And the difference(s), whether or not known, might cause the higher incidence of lung cancer in smokers.

# Experimenting:
# Two Groups

**7**

*By the time you finish reading this chapter, you should be able to answer the following questions:*

What are the two key features of experiments?

What makes experimentation such a powerful technique?

Do experimental and control groups typically start out exactly equal? What procedure is used to produce equal groups?

How do random and systematic error differ? Which type increases the likelihood of getting statistically significant differences, and which type decreases the likelihood?

What is the placebo effect, and what are active placebos?

What is a double-blind study? Are double-blind studies routinely done in psychology? How do researchers often sabotage double-blind studies?

What are the various reasons for experimenting rather than using a different research strategy?

Do well-controlled experiments eliminate all plausible alternative explanations of the data?

Is it reasonable to generalize from the results of laboratory experiments to the world outside the laboratory?

What are field experiments?

What is the difference between between-group and within-group variability?

Why do researchers try to increase between-group and decrease within-group variability?

■　■　■　■　■

*"The observer listens to nature; the experimenter questions and forces her to reveal herself."* George Cuvier, French zoologist

# ■ THE LOGIC OF EXPERIMENTATION

The logic of social science and medical experimentation is straightforward: The experimenter forms two or more groups of subjects that are equivalent in all essential characteristics. He treats the groups exactly alike with one exception—the independent variable. Then, if the groups subsequently differ, he concludes that the IV was responsible for the differences.

# ■ FORM GROUPS

Several possibilities exist for assigning subjects to groups:

1. Assign for convenience, for example, everyone in the front of a room to one group and in the back to another. This is unacceptable. People in the two locations might differ in motivation, personality, eyesight, and so forth. Subjects chosen by any nonrandom procedure may differ, and the differences might obscure the effects of the IV.

2. Use four groups and give two of them a pretest. Give the experimental treatment to one pretested group and one nonpretested group. Then give all groups a posttest. This design lets researchers test the possibility that experimental and control groups were not equivalent initially. But it requires twice as many subjects and more than twice as much work as simple randomization, which, as discussed later, is perfectly satisfactory.

3. Match subjects, for example, by randomly assigning one each of several pairs of identical twins to the experimental group and the other to the control. Identical twins are hard to find, but other matching possibilities exist. To study the effects of exercise on cholesterol level, subjects could be matched on initial cholesterol levels. Matching raises three concerns. First, the matching process might affect the final measurement. Subjects matched on intelligence test scores might improve on a subsequent intelligence test because of practice or do worse because of fatigue or loss of interest. Second, if the variable used for matching is not highly correlated with the dependent variable, the matching is a waste of time. It would make little sense to match subjects on intelligence test scores if the goal were to see whether exercise reduces cholesterol level. Third, matching requires extra work, and costs often exceed benefits.

4. Test each subject under each experimental condition. Experiments in which subjects serve as their own controls are called within-subject designs, and many researchers use such designs exclusively. Advantages and disadvantages are discussed on p. 116.

5. Assign subjects randomly to groups. The experimenter flips coins or uses some equivalent procedure to decide which subjects get which treatments. The coin, not the experimenter or subjects, decides. Randomly assigning subjects to groups is one of the key characteristics of experiments. Note that subjects need not (and usually cannot) be randomly selected. Rats bought from a particular supplier or volunteers from a psychology class are not a random selection of all possible subjects. But neither they nor the experimenter should have any choice about who is assigned to which group.

Random assignment is often impossible (as when comparing characteristics of first and later born children), unsuitable, or infeasible. Cook and Campbell (1979) gave the hypothetical example of a researcher wishing to compare job placements and income supplements as methods for reducing recidivism rates of ex-convicts. A randomized experiment would give the clearest answers but would take a long time. Instead, records of people who had already been given jobs or income supplements upon release from prison could be compared. The alternative approach would not conclusively establish cause, but its inability to do so might be outweighed by the advantage of accumulating data rapidly.

Random assignment does not guarantee initial equivalence of groups. Perhaps, purely by chance, all the men are assigned to one group and all the women to another; or people with an average 7th grade educational level go to one group and college graduates to the other. Random assignment minimizes such occurrences but cannot eliminate them entirely. However, in the typical published study, pretreatment group differences are an unlikely explanation for posttreatment differences. (Statistical analyses take into account the possibility of unequal group formation.) If a substantial inequality between experimental and control groups is noticed before administration of the IV, the experimenter should rerandomize or else the experiment will be compromised.

## ■ TREAT SUBJECTS EXACTLY THE SAME EXCEPT FOR THE INDEPENDENT VARIABLE

The key feature that distinguishes experiments from other types of research is some form of random assignment. The groups thus formed must then be treated differently in one and only one respect. But even excluding the independent variable, subjects are never treated exactly alike. Unequal treatments can be divided into two types: random and systematic.

## Random Error

Social scientists, no less than medical researchers and chemists, should keep their laboratories free from contaminants. They should strive to make testing conditions identical for all subjects, but that is an unattainable ideal. Two objects cannot be in the same place at the same time, so subjects cannot be treated exactly alike. Some will be tested at 8:15, others at 8:22; some on Tuesday, others on Friday; some by a 60-year-old man, others by a 25-year-old woman; some in complete silence, others while an argument rages outside the laboratory. Random errors occur unpredictably and do not favor subjects in any group. However, the errors tend to obscure the effects of the independent variable. Suppose that a new diet pill is given just before lunch to some people and just after to others, and they are then offered food platters. What is already in people's stomachs might have a greater impact on the amount of food they eat than the effects of the diet pill.

Although they cannot attain perfect uniformity, experimenters should identify relevant details and keep them the same for everybody. Such details vary from study to study. Uniformity would be lacking if subjects were tested at different times before and after a brutal, well-publicized boxing match; but outcomes would probably not be affected unless the DV were related to aggression—and even then, not if the subjects were rats. As a matter of routine, try to standardize lighting conditions, noise level, presence of people other than the subjects, time of testing, explicit wording of instructions, manner of presenting instructions, and the experimenter. (An experimenter's gender, age, attitude, and clothing may all influence behavior.) Other factors, such as the size and color of the laboratory and even the odors coming from a nearby restaurant, may influence certain behaviors. Be sensitive to the possibilities.

## Systematic Error

Even if rats injected with a drug become more active than uninjected controls, the drug might not be responsible. A plausible alternative would be that needle insertion caused the hyperactivity. Any variable not deliberately manipulated by an experimenter that acts unequally on experimental and control groups might influence outcomes. Such variables are called *confounds*. All the sources of random error mentioned earlier have the potential to be confounds. Everybody in the experimental group might be tested at 8:15, all of the controls at 8:22; one group on Tuesday, the other on Friday;

one by a 60-year-old man, the other by a 25-year-old woman; one in complete silence, the other while an argument rages outside the laboratory.

Several studies suggested that athletes who combine mental and physical practice outperform those who engage in physical practice only, but Murphy (1990) noted that all had a confound. Mental practice periods act to space out physical practice periods. Murphy speculated that the spacing, rather than the mental practice, accounted for improved performance. He did not find a single study that eliminated spacing as a possibility.

Two potential confounds always exist when evaluating the effectiveness of a treatment with human subjects: differential expectations of people in the treatment and control groups, and the rituals associated with the treatment (arranging an appointment with a psychotherapist, swallowing a pill, being put under anesthesia prior to surgery). Drug researchers try to avoid the problem by giving control subjects placebos (sugar pills—more precisely, substances without specific activity for the condition being treated). All researchers should use comparable safeguards.

Shapiro and Morris (1978) wrote, "The placebo effect may have greater implications for psychotherapy than any other form of treatment because both psychotherapy and the placebo effect function primarily through psychological mechanisms." That probably explains why clients who pay for psychotherapy have better outcomes than those who do not (Yoken & Berman, 1984) and why patients who received diagnostic tests following their complaints of chest pain were less likely to claim short-term disability than patients who did not receive the tests (Sox et al., 1981). An experimenter may be more solicitous toward a subject who has received a powerful drug than to one in the placebo group. That would violate the principle of uniform treatment. The best solution is to conduct double-blind experiments, in which neither experimenter nor subjects know which values of the IV have been assigned to which subject. Thus, presumably, all subjects are treated equally. Still, problems remain.

Both experimenters and subjects often figure out who has received which treatment (cf. Margraf et al., 1991). A solution in drug studies is to give drugs with discriminable side effects but neutral with respect to the condition being treated. But these drugs, called active placebos, sometimes produce negative effects; then patients who receive an ineffective treatment will be comparatively better, and the erroneous conclusion may be drawn that the drug is therapeutic (Lipman, Park, & Rickels, 1966).

Schulz (1995) and his colleagues investigated the actual conduct of double-blind experiments. When the codes indicating group assignment were poorly concealed—for example, pinned on a wall in the researcher's office—the experimental treatment was reported effective by an average of 30% more than when codes were kept strictly confidential. Schulz quizzed 400 researchers after promising them anonymity. More than half admitted opening unsealed envelopes containing the assignments, or cracking simple codes meant to hide the identity of the two groups, or searching for a master list of codes, or holding sealed envelopes up to the light.*

Hart, Turturro, Leakey, and Allaben (1995) reported a different sort of control group problem. Most laboratory rats are given unrestricted diets and grow fat and unhealthy. Mildly toxic substances typically suppress appetite, causing weight loss and, as a side effect, increasing life span. Thus, experimental subjects outlive controls and the substance seems beneficial.

Telling laboratory subjects that they might receive a placebo (as ethical guidelines advise) creates different expectations for them than for patients in clinics. Kirsch and Weixel (1988) simulated the procedure in clinical situations by telling one group of volunteers that they would receive caffeine. Other subjects were told they would receive either caffeine or a placebo, which simulated standard research laboratory conditions. All subjects were given placebos but the two groups responded differently and, on some measures, in opposite directions.

Robert Rosenthal has been at the forefront of research on experimenter bias. In one study (1966), half of a group of student experimenters had their hypotheses confirmed and half had them disconfirmed by their first few participants, who were actually confederates of the real experimenter. The rest of the participants were genuine subjects. The two groups of student experimenters got different responses from the genuine subjects on the experimental task and on standard tests of personality.

## Summary of the Logic of Experimentation

Subjects are randomly assigned to one of two or more groups. Random assignment makes it highly unlikely—although possible—that the groups differ appreciably on whichever variables the experimenter plans to measure. The groups are then treated exactly the same except for the independent variable. If posttreatment differences emerge, the reasonable conclusion is that the IV caused the difference.

---

*Virtually all methodology books assert the importance of double-blind experiments. In 1987 and again in 1996, I sampled the most recent issues of 18 peer-reviewed American Psychological Association journals available in my school library. In only 4 of 52 cases in 1987, and in 9 of 98 in 1996, were double-blind procedures mentioned in the methods, procedure, or data analysis sections. (When several studies were discussed in one article, I considered only the first.) Double-blind studies are expensive and time-consuming and, when phenomena are robust, perhaps unnecessary. At least researchers (if not textbook writers) seem to think so.

# ■ REASONS FOR EXPERIMENTING

## Experimenters Seek Answers to "What Would Happen If ... ?" Questions

Scientists cannot wait for interesting phenomena to occur naturally. Only by carefully arranging circumstances will they see rats press bars for food rewards and people lower their blood pressures by attending to feedback. In the 16th century, Francis Bacon recognized the need of scientists to indulge in experiential play, and he called the invented experiences experiments. Experiments allow scientists to answer "What would happen if ... ?" questions and extend the range of phenomena that can be studied.

## Experimenters Test Logically Deduced Consequences from Theories

Experimentation is the most powerful method ever devised for testing logically deduced consequences of scientific theories. Given the prediction that event $Y$ will occur under circumstance $X$, experimenters produce $X$ and see if $Y$ occurs.

## Experimenters Can Control Variables

A researcher might study the relationship between stress and aggressiveness nonexperimentally, but she would have to wait for the two variables to change spontaneously and would have no control over other variables that might affect them. A great virtue of experiments is that they allow control over both the independent variable and extraneous variables.

## Experimenters Can Eliminate Otherwise Plausible Alternatives to Their Interpretations of Data

Nonexperimental research generally fails to eliminate plausible alternative explanations of results. By contrast, the logic of experimentation forces the conclusion that the IV has (has not) influenced the DV. Contrast (a) and (b):

a. During the course of a night, while campers sleep, a tape recorder plays a continuous message telling them to drink milk at breakfast time. The next morning, each camper drinks a large glass of milk.
b. Campers are randomly assigned to be exposed to either continuous music or the message to drink milk. The next morning, campers in the second group drink significantly more milk on average than do those in the first group.

Study a is not an experiment. Even if every camper guzzled a quart of milk the next morning, the reason would be unclear. The message might have affected them, but they might have normally drunk lots of milk. Study b is an experiment. If campers exposed to the message and otherwise treated just like the music group drank significantly more milk, a conclusion that the message was responsible would be on much firmer grounds.

Several nonexperiments and faulty conclusions derived from them are listed in Box 7.1 (based on the work of Campbell & Stanley, 1996). Try to think of an alternative explanation for each.

---

**BOX**

## Alternative Interpretations Exist for Nonexperimental Data

The conclusions drawn from the following studies might be correct, but there are plausible alternatives. Think of one for each study.

1. A teacher tries a new teaching method with her second grade class. The class does better on an achievement test at the end of the year than on a similar test at the beginning of the year. She concludes that the new method works.

2. In the month following a well-publicized campaign to crack down on speeders, car fatalities decline substantially from the previous month; the highway patrol attributes the decline to the campaign.

3. In Prussia, until 1883, suicides were recorded by local police stations. In that year, recording was made the responsibility of a national bureau and 20% more suicides were reported. The conclusion was that the suicide rate, for reasons unknown, had increased 20%.

4. At 6:00 P.M., volunteers are seated in comfortable stuffed chairs in a dark room. At 11:00 P.M., soft music is piped into the room, and by midnight most of the volunteers are asleep. The researcher concludes that the music is an effective way to put people to sleep.

5. Fifty volunteers receive a series of painful electric shocks while 50 control subjects listen to a motivational tape. Half the people in the shock group quit before the experiment is over. The remaining 25 do better on average than the control group at a motor coordination task. The experimenter concludes that electric shock, properly applied, improves motor coordination.

6. Fifty volunteers receive a powerful drug, and their scores on a memory test are compared with those of 50 nonvolunteers. The drug takers do better, leading to the conclusion that the drug improves memory.

**Answers**

1. *Maturation.* Older children do better on average than younger ones, and the children in this study aged 9 months during the school year. Maturation effects refer to any changes that occur because of the passage of time (fatigue, increased or reduced motivation, changes in health, etc.).

2. *History.* The weather may have been exceptionally good during the second month. The first month may have been a holiday season when fatalities are normally high. History refers to events besides the independent variable that take place between measurements and may affect them.

3. *Instrumentation.* The local stations and the national bureau used different criteria for suicide. Instrumentation effects refer to any changes in the measuring instrument that affect scores.

4. This is also a maturation effect.

5. *Mortality.* Drop-outs often differ in relevant ways from subjects who remain in experiments, so if groups differ in drop-out rates (called mortality or attrition), conclusions are suspect. (Differential mortality presents problems of interpretation to experimenters as well as to other researchers.)

6. *Selection.* Those who volunteer to take a powerful drug differ in many ways from nonvolunteers. A researcher, observing the differences after administering a drug, might falsely attribute them to the drug. Selection effects are caused by nonrandom assignment to groups.

## Experiments Can Establish That One Event Has Caused Another

Experimenting is the best way to determine if one event causes another. Readers of scientific articles should always examine methods sections to see whether the research described has the two key features of experiments. If not, they should be wary about attributions of causes. Note: Many words imply the same thing as "cause" and require equal caution: influence, affect, modify, increase, decrease, change, alter, induce, elicit, and so on.

## ■ EXPERIMENTS DO NOT ELIMINATE THE NEED FOR JUDGMENT

## Plausible Alternative Explanations May Remain

Although randomization makes it unlikely that subjects will differ much at the start of an experiment, they might drop out nonrandomly for any of several reasons. One group might (a) be exposed to more unpleasant conditions, (b) experience more benefits, or (c) receive more attention. Certain types of subjects might drop out in greater numbers; for example, people with less (more) severe symptoms or who are hurt more easily by criticism. *Attrition* refers to the number of dropouts from an experiment. Even if nobody drops out, data might be harder to collect on one group than another. Experiments render each alternative of Box 7.1 other than nonrandom attrition implausible. A historical event or change in a measuring instrument might affect subjects during the course of an experiment but is unlikely to affect groups unequally. However, nonrandom attrition is not rare. Goldwater and Collins (1985) and Hughes, Casal, and Leon (1986) studied the effects of exercise on mood, but many of the exercising groups dropped out. McCrady et al. (1986) collected complete data on only 101 of the 174 patients who started their study. Riley, Sobell, Leo et al. (1987) reviewed 68 studies on the treatment of alcohol problems. An average of 24% of patients who completed treatment were lost to follow-up.

Because missing data complicate interpretations, researchers should do everything possible to keep all subjects in their study and minimize losses to follow-up. Armitage (1983) imagined a study in which patients with lung cancer were randomly assigned to receive either surgery or radiotherapy. Patients with inoperable tumors, if they were in the surgery group, would be identified and probably excluded from the study; however, patients assigned to the radiotherapy group would not have inoperable tumors discovered. Then, patients remaining in the surgery group would have a better prognosis than the intact radiotherapy group. So Armitage advised comparing the total groups assigned to the two conditions. Readers who wish to pursue the matter further should read Little and Schenker (1995) for statistical advice on handling missing data.

## Results Must Be Interpreted Within the Framework of Existing Knowledge

Study c is analogous in form to the previous nonexperimental study a.

   c. During the course of a night, while campers sleep, a tape recorder plays a continuous message telling them to grow taller. In the morning, their average height has increased by 6 inches.

Such extraordinary results would not be dismissed on the grounds that c lacked a control group; and the addition of a control group would make little difference. The alternatives of Box 7.1 would not apply, but others would—specifically, fraud and measurement errors. If the study inspired further research, the goal would be to rule out those possibilities.

Why scientists accept one interpretation rather than another is not susceptible to simple analysis. An important requirement is that acceptable explanations be compatible with previously established facts; but even well-established facts often prove incorrect. Here, as in all aspects of scientific investigation, rules cannot be applied mechanically.

## Experimenters Must Be Sensitive to the Complexity of Variables

When posttreatment differences are found between experimental and control groups, investigators typically attribute them to the actions of a specific IV. But, as in the earlier examples of confounding, IVs as experimenters conceive them may differ from IVs as subjects receive them. The IV may be entirely responsible for differences between groups, but not in the way interpreted by the experimenter. She may keep rats in a hot room because a theory predicts that increases in body temperature promote aggression. The heat may produce the predicted consequences, but only because it attracts fleas that irritate the rats.

## Generalizations Cannot Be Made Routinely

Subjects and settings for experiments are rarely chosen randomly, so generalizations cannot be made by formula. They require careful judgments and must be considered unproven until tested.

**Generalizations to Other Subjects Cannot Be Made Routinely.** The subjects in a study constitute the sample. Experimenters hope that the sample is representative of a larger group, the population, so that what is learned about the sample holds for the population as well. But that expectation is often unjustified. For example, most studies of antidepressant drugs exclude people with mild depression, but most people treated with antidepressants are mildly depressed (Munoz, Hollon, McGrath et al., 1994). Most studies on drugs for treating heart attacks exclude people over the age of 75 years, who are the ones most likely to die from heart attacks, and they also have a small percentage of women (Gurwitz, Col, & Avorn, 1992).

If the goal of a research project is to discover general laws of behavior, then the population is all of humanity and representative samples are beyond the reach of even the most dedicated scientists. Many samples are comprised of student volunteers (most frequently male) from psychology classes or Norway rats. Valid generalizations from these are possible, but the only way to know is to test them on the appropriate populations. Contrast (d) and (e).

d. Student volunteers randomly assigned to an experimental group receive painful electric shocks. Students in a control group have electrodes attached to their wrists, but no current is passed through. The heart rates of experimentals change more than do those of controls.

e. Student volunteers randomly assigned to an experimental group hear a speech about the need for a doubling of tuition costs. Students in a control group watch a short film on crocheting. Heart rates change more in the experimental group.

It would be reasonable to generalize from the student sample to the general population about the effects of shock on heart rate, and unreasonable to generalize about the effects of speeches on tuition hikes. No plausible explanation comes to mind why students differ from other people in the first case, but an explanation is available for the second case.

Volunteers and nonvolunteers differ (Rosenthal & Rosnow, 1975). Women who had previously completed a questionnaire about sexual activities and sex guilt were asked to volunteer for a study on psychophysiological measurement of sexual arousal. The volunteers had reported less sexual inhibition and more experience with a variety of sexual practices (Morokoff, 1986). Volunteers even differ among themselves. Several differences were found between volunteers for a study labeled "Personality Assessment" and another called "Color Preferences" (Silverman & Margulis, 1973).

## Generalizations to Other Situations Cannot Be Made Routinely.

Experimenters generally investigate their variables in one particular context, the laboratory. But people's perceptions of the experimenter's purpose affect their behaviors in laboratory settings (Orne, 1962). Other settings influence behaviors in their own unique ways. Bruner (1965) wrote: "I am still struck by Roger Barker's ironic truism that the best way to predict the behavior of a human being is to know where he is: In a post office he behaves post office, at a church he behaves church."

Critics have argued that by demanding rigorous control, experimenters create artificial settings with little relevance to conventional ones. Gergen (1978) wrote,

> In the attempt to isolate a given stimulus from the complex in which it is normally embedded, its meaning within the normative cultural framework is often obscured or destroyed. When subjects are exposed to an event out of its normal context they may be forced into reactions that are unique to the situation and have little or no relationship to their behavior in the normal setting.

Critics say that laboratories distort the normal actions of experimental variables and, as a result, findings often fail to generalize to nonlaboratory settings. But all distinct settings, by definition, are unique. Laboratories differ from schools, which differ from churches, hospitals, and homes. Generalizations from one to another often do not apply. However, unless the settings and relevant variables are specified, meaningful generalizations are not even possible. Then, if the generalizations do not hold up, experimenters can search for reasons in the differences between the settings. Isolation of variables serves two distinct purposes. First, it enables scientists to specify the precise conditions under which phenomena occur. Second, simple systems often provide clues to the workings of more complex ones. Social scientists are not alone in dealing with the context-specific properties of variables. Organic chemistry is the study of carbon compounds, that is, of the immense number of contexts (molecular configurations, including many found only in laboratories) in which the element carbon is found. Organic chemists owe much of their success to the development of procedures for isolating and purifying these compounds.

Laboratory subjects are aware they are being studied, and that affects their behavior. But they are made aware because of ethical considerations, not because the logic of experimentation requires it. People who use other research designs must also either deceive about the nature of their work or risk influencing the behaviors of subjects by explaining it.

More than 200 studies show that psychotherapy is beneficial with children and adolescents. Weisz, Weiss, and Donenberg (1992) noted that most were experiments, which differ from conventional clinic therapy in several ways. Yet although studies on clinic-based therapy show much smaller effects than experiments, Weisz et al. (1992, p. 1584) concluded that the latter

> suggest that under proper conditions child therapy may be very effective. When the findings are viewed in this light, a key task for researchers becomes that of identifying those proper conditions under which effects of child therapy may be optimized. Identifying such conditions may require adapting research therapies to actual clinical conditions with referred clients, then testing the efficacy of research-based therapies in clinic settings.

Some scientists experiment in natural settings to test the generality of laboratory findings. Laboratory studies had supported the proposition that happy people are more likely than unhappy ones to help others. Mood in the laboratory had been manipulated by having subjects read either cheerful or unpleasant materials, and helping had been measured by their responses to requests for donations of money. Underwood et al. (1977) tested the proposition with a field experiment. After having moviegoers rate several popular films, Underwood et al. picked three double features playing at the time. One film pair was rated as inducing negative emotions and two were rated as neutral. The investigators set up collection boxes for a well-known charity outside the theater lobbies. Less money was collected after the sad movies, which corresponded with the laboratory findings.

■ ■ ■

Q1: Was the rating procedure necessary? Could the experimenters have picked the movies on the basis of their own reactions?

Q2: Subjects were not randomly assigned to watch the sad or neutral movies. Might that have affected results?

Q3: Can you think of any strategy to overcome the problem of nonrandom assignment?

Q4: Subjects can be randomly assigned to conditions in field experiments. Suppose you wanted to see if helping behaviors of bystanders toward victims of falls are influenced by the victim's race. Can you design a field experiment with random assignment?

See p. 106 for answers.

■ ■ ■

Memory researchers have debated the value of field experiments, which, for them, involve the study of memory for events occurring in the everyday worlds of subjects. Banaji and Crowder (1989) wrote that such research has produced no powerful theories, led to the discovery of no new principles of memory, and developed no new methods of data collection. They argued that scientists working in laboratories are better able to control variables and thus to discover generalizable principles. Their article, entitled "The bankruptcy of everyday memory," elicited a flood of responses.

Bahrick (1991, p. 76) wrote: "It is acceptable to sacrifice some control over critical variables in order to investigate ecologically important phenomena that would otherwise be neglected." Ceci and Bronfenbrenner (1991) advised psychologists not to think about research in terms of available equipment and laboratory paradigms: "The choice of experimental versus nonexperimental or field versus lab ought to be made in the context of the particular research question. No a priori rule can satisfy what is certainly a case-by-case judgment call on the part of the researcher." Neisser (1991, p. 35) wrote, "Benaji and Crowder asked their readers, mockingly, to imagine doing chemistry without laboratory controls. Can they imagine evolutionary biology, or ecology, or ethology without field studies?"

Several respondents referred to field studies that had advanced scientific knowledge. For example, Bahrick (1984) discovered surprising retention curves when he studied people's memories for Spanish lessons taken 50 years earlier. Neisser described Nelson's (1986) studies showing that 2-year-olds recall familiar routines and are rarely wrong.

Roediger (1991, p. 39) defended Banaji and Crowder: "The traditional role of naturalistic observation is to draw attention to significant phenomena and to suggest interesting ideas. Researchers will then typically create a laboratory analog of the natural situation in which potentially relevant variables can be brought under control and studied."

Banaji and Crowder (1991) were given the last word. They distinguished between two dimensions in scientific research—the ecological validity of the method used and the generality of the conclusions permitted. They argued that the only real problem occurs when one dimension must be sacrificed in favor of the other. They believe it is more important to be able to generalize findings, even when that means sacrificing valid investigation methods.

## ■ VARIABILITY IN EXPERIMENTS

Suppose subjects are randomly assigned to experimental and control groups and then, before being exposed to an IV, given a test. Almost certainly, their scores will vary. The following sections explain why and in so doing prepare the way for learning how to improve experiments and analyze them statistically. Three sources of variation are inherent in any measurement situation involving living subjects. First, subjects come in assorted sizes, shapes, histories, and ages, and with different motivation and ability levels. Second, as discussed earlier, it is impossible to treat all subjects exactly alike. Third, measuring devices are imperfect and imperfectly used. That is, errors occur. For these three reasons, variation occurs even among subjects assigned to the same group; it is called within-group variability.

If equivalent groups are formed by random assignment, then prior to the administration of an IV the variability between the groups will approximate the within-group variability. That is, the ratio *between-group variability/within-group variability* will approximate 1. If an effective IV is given to only one of the groups, or given in different doses, between-group variability will increase. But since everybody within a group receives the same level of the IV, within-group variability will not change. Thus, the ratio *between-group variability/within-group variability* will become greater than 1. The stronger the effect of the IV, the greater will be the posttreatment ratio *between-group/within-group variability*. Shown in Table 7.1 are the DV scores of subjects in two fictitious experiments. In the first, subjects were randomly assigned to receive either treatment A or B; in the second, they received either C or D. In both cases the mean of the first group is 10 and of the second, 7. Yet only experiment 1 yields statistically significant results, because the ratio *between-group/within-group variability* is much larger in experiment 1. Experimenters try to increase the ratio by minimizing within-group and maximizing between-group variability.

**TABLE 7.1**  Results of Two Fictitious Experiments

| A | B | C | D |
|---|---|---|---|
| 10 | 7 | 20 | 10 |
| 11 | 6 | 0 | 4 |
| 9 | 8 | 18 | 14 |
| 12 | 8 | 2 | 0 |
| 9 | 6 | 15 | 13 |
| 9 | 7 | 5 | 12 |
| 10 | 7 | 19 | 1 |
| 10 | 7 | 1 | 2 |

## Increasing Between-Group Variability

Between-group variability increases with increasing treatment effect, so experimenters should select their IVs carefully. Concepts can be operationalized in many ways, each with a different potential impact on behavior. Creating stress by giving an electric shock will probably produce a stronger effect than saying "Boo." Once a concept is operationally defined, it should be pretested and then given at a level to maximize the difference between experimental and control groups. For example, people who set specific goals generally outperform people who simply try to do their best. But if the goals are too easy, the groups do not differ.

Manipulations sometimes fail. Two subjects who were asked to imagine failure experiences before attempting a motor skills task reported that they had imagined a success experience instead (Woolfolk, Parrish, & Murphy, 1985). Despite being instructed to do their best, many subjects set specific goals for themselves (Locke, Cartledge & Koeppel, 1968). So researchers should verify that their IVs worked as intended; that is, they should do manipulation checks. When scientists were asked to evaluate the methodology of important and unimportant studies (Wilson, DePaulo, Mook, & Klaaren, 1993, see p. 41), they also rated the importance of the studies. The ratings confirmed the effectiveness of the manipulation.

Note: Systematic errors increase between-group variability and hence increase the likelihood of making a Type I error (reporting statistically significant results although the treatment has been without effect; see p. 212).

## Decreasing Within-Group Variability

Random error increases within-group variability and so increases the likelihood of making a type II error (failing to find statistically significant results although the treatment has had an effect). Strategies exist for minimizing each of the three sources of within-group variability.

**Selecting Subjects.** Within-group variability can be reduced by restricting the experiment to only a certain type of subject. Researchers who use human subjects try to make their samples as homogeneous as possible. They may open an experiment only to male volunteers from an introductory psychology class who have not previously participated in a learning study, or to inmates of a particular institution, or to girls in a day care center. Researchers who work with animals are even more demanding. Unless their specific goal is to compare, they typically use only a single species. More than that, they use inbred animals of the same age and weight, from the same supplier, housed and fed under identical conditions. Denenberg (1982) argued that the animals are for all practical purposes the same individual.

Unfortunately, researchers who use homogeneous samples often focus on certain types of subjects and exclude others. The much greater use of males than females in both animal and human research has resulted in theories that apply to only one gender (Carlson, 1971; Hyde & Rosenberg, 1976). For example, Kohlberg's (1976) data seemed to support his view that men are more likely than women to reach the highest levels of morality. But he initially studied only boys and young men, so male responses defined the highest levels. Girls and women may base their moral decisions on other factors (compassion rather than abstract principles of justice—see Gilligan, 1982).

Blanchard et al. (1995) summarized evidence for (a) a large gender difference in response to stressful situations, and (b) an important role of the neurotransmitter serotonin in such behaviors. Yet, in the years between 1973 and 1994, fewer than 5% of serotonin/anxiety studies used either females alone or both males and females as subjects. Most of the few comparisons between males and females indicated that they respond differently to drug treatment in a threatening situation.

**Treating Subjects Uniformly Except for the IV.** This is discussed on pp. 92–95.

**Reducing Measurement Errors.** Random errors increase variability. Reduce errors by practicing your scoring systems. If two or more people share the responsibility of scoring, run periodic reliability checks and double-check all computations.

## ANSWERS

Q1: Researchers should directly test, rather than rely on intuition, that their manipulations produce the desired effects. Laboratory researchers use the same manipulations repeatedly and need not test each time; field experimenters should test.

Q2: Any time subjects are not randomly assigned to groups, there may be a problem. See the next answer for strategies to deal with this.

Q3: Underwood et al. (1977) exposed subjects to the collection boxes at different times: either as they entered the theaters or as they left. Had the entering subjects donated differently depending on choice of movie, the results would have been difficult to interpret. As there were no differences, the authors concluded that with respect to giving to charity, people who chose sad and neutral movies were similar. Thus, differences in giving behavior of people as they left the theater were caused by the movies, not by pretreatment differences. Random assignment could have been implemented had it been thought essential. For example, people in a large apartment building could have been randomly assigned to receive free tickets to one showing or the other. (If the tickets named the films, differential attrition and trading of tickets would have become problems.)

Q4: There are many possibilities. Here is one: Piliavin, Rodin, and Piliavin (1970) had accomplices pretend to collapse on New York City subway trains. Some of the "victims" were black, some white, and they pretended to be either crippled or drunk. The investigators found that riders helped cripples irrespective of race but were more likely to help drunks if they were of the same race.

# Variations on the Simple Experiment

*By the time you finish reading this chapter, you should be able to answer the following questions:*

What are the advantages of using more than one level of an independent variable?

What is a factorial design?

What is an interaction?

What is a subject variable?

What are the advantages and disadvantages of using subjects as their own controls?

■  ■  ■  ■  ■

*"To predict a subject's voluntary delay of gratification, one may have to know how old he is, his sex, the experimenter's sex, the particular objects for which he is waiting, the consequences of not waiting, the models to whom he was just exposed, his immediately prior experience—the list gets almost endless."* Mischel (1973)

The type of experiment described thus far involves randomly assigning each subject to one of two groups and then treating subjects exactly the same except for the independent variable. Three variations of the two-group design are considered.

## ■ STUDYING AN INDEPENDENT VARIABLE AT MORE THAN ONE LEVEL OR STUDYING MORE THAN ONE IV

An IV given at too low a dose will have negligible effects, whereas high doses may be expensive, painful, or even deadly. Maximum between-group variability often occurs at moderate doses. Figure 8.1 shows that performance is better when subjects' levels of anxiety are moderate rather than high or low. Probably all treatments that enhance a particular behavior will, if sufficiently intense, impair the same behavior.

Since the actions of IVs are not known in advance of testing, experimenters must guess at effective levels. They can search the scientific literature for clues and they can do pilot tests. In addition, they can administer more than two levels of the IV, each to a different group of randomly assigned subjects. This increases the likelihood of finding meaningful differ-

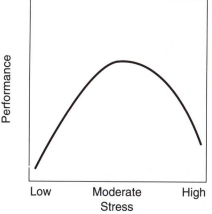

**FIGURE 8.1**
The relationship between stress and performance is complex.

ences and also shows how the DV changes throughout the tested range of the IV. A good strategy is to use levels that are constant multiples of each other, for instance, 4, 8, 16, and 32 hours of food deprivation.

Experimenters can compare different IVs. To test the effectiveness of various treatments for depression, group 1 might be given a drug, group 2 cognitive behavior therapy, group 3 psychoanalysis, group 4 hypnotic suggestions, and group 5 exercise. The single five-group experiment would accomplish as much as a series of two-group experiments and do it more efficiently. (To evaluate the effects of each of five IVs against the effects of each of the other four, 10 two-group experiments would be needed. This would entail 20 groups of subjects and 10 different times and conditions of testing.)

## ■ FACTORIAL DESIGNS

The answers to many questions depend on circumstances: "Which sport, basketball or hockey, is more popular?" The answer depends on whether the question is asked in the United States or Sweden. "Is a daily 5-mile run good for health?" Maybe, if the subjects are 20; highly unlikely if they are 90. "Is sexual attractiveness increased when a person changes from faded jeans to an expensive dress?" Maybe, for Daryl Hannah; no, for Denzel Washington. (Even then, the answer depends on the judges.)

When the effects of one variable depend on the value of a second, the two are said to interact. A recurring criticism of social science experiments is that they isolate variables from stimulus complexes in which the variables normally occur. Outside laboratories, the variables interact in so many different ways and with so many other variables that the laboratory-based laws do not apply. Cronbach (1975) suggested that social scientists devote more time to the study of interactions. Rather than trying to discover general behavioral laws, they should accept the more modest goals of describing the conditions under which their data are collected and analyzing the data for local effects.

With a single study called a *factorial design,* experimenters can test not only the separate effects of each of two or more variables (factors) but also how they interact, with fewer computations and subjects than separate experiments would require. Factors can be administered at several levels, for example, low, medium, and high intensity. If one factor has three levels and the other five, the design is called a 3 × 5 factorial. If there are five factors, one with three levels and all the others with two, the design is called a 3 × 2 × 2 × 2 × 2. Experimenters rarely use more than three factors or five levels of any one factor. As the number of factors increases, so does the number of potential interactions.

If two IVs in an experiment are each administered at two levels, the design is a 2 × 2. Two × two factorial designs give rise to six possible combinations of main effects (effects of the IVs) and interactions.

## Six Possible Outcomes of a 2 × 2 Factorial Study

1. Neither variable affects the DV and there is no interaction: Results of this type rarely get published.

2. Neither IV has a significant effect, but there is an interaction. See Figure 8.2. Shute (1994) randomly assigned subjects to work at a computer under one of two conditions for learning about electricity: (a) information was spoon-fed or (b) learners were required to derive concepts and rules on their own. Subjects in both conditions had the option of exploring other information in addition to the lesson. Then Shute measured learning. She found that neither learning environment was better overall than the other and frequent and infrequent explorers did equally well, but there was an interaction. Frequent explorers did better in the environment requiring that they derive concepts; infrequent explorers did better in the spoon-fed environment. A researcher who had run two separate two-group experiments on learning environment and exploratory behavior would have concluded, probably unhappily, that her results had no educational policy implications; neither factor seemed to make a difference. The factorial design shows that the conclusion would have been mistaken.

3. There is one significant main effect. That is, one IV significantly affects the DV: A low dose produces a different effect than a high dose. The other IV does not affect the DV: that is, no matter what its level, the DV score is the same. There is no interaction. This pattern is diagrammed in Figure 8.3. Burleson, Kunkel, Samter, and Werking (1996) asked college students to judge the importance of various communication skills in relationships: One group judged opposite-sex romantic relationships; one group judged same-

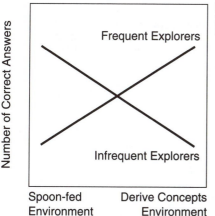

**FIGURE 8.2**
Neither IV has a significant effect, but there is an interaction.

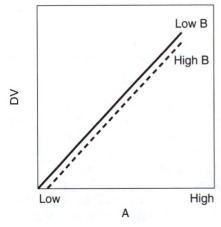

**FIGURE 8.3** One IV, in this case A, significantly affects the DV, and there is no interaction.

sex friendships. There was one main effect—communication skills were seen as more important in romances than in friendships. The main effect for gender was not significant; that is, men and women did not differ in their judgments. The interaction between relationship type and sex was not significant.

■ ■ ■

Q1: Was this study an experiment? (Answer on p. 117.)

■ ■ ■

4. In this pattern, an IV that does not act directly nevertheless modifies the actions of another IV. The drug naloxone, administered alone, has negligible effects. But when naloxone-treated subjects are exposed to music that normally moves them, they do not enjoy the music as much (Goldstein, 1980). See Figure 8.4.

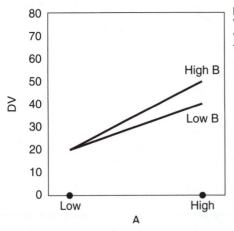

**FIGURE 8.4** Variable *A* significantly affects the DV, variable *B* does not, and there is an interaction.

5. Both IVs significantly affect the DV, but the influence of each is independent of the value of the other; that is, there is no interaction (see Figure 8.5). Lee and Clemons (1985) asked college students to make decisions about written memos describing hypothetical work situations. The students had to give their probability of approving (a) a 65-year-old employee's request to attend a conference and (b) requests from two workers, a 32-year-old and a 61-year-old, competing to be in a training program. Half of the subjects received job descriptions and moderately positive performance reports about the employees and half did not. There were two main effects. Students gave more favorable decisions to the older workers when (a) the situation did not require a choice between older and younger, and (b) performance information about the older worker was provided. There were no interactions.

6. Both IVs affect the DV and there is an interaction. Note that interactions can occur in more than one way (see Figures 8.6 and 8.7). Subjects who inhaled cocaine and drank ethanol-containing beverages had heart rate increases that were significantly larger than the sum of the increases when the drugs were taken separately. Combinations of cocaine and marijuana also increased heart rate above the simple summed effects (Foltin, Fischman, & Levin, 1995).

## Interpretation of Interactions

The type of interaction between two IVs is likely to differ for each DV measured. Interactions restrict generalizations, as can be seen by considering the results depicted in Figure 8.2. Teaching by spoon-feeding works best, but

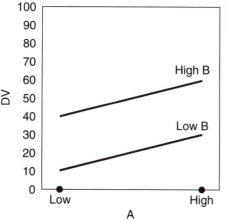

**FIGURE 8.5**
Both IVs significantly affect the DV, but there is no interaction.

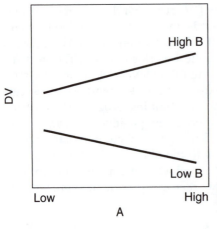

**FIGURE 8.6**
Both IVs significantly affect the DV, and there is an interaction.

only with learners who do not explore much. Findings of the type shown in Figure 8.2, with an interaction but no significant main effects, should not disappoint. The *A* results are not significant only because *A* acts in opposite directions at low and high levels of *B*, so the effects cancel each other out. If *A* were tested at only one level of *B*, significance would be reached; and *B*, likewise, would be significant if tested at only one level of *A*. More generally, a significant interaction tells that variables work better under certain conditions and would have significant effects if tested under the right conditions. Graphs clarify the nature of interactions, so they should be routinely drawn and analyzed. If two lines are drawn, as in Figures 8.2 to 8.7, parallel lines indicate that the variables do not interact. If the lines are not parallel, the variables do interact.

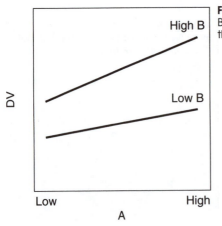

**FIGURE 8.7**
Both IVs significantly affect the DV, and there is an interaction.

## Subject Variables

Males and females often respond differently, as do old and young, soldiers and civilians, and normals and schizophrenics. To learn if an IV affects both sexes similarly, a researcher might use gender as one of her factors in a 2 × 2 design. Her four groups would be (a) males, level one of the IV, (b) males, level two, (c) females, level one, and (d) females, level two. All subjects would be assigned randomly to the IV or control condition. But because they cannot be assigned randomly to gender, that aspect of the study would be correlational. The same restrictions on causal inferences would apply as in all correlational research.

Genotype (the genetic constitution of an organism) is a subject variable. Behavior geneticists frequently publish estimates of the extent to which individual differences in behaviors are due to different genotypes. Wahlsten (1994) criticized such heritability analyses on several accounts, the most important being that genotype interacts with environment. He summarized studies on inbred mouse strains tested for motor activity in different laboratories. The interactions of genes and the environment were numerous. Treatments that increased activity in some strains decreased it in others, and whether one strain was more or less active than another depended on the laboratory in which they were tested.

## Blocking

As subjects become increasingly dissimilar in characteristics relevant to the dependent variable, within-group variability increases. And the greater the within-group variability, the smaller the likelihood of getting statistically significant results. But to have a large enough sample, investigators must often use subjects who differ, such as males and females or students from two distinct school districts. If the trait on which they differ is identified beforehand and correlates reasonably well with the DV, it can be used as one of the factors in a factorial design. Suppose, for example, that gender correlated positively with math scores. An investigator interested in the effects of teaching methods X and Y on math scores, even though not interested in gender differences, might benefit from using a 2 × 2 factorial design with gender as one of the factors. Within-group variability would be reduced by this approach, called *blocking*. Subjects within a block would be randomly assigned to methods X or Y.

## The Experimenter as a Variable

Two experimenters following identical protocols may get substantially different results. Two examples follow:

- Two experimenters, a young, petite woman and a mature, large man, reinforced subjects for saying hostile words. Significantly more were emitted in the presence of the woman (Binder et al., 1957).
- Psychotherapists were divided into two groups on the basis of their perception of movement in Rorschach inkblots. Later, they administered Rorschachs. Those who had perceived lots of movement scored their patients as perceiving significantly more movements (Graham, 1960).

## ■ WITHIN-SUBJECT DESIGNS

If each subject is exposed to each experimental condition, within-group variability can be reduced to a minimum. Experiments in which subjects serve as their own controls, called within-subject designs, are discussed further in chapter 11. A researcher wishing to compare teaching methods X and Y could randomly assign subjects to one or the other condition or, alternatively, could expose each subject to both conditions. The savings in subjects of the latter approach is considerable and a major advantage of within-subject designs. In addition, within-group variability is minimized.

■ ■ ■

Q2: In within-subject designs, each subject serves as her own control. Why does within-group variability not reduce to zero? (See answer on p. 117.)

■ ■ ■

The advantages come with costs. One problem is that the order in which a treatment is given might influence its effects. A solution is to randomly assign subjects, half to receive treatment X first and half to receive treatment Y first. The design becomes a 2 × 2 factorial in which treatment and order are the factors, and the data are analyzed as with any other 2 × 2. Called *counterbalancing*, this procedure with appropriate variations can be used to accommodate more than two factors.

A second disadvantage of within-subject designs is that if subjects drop out before receiving all treatments, the data collected on them are wasted. Even worse, if the various conditions are not equally desirable, subjects receiving the less desirable ones first may drop out in greater numbers and make the final results difficult to interpret.

Within-subject designs are useless for evaluating treatments that cause permanent changes, such as brain lesions, and they are impractical for treatments with long-lasting effects, such as administration of slowly eliminated drugs. They cannot be used to test subject variables. Further consideration of these designs is given in chapter 11.

## ANSWERS

1. Subjects were not randomly assigned to gender, so it was not an experiment and causal conclusions would be unwarranted.

2. Within-subject variability refers to all unintended causes of differences between subjects: slight changes in conditions of testing, measurement errors, and pretreatment differences between subjects. Within-subject designs eliminate only pretreatment differences between subjects.

# Comparing
# Existing Groups

*By the time you finish reading this chapter, you should be able to answer the following questions:*

What are the different reasons for doing comparative studies?

How can comparative studies stimulate research?

How can comparative studies extend the range over which variables are tested?

Why is there a huge concern about sampling procedures in virtually all comparative research?

What are other pitfalls in virtually all comparative research?

If the comparison groups are carefully matched on all relevant variables, is the sampling problem eliminated?

What strategies do behavioral ecologists use?

■ ■ ■ ■ ■

*"The male has more teeth than the female in mankind, and sheep and goats, and swine. This has not been observed in other animals. Those persons which have the greatest number of teeth are the longest lived; those which have them widely separated, smaller, and more scattered, are generally more short lived."* Aristotle

Whereas experimenters assign subjects to groups randomly, some researchers compare existing groups: men with women; people of different races, cultures, or ages; alcoholics with heroin addicts; people who score high on a test of anxiety with people who score low; nonhuman animals with either humans or other nonhumans; and so on. Valid comparisons can be made from data collected by any of the methods discussed in chapter 6, but this chapter focuses on data from existing groups. Many of the reasons for comparing as well as many pitfalls are unique to the groups studied, but many are relevant for all comparative researchers.

## ■ REASONS FOR DOING COMPARATIVE STUDIES

### To Describe

Differences between groups can be explored either as an end in itself or as a prelude to designing research to explain the differences. Do males and females differ in learning abilities? What types of changes occur during the normal course of aging; that is, how do young people compare with old ones? Do schizophrenics differ genetically from nonschizophrenics? Some studies that appear to be about a single group actually involve implied comparisons (see Box 9.1).

### To Learn About Key Variables and Stimulate Research

Although some descriptive researchers publish their work and go no further, differences between groups call out for explanations. Why are there gender differences? Sociobiologists such as Buss (1995) attribute most of them to the different adaptive problems faced by men and women over the history of human evolution. Biological psychologists focus on differences in the brains of men and women that might be caused by exposure to different patterns of sex hormones (Hofman & Swaab, 1991). Derry (1996) and Silverstein (1996) preferred explanations in terms of culture and membership in dominant versus subordinate groups. Others argue for a combination of factors. The issue may never be resolved to everybody's satisfaction, but the documentation of differences stimulated many productive research programs.

**BOX 9.1**

## Implied Comparisons

Zita (1988) wrote that research on premenstrual syndrome (PMS) reflects masculine biases. Women are compared with men, and differences are assumed to be deficiencies. The cyclicity of women is considered deviant when compared with the relative noncyclicity of men. Although cyclicity implies peaks as well as valleys, much PMS research involves women who are seeking help for their symptoms. When subjects are those who have identified themselves as having a problem, the research typically has a negative focus.

Conditions associated with PMS, such as irritability and aggression, are considered deviant when compared with the norm of passive femininity. Dalton (1960) reported that accident rates increase during menstruation, which seems to suggest that women should not drive during that time of month. But Dalton compared accident rates during menstruation and midcycle. She did not compare accident rates of menstruating women and men. Men have higher accident rates.

## To Extend the Range Over Which Variables Can Be Tested

A phenomenon that does not vary much is difficult to study. Experimenters can extend the range of variation; for example, they can deprive laboratory subjects of sleep or food or give them doses of drugs in amounts ranging from zero to lethal. The study of natural variations is also useful. Sigmund Freud theorized that young boys resent their fathers because boys desire their mothers sexually and regard their fathers as rivals for her affection. But his theory of a universal Oedipus complex was derived from observations limited to Western culture, where fathers typically have dual roles as both warm, nurturing male and disciplinarian. Malinowski studied Trobriand Islanders, a culture in which the mother's brother enforces discipline, so the father can be just warm and nurturing. Malinowski reported that Trobriand Islanders showed no signs of an Oedipus complex.

People's sleep patterns vary much less than variations in sleep between species. So, theorists on the function of sleep have compared animals. Predatory animals generally sleep more than prey, small animals more than large animals, and among similarly sized animals, those with low metabolic rates sleep more than those with high metabolic rates. Infants of all species sleep more than adults. Theorists who incorporate the comparative data are more likely to be successful.

## ■ PITFALLS IN COMPARATIVE RESEARCH

Many predictions based on comparisons are borne out daily. Babies cry more than adults, nonschizophrenics are more lucid than schizophrenics, and boisterous activity occurs more often in college dorms than in nursing homes. Nevertheless, the interpretive pitfalls of comparative research are considerable. Suppose an investigator wanted to find out whether 20- or 70-year-olds have larger vocabularies. He might randomly select 50 people from each age group, randomly pair them, and have each pair sit at a table while he slowly read a set of 100 vocabulary words. The first subject to call out an accurate synonym for each word would earn one point, and the winner would be the one with the most total points. If 20-year-olds won significantly more of the contests, the investigator might conclude that vocabulary declines with age. But his conclusion would be premature. Cross-sectional studies, that is, studies in which two or more age groups are compared at the same time, never completely rule out plausible alternative explanations.

### Sampling

One problem in comparative research relates to sampling. Suppose the investigator went to a college campus for the 20-year-olds and a nursing home for the 70-year-olds. Neither setting would yield a representative sample. He might find enough 70-year-olds on college campuses to fill his quota, but they would not be typical 70-year-olds; and no other selection method would eliminate the potential for bias. Since many 20-year-olds die before reaching 70, the survivors are always a biased sample. So, for example, if all 20- and 70-year-olds were given a test to measure masculine versus feminine tendencies, 70-year-olds would almost certainly receive higher average femininity scores. That does not prove that individuals become more feminine with age. A greater proportion of males than females die at every age, so the ratio of females to males continually increases.

Some investigators compare people to themselves; that is, they give repeated tests over many years on the dependent variables of interest. Studying the same people over time, called *longitudinal research,* is an interesting alternative to cross-sectional research but does not eliminate sampling problems. Some subjects in longitudinal research invariably lose interest, move, or die. Even if none dropped out, the subjects would be a biased sample. Imagine a study in which all 20-year-old subjects lived and continued to participate until they reached age 70. They could hardly be considered representative of all 20-year-olds.

Sampling problems extend beyond age issues. Suppose a cross-cultural researcher compares young adults in the United States and Turkey. He recruits his sample by posting notices at Cal State University in Hayward, UC-Berkeley, the University of Michigan, and Bogazici University in Turkey. He would have to make several assumptions: that U.S. and Turkish citizens are equally likely to attend college; that the colleges picked are representative of that country's colleges; that they offer similar courses of study; that students in the two countries start college at about the same age; and that they will be equally willing to participate in his study. If even one of the assumptions were wrong, his conclusions might mislead.

Edgerton (1965) reported that herdsmen and farmers differ in personality characteristics. Farmers make more group decisions than herders, place greater value on hard work, and are more suspicious and hostile toward others. Edgerton related the traits to the methods of earning a living. But although his sample was large, he based his conclusions on observations of four tribes in East Africa. Herdsmen and farmers from different tribes might have given a different picture.

If every individual in each group to be compared is tested, sampling problems are small. More typically, however, members of each group are located in different ways and may differ in proportions of males and females, adults and juveniles, healthy and sick, and so on. Comparative studies seem to show that heroin addicts have less severe psychological problems and greater antisocial tendencies than alcoholics, but the conclusion is probably an artifact due to sampling. Alcoholics tend to be older when first identified, and they come to the attention of investigators through consequences of use such as cirrhosis of the liver, a failing marriage, or high absenteeism from work. Heroin addicts are more often recognized following arrest for a crime committed to get money for buying heroin.

A researcher whose stated goal is to compare annual incomes of drug abusers and nonusers might visit a free clinic or homeless shelter for his sample of abusers. Alternatively, he might recruit from the Betty Ford Treatment Center. Treatment at the Betty Ford Center takes approximately 28 days and, for inpatients, costs more than $13,000. Political rather than scientific reasons might govern his choice of sample.

## Stimuli

Just because the same stimulus is presented to all subjects does not mean all will perceive it similarly. A cat is a different stimulus to a mouse than to a Doberman. Twenty-year-olds might respond faster to vocabulary words not because they know more but because they hear the words better or their reaction times are quicker. Subtle changes in stimuli may affect only one of the comparison groups. The scores of African Americans increase on IQ tests and the scores of women increase on map-reading tests when the tests are not labeled as such (Sharps, Welton, & Price, 1993; Steele & Aronson, 1995). The investigator is part of the stimulus complex, and test scores often depend on whether investigator and subject are of the same race, gender, age, and so forth.

In longitudinal studies, the nature of the stimulus may change over time. Repeated testing may yield improvements because of practice or decrements due to boredom, nervousness, or resentment at having to fulfill an annoying obligation.

## Motivation

Animals in comparative studies of learning have been motivated with food rewards, but it is difficult to equate motivations. For example, laboratory rats eat daily whereas some snakes go months between meals. Motivational differences between 20- and 70-year-olds, though less extreme than between lab rats and snakes, are far from negligible. The two groups almost certainly differ in both motivation to perform and cautiousness in calling out uncertain answers.

## Experiences

People of different age groups have had different experiences. School environments and styles of parenting changed during the past half-century. There were important medical developments; wars; riots; assassinations; changes in the quality of the air; and new trends in art, music, motion pictures, diet, size of families, and in virtually every other facet of life. Twenty- and 70-year-olds may differ because of any of these rather than because of age-related changes. The inability to isolate aging as the crucial factor applies equally to longitudinal and cross-sectional studies.

Most members of each race, species, gender, and culture also share unique experiences. During the past several decades, U.S. citizens lived through the assassination of one president and resignation of another, the first Super Bowl, and the debut of rock-n-roll. During the same time period, the beloved founder of modern Turkey died, a military coup shook the country, and easing of foreign import restrictions opened Turkey to Western influences. Differences between U.S. and Turkish citizens might reflect each group's specific experiences rather than inherent differences between them.

## A Nonsolution to the Sampling Problem

Suppose a researcher wants to compare mathematics performance in smokers and nonsmokers. She might match each smoker subject with a nonsmoker of the same age, gender, socioeconomic status, years of schooling, and all other variables thought relevant to mathematics ability. Such matching procedures are common in medical and social science research, but they are invalid because subjects in nonrandomly formed groups *must* differ even before the groups come into existence. To argue otherwise is to claim that membership in the group, for example, becoming a smoker or nonsmoker, is uncaused. But if the groups differ to begin with, then matching makes at least one group unrepresentative (Meehl, 1970a). It would be easy to match men and women in height, but the men would have to be unusually short for men or the women unusually tall for women.

## ■ SYSTEMATIC COMPARISONS

Biologists and psychologists interested in the evolutionary histories and functions of behaviors ask questions about ultimate causes that focus on evolutionary origin and survival value, rather than seeking proximate causes such as current physiological and psychological controlling mechanisms. (A question about ultimate cause might be, "Why are monkeys more likely to reproduce if they eat ripe rather than unripe fruits?" A question about proximate cause might be, "What area of the brain controls a monkey's preference for ripe over unripe fruit?") Scientists who focus on ultimate questions sometimes conduct experiments, but their primary methods are observational, comparative, and correlational. They systematically compare many different species and often gain insights that apply broadly. Although they must confront the same problems that face all comparative researchers, they minimize the problems by comparing many species rather than just one or two. In Crook's (1964) work (described later), 90 species were compared. Closely related species that behave similarly probably do not differ greatly in motivation, perception, or experience. Any species that displays unique behavior patterns stands out and is likely to suggest testable hypotheses to explain the patterns.

Behavior ecologists compare related species living in diverse environments and unrelated species in congruent ones. Close relatives that behave similarly despite living under different conditions provide evidence for a strong genetic component to the behaviors, whereas close relatives that differ behaviorally stimulate speculations about possibly important environmental variables. For example, most gull species nest on the ground, but kittiwake gulls build their nests on narrow ledges of high cliffs. So kittiwakes, unlike other gulls, have few predators. If a crow or fox intrudes on a ground-nesting gull colony, groups of birds fly toward it screaming and dive bombing. But kittiwakes do not mob predators. Cullen (1957) related this and many other behavioral differences to the contrasting nesting sites. The name for this phenomenon is *divergent evolution.*

Conversely, unrelated species that face similar selection pressures often show similar behavior patterns. This is called *convergent evolution.* Bank swallows and ground squirrels, like most gulls, live in colonies and mob predators. Gannets nest in places inaccessible to most predators and behave in many ways like kittiwakes.

When comparisons are made across many species, patterns may emerge and suggest testable hypotheses. For example, monogamy is one of several different mating systems that arise in human societies and throughout the animal kingdom. Observations of individual groups did not suggest reasons for the diversity, but when Orians (1969) compared many species he concluded that monogamy is most likely when any of the following conditions are met:

1. Receptive females are scarce and widely distributed.
2. Successful reproduction requires the cooperation of both parents.
3. A valuable resource such as a nesting site or food source is scarce and must be defended.

Crook (1964) observed about 90 species of weaver birds in both forest and savannah habitats. Food in the forest is dispersed and difficult to find, whereas seeds in the savannah are clumped in rich patches. Forest nests can be carefully hidden but savannah nests are exposed. Crook hypothesized that many behavioral differences between forest and savannah dwellers can be explained by food availability and exposure to predation.

Because the food supply of forest dwellers is limited, single females cannot easily feed their young. Males must contribute, which favors a monogamous breeding system. Males frequently visit the nests, so dull colored ones are less likely to attract predators and have a selective advantage. The nests are spaced far apart, which is another adaptation for avoiding predators. One result of spacing is increased likelihood that territoriality will evolve.

Seed-eating savannah females can feed their young alone, so males are not needed and show no parental care. They are brightly colored and constantly compete for females. Once a seed clump is located, the entire flock can feed; so, unlike forest birds, savannah dwellers forage in groups. Because they cannot hide their nests, they build them in protected sites, such as spiny acacia trees. These trees are relatively rare, so many birds build nests in a single tree.

Crook's insights about the correlation between behavioral and ecological variables may have broad application. Behavioral differences between African ungulates (hoofed mammals) have also been related to dietary and predator pressures (Jarman, 1974).

# 10

# Correlational Strategies to Predict and Assess Relationships

*By the time you finish reading this chapter, you should be able to answer the following questions:*

Why do scientists do correlational studies?

What is the range of values for a correlation coefficient?

Does a high correlation between two variables mean that the variables are related? Does a low correlation mean that they are unrelated?

How does the correlation between height and weight among basketball players compare with the correlation between height and weight in the population as a whole?

Do correlational studies provide any evidence about causes?

Why are there several different correlation coefficients?

Which shows the stronger relationship, a correlation of +.3 or −.8?

■   ■   ■   ■   ■

*"It is proven that the celebration of birthdays is healthy. Statistics show that those people who celebrate the most birthdays become the oldest."* S. den Hartog, PhD. thesis, University of Groningen

In comparative research, the major variable is typically measured with a nominal scale; that is, the different categories are labels and nothing more. The major variable is divided into no more than a few and often only two categories—men/women, schizophrenics/nonschizophrenics, farmers/herdsmen, seven species of the genus Rodentia, and so on. The categories are of the same type, for example, all rodents. Comparative questions concern both similarities and differences.

Correlational studies answer questions about how any two variables are related, specifically, how changes in one variable are associated with changes in the other. Although they are of limited value for establishing causality, correlational studies cover a lot of territory. Correlations may be obtained between any variables measured simultaneously or years apart. To take two examples, McClelland (1967) reported significant correlations between the need for achievement within different cultures, as measured by a complex scoring system applied to popular songs and stories, and several indicators of economic and social development of those cultures. And Livson (1977), in a study spanning almost 30 years, found that the physical attractiveness of 40-year-old women correlated less highly with their attractiveness at age 12 (correlation of .29) than with their direct expression of hostile feelings at age 12 (correlation of –.31). Correlation coefficients are calculated in a variety of ways depending on how the variables have been measured, and they serve many functions besides evaluating correlational research designs.

## ■ INTERPRETING CORRELATION COEFFICIENTS

Correlation coefficients range from –1.0 through 0 to +1.0. The stronger the relationship is between variables, the more the coefficient will deviate from 0. A positive correlation means that increases in one variable are associated with increases in the other, and a negative correlation means the reverse. For example, since tall people tend to outweigh short ones, height and weight are positively correlated; and the correlation is probably negative between hours of television watching per week and overall health. Correlations higher than .8, positive or negative, are rare in social science research.

■ ■ ■

Q: Do you think the heights of daughters correlate more highly with their mothers' heights than with their fathers'? Why or why not? (See answer on p. 134.)

■ ■ ■

Figure 10.1a is a graph showing Celsius scale temperatures on the X-axis and corresponding Fahrenheit temperatures on the Y-axis. The relationship between Fahrenheit and Celsius is perfect; that is, the correlation between them is +1.0. A linear equation can be found that summarizes the relationship: $Y = 32 + 1.8X$. Because the correlation is perfect, each data point fits right on the line.

A fictitious relationship between two personality traits, A and B, is graphed in Figure 10.1b. The best summary of the linear relationship between the traits is again $Y = 32 + 1.8X$. But because A and B are not perfectly correlated, there are many deviant scores.

A fictitious relationship between two personality traits, C and D, is graphed in Figure 10.1c. There is no good straight line fit, but the equation $Y = X^4 - 7X^3 + 50$ describes the relationship perfectly. Many strong relationships cannot be fit to straight lines. For example, the relationship between age and running speed is curvilinear (young adults run faster than both toddlers and elderly people). So be aware that a low or zero correlation means only that the variables show no linear relationship.

Figures 10.1a, 10.1b, and 10.1c are examples of scatter plots, although simple ones. Scatter plots display data relating two variables, with each pair

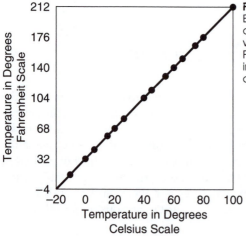

**FIGURE 10.1a**
Each dot on the straight line indicates a data point, where temperatures were converted from Celsius to Fahrenheit. Temperatures are plotted in degrees Celsius on the X-axis and degrees Fahrenheit on the Y-axis.

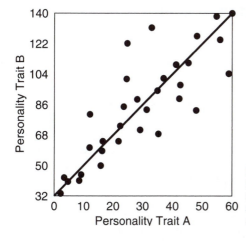

**FIGURE 10.1b**
Each dot represents a single person's score on two tests, one to measure personality trait A and one to measure personality trait B.

of data points represented by a single dot. The dots are plotted on paper with a vertical (*Y*) and horizontal (*X*) axis. Scatter plots should be drawn routinely prior to doing computations, because they provide lots of potential information:

■ Is the relationship more or less linear or is it curved?
■ Does *Y* tend to increase or decrease as *X* increases?
■ Is the relationship monotonic; that is, are increases in *X* consistently associated with increases or consistently associated with decreases in *Y*?
■ Are there any unusual data points (outliers)?

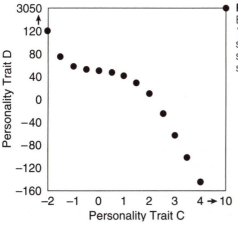

**FIGURE 10.1c**
Each dot, including the one at *X* = 10, *Y* = 3050, represents a single person's score on two tests, one to measure personality trait C and one to measure personality trait D.

## ■ WHEN SHOULD A CORRELATIONAL STUDY BE CONSIDERED?

### To Test Theories

Some correlations have theoretical importance. Sheldon (1942) argued that people's body types determine their personalities. He found correlations of about .80 between endomorphy (softness and spherical appearance) and viscerotonia (love of comfort, sociability, and gluttony); between mesomorphy (hard, muscular body) and somatotonia (love of physical adventure and risk taking); and between ectomorphy (flat chest, fragile) and cerebrotonia (restraint and inhibition). Sheldon was justly criticized on the grounds that he knew the body types of the people whose personalities he judged. Yet his work has many interesting implications and is still reported in textbooks.

### Because Experimental Manipulation Is Impractical or Impossible

Ethical and practical considerations preclude the manipulation of some variables. To study how alcohol affects memory, an experimenter could ask subjects to voluntarily elevate their blood alcohol concentrations; but an investigator studying the relationship between gender and memory could not manipulate genders (unless he had a *very* large budget and the subjects were *very* adventurous). Traits that people carry with them (gender, age, race, country of origin, species, test scores, political attitudes, favorite songs, etc.) cannot be manipulated but can be studied correlationally. (But recall that correlational studies answer different questions than do experiments.)

### To Pretest a Causal Hypothesis

If one variable causes a reliable change in another, they must be correlated. So correlational studies can pretest causal hypotheses inexpensively. For example, it would be enormously expensive to experimentally test the hypothesis that long periods of overcrowding increase human aggression. But a researcher could easily compute the correlation between population densities of different cities and incidences of violent crimes within the cities. Relevant data are available. Only if the correlation were high enough would the researcher follow up with rigorous experimental tests.

Note, however, that correlational studies can easily mislead about causes. Several investigators had reported that heavy coffee drinking is associated with an increased risk of coronary heart disease, and a causal connection between the two seemed plausible. So Puccio, McPhillips, Barrett, and Ganiats (1990) interviewed 2,304 men and women. Compared with non–coffee drinkers, the coffee drinkers drank more alcohol, consumed more dietary saturated fats and cholesterol, and were more likely to smoke and less likely to exercise. All those factors also correlate with heart disease. Confounding (and often unknown) factors are unavoidable in correlational studies.

## To Seek Nonobvious Connections Between Variables

Epidemiologists study diseases around the world and among people with different lifestyles, searching for connections (correlations) between particular lifestyles and the likelihood of contracting a disease. Their observations suggested links between cigarette smoking and lung cancer, cholesterol level and heart disease, obesity and high blood pressure, and intravenous drug use and AIDS. Experiments were crucial for testing the suspected causes against possible alternatives, but the correlational data came first and provided a rationale for the specific experiments.

## For Predicting

Regression analysis, a technique closely related to correlation analysis, can improve the accuracy of predictions. The closer the absolute value of the correlation coefficient is to 1.0, the more accurate the regression equation will be in predicting from $X$ to $Y$. If the correlation between $X$ and $Y$ is 0, the best prediction for a new $Y$ value is the mean of $Y$. But for nonzero correlations, computing the regression equation and plugging in the new $X$ value will improve predictive accuracy. Given the fictitious relationship described by Figure 10.1b, if personality trait $A$ were measured and the value plugged into the equation $Y = 32 + 1.8X$, the value of $B$ could be accurately calculated. College admissions officers use regression equations to estimate the likelihood of a freshman's academic success given his SAT scores.

## To Evaluate the Properties of Tests

Correlations are computed to evaluate the reliability of tests. For example, the test may be given at two separate times and the correlation between scores computed. Correlations between tests indicate whether the tests measure the same thing. The correlation of scores on a test with scores on a criterion indicates whether the test accurately predicts criterion performance.

## ■ THREE POTENTIAL PROBLEMS

### Bias

An investigator who is aware of a subject's score on one variable while measuring a second may allow his biases to influence the results. (See the comment on p. 130 on Sheldon's research.) Avoid the problem by having different people collect data for each variable.

### Reliability of Measures Is a Limiting Factor

Unless each variable is measured reliably, the correlation between them cannot be high. A low reliability means that a variable does not correlate well even with itself. To find the maximum correlation between two variables, multiply their separate reliabilities and find the square root of the product. If activity level and verbal aggression were measured with .72 and .50 reliabilities, respectively, the highest possible correlation between them would be

$$\sqrt{.72 \times .50} = .60$$

### Results Vary With Samples

The strength of a correlation is tied to the specific sample tested. A high positive correlation means that subjects who rank high on one variable tend to rank high on the other. Consider the correlation between height and weight. Tall people (those who rank high on height) tend to outweigh (rank higher than) short ones. Now consider the heights of two groups of three people:

Group 1: 3'0", 5'0", and 7'0"
Group 2: 5'10", 5'10½", and 5'11"

The vast majority of seven-footers outweigh the vast majority of three-footers, but many 5'10" people outweigh those who are 5'11". The rankings would be more likely to be preserved in the first case, and thus the correlation would be higher. More generally, samples that are relatively homogeneous with respect to one or both variables will have relatively low correlations between the variables. The correlation between height and weight is lower among basketball players than in the population as a whole. The correlation between reading ability and school performance is lower for college students than for grade school students (because poor readers are likely to drop out of school before reaching college). The correlation between scores on a screening test and job performance is lower when only those who pass the test, rather than all testees, are considered. So be careful about generalizations.

# ■ SEVERAL CORRELATION COEFFICIENTS

There are a variety of correlation coefficients because data come in many forms and must be handled in different ways. Refer to a statistics book for computational procedures for the correlation coefficients described here.

1. When variables are measured on an interval scale (a scale that tells not only the rank order of subjects but also by how much they differ), the product-moment correlation is most likely to detect a linear relationship between them.

2. If both variables are measured nominally (subjects are assigned to categories that serve as labels and nothing more) and each has only two possible values, use the phi coefficient. Phi would be used to test the correlation between gender and attitude toward abortion (pro-choice or pro-life).

3. If both variables are measured nominally and either or both can be assigned to more than two categories, use the contingency coefficient. The contingency coefficient would test for a correlation between gender and attitude toward abortion (pro-choice, pro-life, undecided, depends on the circumstances).

4. Use the Spearman rank order correlation for two variables measured ordinally (subjects are rank ordered but the degree of difference between ranks is not considered). Some professors at Cal State make a $1 bet each year on the final baseball standings. We predict the rank order of finish for each team. The winner is the one whose Spearman is highest between predicted and actual final standings.

5. If one variable is measured on an interval and one on a nominal scale, use the point-biserial correlation coefficient (see Table 17.3).

# ■ PARTIAL CORRELATION

Because almost all of the evidence for a relationship between cigarette smoking and cancer is correlational, tobacco company spokespeople argued that a third factor such as anxiety might cause both cancer and smoking. Suppose a correlational study indicated that level of anxiety correlates .60 and smoking .50 with incidence of cancer. Could they justifiably claim that the effects of smoking are largely irrelevant to the genesis of cancer? The technique of partial correlation helps answer such questions. For the example, an investigator would find the correlation between level of smoking and anxiety. Then the correlations between smoking and anxiety and between anxiety and cancer could be statistically eliminated and the partial correlation between smoking and cancer determined.

# ■ CORRELATION AND CAUSATION— ADDITIONAL COMMENTS

*Correlation does not prove causation.* Those words, drummed into the brains of social science majors from their first exposure to methodological issues, are discouraging; scientists generally seek causes yet must often rely on correlational data. If a high, reliable correlation exists between $X$ and $Y$, then $X$ may cause $Y$ or $Y$ may cause $X$ or another variable or variables may cause both. ($X$ and $Y$ may be interdependent such that $X$ causes $Y$ and then $Y$ causes a stronger $X$; for example, if a depressed person sits home and avoids friends, the depression may deepen.) Simple reflection may eliminate one or more possibilities. High school and college grade point averages correlate significantly. It is unlikely that high school grades affect college grades to any great extent, and inconceivable that the causal arrow is in the opposite direction. But why?

The conclusion that high school grades do not appreciably influence college grades comes from the belief that academic performance at all levels is determined primarily by factors such as intelligence, motivation, and work habits. Nevertheless, Rosenthal and Jacobson's research (1968; see p. 36) suggests that a student's transcript may bias teachers' ratings of the student. Also, both self-esteem and aspiration level are influenced by grades and probably affect subsequent performance (Wattenberg & Clifford, 1964). The statement that college grades do not affect high school grades would be made with certainty even if nothing were known about the roles of intelligence, motivation, and work habits. Our logic requires causes to precede effects. An extension of the logic forms the basis for techniques in which correlations are analyzed for causes. See Shaffer (1992) for further discussions.

# ANSWER

It might seem that correlations would be higher between mothers and daughters and between fathers and sons, but that is not so. The difference in average height between men and women is irrelevant. If tall mothers tend to have tall sons and short mothers short sons, the correlation between mothers and sons will be high, and similarly for fathers and daughters.

# Case Studies

*By the time you finish reading this chapter, you should be able to answer the following questions:*

What are the different reasons for doing case studies?

How many subjects can be in a case study?

Can a case study have theoretical significance?

Why are most case studies inadequate for showing causes?

Why are most case studies inadequate for showing relationships between variables?

Why do advertisers and politicians make frequent use of case studies?

Why have the results of social programs often been misinterpreted?

What are quasi-experiments?

Why do some scientists argue that generalizations from just a few subjects studied intensively may be more accurate than generalizations from experiments with two large groups of subjects?

What is dimensional sampling?

Why should researchers consider using themselves as subjects?

■　■　■　■　■

*"Here was a first principle not formally recognized by scientific methodologists: when you run onto something interesting, drop everything else and study it."* B. F. Skinner (1956)

Runkel (1990) contrasted two ways of doing research. Some researchers seek to find common relationships, so they cast nets to catch many cases. Others test single specimens to find out how an individual case works. The primary method of case study research is to test specimens. *Case studies* are investigations of people, events, institutions, or other phenomena. Sometimes a single case is studied; sometimes multiple instances of similar ones are studied; but the focus is always on the individual case(s) rather than on grouped data. Three types of case studies, each distinct in purpose and quality, are discussed in this chapter.

# ■ UNPLANNED, ISOLATED CASES

All scientific research begins with the observation of phenomena, and unusual cases provide unique opportunities. For example, a man known in the scientific literature as H. M. had the hippocampus on both sides of his brain removed to treat his severe grand mal epilepsy. Following the surgery, H. M. could remember things he had already learned but could not learn anything new. H. M.'s case gave scientists many insights into the biological bases of memory. Other medical milestones also began with unusual cases: an obese person found to have a tumor near the hypothalamus, an aphasic with a lesion in Broca's area, a child with a defective adrenal gland who ate handfuls of salt with each meal, and people who slept excessively because of lesions or tumors of the reticular formation.

Some cases vividly exemplify abstract principles, so are used for demonstrations. Skinner's quote at the top of this page comes from an instructional article on scientific strategizing that he titled "A case history in scientific method." Cases can have theoretical implications, as in Lenneberg's (1962) description of a boy who lacked the necessary motor apparatus to babble, yet nevertheless understood language. This single negative case overthrew the belief that babbling is essential to later understanding of language. Cases of heterosexual men and women with AIDS demolished the previously held view that AIDS was restricted to homosexual men.

But investigators frequently analyze cases only after the essential features have occurred, then draw conclusions beyond what the data warrant. For example, Kolansky and Moore (1971) asserted that "moderate to heavy use of marijuana in adolescents and young people without predisposition to psychotic illness may lead to ego decompensation ranging from mild ego disturbance to psychosis." The conclusion was based on 38 cases of people who had appeared psychologically healthy until they smoked marijuana and had then shown symptoms serious enough to require psychiatric services.

The evidence was inadequate for two reasons. First, the subjects were not randomly assigned to groups. Instead, only smokers were studied and they were taken as they came. Marijuana smokers and nonsmokers differ in political attitudes, use of other drugs, respect for authority, hair length, music preferences, and many other traits. They differ even before any have ever tried marijuana. They must, on logical grounds—the alternative is that the decision to smoke is arbitrary and uncaused. Any of those other factors rather than the marijuana might explain the accelerated rate of ego decompensation.

And there may not have been an accelerated rate. The second problem with case studies is that they provide only partial information. Kolansky and Moore did not know how many marijuana smokers were symptom free, or how many nonsmokers did and did not show symptoms. Suppose the numbers were

marijuana and subsequent symptoms—38
marijuana, no subsequent symptoms—1 million
no marijuana and subsequent symptoms—1 million
no marijuana, no subsequent symptoms—5

So the conclusion that marijuana causes ego decompensation was unjustified, because other factors may have been responsible. The conclusion that ego decompensation is more common among marijuana smokers was unjustified, because figures for comparison groups were not presented. For a second example in which case studies led to unwarranted conclusions, see Box 11.1.

Despite their limitations, case studies focus on real individuals rather than dry, abstract numbers, and that makes them powerful tools of persuasion. Product testimonials are a type of case study, with each satisfied customer a single case. But even if 100 customers each swear under oath that he or she lost 200 pounds on the sponsor's special diet, the diet may not be useful. Additional data would be needed: the total number of customers, their average weight loss, and the average weight loss of comparably overweight people not on the special diet.

Do some welfare mothers cheat? Yes. Do some students default on government loans? Yes. Do children who grow up under conditions of deprivation ever achieve more than children of privilege? Yes. Do politicians exploit such cases to manipulate voters? Absolutely. People who understand about randomization and control groups know the limitations of such evidence, so they are harder to manipulate. Yet they also appreciate that

## BOX

### Sex Between Psychotherapists and Patients

Brown et al. (1992) cited evidence from clinical reports (case studies) to show that sex between psychotherapists and their patients harms the patients, and Pope and Bouhoutsos (1986) identified a cluster of symptoms (Therapist-Patient Sex Syndrome) that may result from sexual involvement between therapists and patients. The studies have legal ramifications, as lawsuits brought by patients against their former psychotherapists have become commonplace. But clinical reports, while they establish that some therapists have become sexually involved with patients, suffer the same limitations as all case studies. Williams (1995) described the problems (though he also deplored the willingness of some psychotherapists to abuse their positions and acknowledged that therapist-patient sexual involvement may cause harm).

- ■ Without data on the number of patients unharmed by sexual involvement with a therapist, which is unavailable and probably impossible to get, reports of harm cannot be meaningfully interpreted. Harm may occur in only a tiny proportion of cases or be almost inevitable.
- ■ To determine if a prior sexual relationship has caused harm, a new therapist must (a) infer the patient's condition prior to that relationship, and (b) assume what the current condition would have been had no relationship occurred. The new therapist may occasionally gain access to treatment records predating the sexual episode but typically uses only the history provided by the patient (Williams, 1995).
- ■ The sexual relationship might have had little effect on the patient's current condition, which might stem from childhood sexual abuse. Or, the patient might suffer from a long-standing personality disorder. Or, the patient might have suffered equally from any interpersonal intimacy: "The causal link is often completely without substantiation. A therapist interviews a woman who states that she arrived at her current distressed and dysfunctional state by virtue of sexual abuse by a prior therapist, and her report is taken at face value."
- ■ People with borderline and histrionic personality disorders are at great risk for therapist-patient sexual involvement—and also show many symptoms resembling those of the Therapist-Patient Sex Syndrome. So, many people with the symptoms must have had them prior to sexual relations with a therapist.

case study conclusions should not be summarily rejected. In none of the fictitious examples of Box 11.2 are variables isolated or subjects randomly assigned, yet some conclusions would be persuasive.

Box 11.2 is given for several reasons:

## BOX

### Green Faces

Suppose a man enters a physician's office with his face shimmering bright green. The physician, trying to establish a cause, would probably ask his new patient if he had recently done anything unusual. Evaluate each of the following responses for their probable relevance:

1. I don't normally eat tuna fish, but I tried a tuna sandwich this morning. My face changed color 10 minutes later.
2. I'm a registered Democrat, but I went to the ballot box this morning and voted Republican. My face changed color 10 minutes later.

Last year I smuggled in a new species of mushrooms from the Amazon rain forest and

3. ate them this morning. My face immediately changed color.
4. ate them last month.
5. my family and I all ate them last month. My wife's face turned green last week, my younger daughter's on Tuesday, my older daughter's yesterday, and mine this morning.
6. my family and I ate them last month, except for my son. My wife's face turned green last week, my younger daughter's on Tuesday, my older daughter's yesterday, and mine this morning. My son has shown no symptoms.
7. presented them yesterday at a large gathering of mycologists. I didn't have enough for everybody so I gave them on a first-come, first-served basis. The face of each of the 100 guests who ate a mushroom turned green immediately. None of the others developed symptoms.

■ To emphasize Skinner's point that unusual cases present unique opportunities. A good scientist, even if he specialized in faces that turned magenta, would probably be interested.

■ To show that hypotheses are developed and evaluated in terms of background knowledge. Cases 1, 2, and 3 are similar in form, but few people would attribute changes in facial color to voting Republican. They might speculate that tuna fish was the cause and would almost certainly blame the mushrooms. Case 4 would be considered weak evidence for a mushroom hypothesis, because we expect causes and effects to be linked closely in time.

■ To emphasize the major strength and weakness of unplanned, isolated case studies. The strength is that they suggest promising leads for further research. Case 2 suggests the hypothesis that eating tuna fish caused the change in face color. Although it would make sense to investigate further, the initial evidence is far from conclusive. The weakness is that one-shot case studies may seem conclusive.

Once a hypothesis is developed, scientists should test it against competing hypotheses. Cases 5 through 7 are progressively stronger, because each rules out a greater number of plausible competitors than its predecessor. Case 5 rules out hypotheses related to unique events in the life of a single individual. Case 6 weakens genetic explanations. By providing a rudimentary (even though not randomly chosen) control group, case 6 rules out hypotheses that might have occurred if, for example, the entire family lived near a power line or had recently gone on a cruise together or eaten a different unusual food. Some case studies, such as number 7, rule out all plausible competing hypotheses and produce evidence as compelling as that from any experiment.

## ■ CASE STUDIES AS PLANNED, AFTER-THE-FACT RESEARCH DESIGNS

Case studies are uniquely suited for studying certain "how" and "why" questions. Yin (1994) cited the book *All the President's Men* about the Watergate burglary and cover-up during President Richard Nixon's administration that ultimately led to his resignation. The authors, Bernstein and Woodward, pieced together fact after fact to explain how and why it occurred. They were journalists, not scientists, but their conclusions are convincing.

Planned case studies investigate contemporary phenomena within their real-life contexts. Yin contrasted this with historical studies, which focus on the past, and experiments, which use laboratories as their typical setting. As with all good research, a case study should begin with a clear statement of the research question; for example, how and why did the Watergate cover-up occur? Then the investigator should speculate about possible answers. Was the cover-up ordered to protect the president's top advisors from criminal prosecution? To keep Democrats unaware that the president knew their campaign plans? To safeguard Patricia Nixon's secret recipe for peach cobbler? Each speculation would have sent the inquiry in a different direction. The research design should show how the data to be collected will link to the speculations and should provide criteria for evaluating whether the speculations are supported. Case studies, unlike experiments and surveys, do not limit the number of variables to be analyzed.

The unit of analysis, that is, the case, can be an individual, such as a medical patient with an unusual condition or a politician with a distinctive style. Several individuals can be compared in a multiple-case study. The unit can be a country or a country's music, a verdict, a baseball team, an invention, or an event—virtually any type of unit is acceptable if it is made explicit.

## Treatment Programs

Social programs can be considered as cases and should be rigorously evaluated. Unfortunately, instead of assigning people randomly to treatment or control groups, many program administrators have assigned the neediest participants to receive treatment. The strategy, although stemming from noble reasons, has led to serious and counterproductive misinterpretations. Specifically, treatment effects have been underestimated, especially for children's programs. Campbell and Boruch (1975) gave several reasons:

■ If two tests are positively correlated, people who score extremely well or poorly on one tend to score closer to the mean on the other. (The phenomenon, called *regression to the mean,* is explained in introductory statistics books.) When disadvantaged people are given a pretreatment test, others in the general population who score equally poorly are often picked as controls. But each subgroup regresses to the mean of its own group, so the controls can be expected to regress more; in the absence of treatment effects, they will score higher on a posttest.

■ Differences in children's scores on pretests are caused in part by differences in their growth rates in previous years. If differential rates continue at least for a time, children from disadvantaged groups will show the smallest pretest/posttest growth changes; this will obscure effects resulting from treatments.

■ Differences between groups are demonstrated best with reliable tests, and test reliability increases as children get older. In the absence of treatment effects, posttreatment tests will show greater differences between advantaged and disadvantaged groups.

■ Test reliabilities are generally lower for disadvantaged groups, so their gains are harder to detect and seem smaller.

■ Behaviors have multiple causes. Even if a treatment produces positive effects, other environmental features continue to act and may increase the disparity between advantaged and disadvantaged people.

If random assignment is impossible, researchers can use certain nonrandomized designs to rule out most plausible alternative explanations of data. Campbell and Stanley (1966) called the designs quasi-experiments. Although they can be useful and are now featured prominently in many research methods texts, consider this quote from Campbell and Boruch (1975):

It may be that Campbell and Stanley (1966) should feel guilty for having contributed to giving quasi-experimental designs a good name. There are program evaluations in which the authors say proudly, "We used a quasi-experimental design." If responsible, Campbell and Stanley should do penance, because in most social settings there are many equally or more plausible rival hypotheses than the hypothesis that the puny treatment indeed produced an effect.

In one quasi-experimental design, comparisons are made between records just before and just after a reform is put into effect. This is called an interrupted time-series design. A widely cited example is Connecticut Governor Ribicoff's 1956 crackdown on speeding after a record 324 traffic fatalities in that state in 1955. The following year there were 284 fatalities, a drop of 12.3%. Ribicoff attributed the decline to the crackdown. Campbell agreed, but pointed out plausible alternatives. How many can you think of? See pp. 97–98.

The interrupted time-series design has no control group, as everybody within the relevant population receives the experimental treatment. All people who drove in Connecticut were subjected to the new laws against speeders. But a control group, although not assigned at random, can often be found. This quasi-experimental procedure is then called a *control series design*. (But do not try to match experimental and control groups on pretest scores. This common practice leads to artifacts. See pp. 97–98.) Campbell used four neighboring states of Connecticut as controls. They did not show a similar sharp drop in fatalities in 1956, and their fatalities remained higher than those in Connecticut in 1957, 1958, and 1959.

# ■ SINGLE-CASE EXPERIMENTAL DESIGNS

The most popular method for experimentally testing the effects of an independent variable is to assign subjects randomly to groups. Each group receives a different level of the IV, and posttreatment differences are analyzed statistically. This approach has drawbacks. First, behaviors of individuals are swallowed up in group means. Second, researchers who study people with unusual characteristics (rare diseases, special talents, unusual life experiences) may be unable to get enough subjects. Third, applied researchers seek long-term changes, but most group comparison studies would be too expensive to conduct over any but a short time period. So some researchers conduct planned tests with only a few subjects. Each subject is exposed many times to each treatment, and changes in the dependent variable are measured repeatedly. Thus each subject, whether a rat in a Skinner box or a patient receiving behavior modification therapy, serves as its own control. Sidman (1960) wrote: "When an organism's behavior can repeatedly be manipulated in a quantitatively consistent fashion, the phenomenon in question is a real one and the experimenter has relevant variables well under control." He added that the control "can be exercised, at will, over the course of time." In experiments with groups of subjects, such control is lacking.

Single-case experimental designs can provide a satisfactory alternative when financial or other considerations rule out large-scale studies, and they have enriched the field of psychology (Garmezy, 1982). Although single-case experimenters typically use just a few subjects and sometimes only one, large samples are possible. The key is that each subject is studied intensively.

Following two-group experiments, researchers typically conclude that their independent variables either do or do not affect the dependent variables. Successful replications, especially with a diverse group of subjects, seem to indicate great generality for the effect. But unless a sample has been randomly chosen from a population (which is almost impossible to do—if the sample is comprised of rats or volunteers from psychology classes, what is the population?), generalizations are problematic. Even if a truly representative sample could be found, generalizations from data analyzed at the group level would be suspect.

Consider the fictitious data of Table 11.1 on 27 pairs of identical twins. Analyzed in the traditional way, the results show that creativity scores are significantly higher for the group that received special musical training. Now assume that the pairs included women and men with wide ranges in age, education, and socioeconomic status. It would be tempting to conclude that the results apply to a broad population, but doing so would require ignoring pairs 5, 6, 11, 15, 19, and 24. They might have been the only left-handers in the study, or the only women, or the only college graduates. Whatever their special characteristics, they would be swallowed up by grouped data.

Eysenck (1952) contended that psychotherapy is ineffective. He based his position on a statistical analysis that showed little difference in outcomes between clients who had undergone therapy and untreated controls. But the average effect of psychotherapy is small partly because some clients get worse, and the improvements observed in others are obscured when outcomes are averaged (Bergin, 1966). Scientists who focused on individual cases rather than grouped data were able to identify client and therapist characteristics associated with positive outcomes; they showed that outcomes depend on an interaction between type of therapy and type of disorder (Nietzel & Bernstein, 1987; Strupp & Hadley, 1979).

When a few subjects are studied intensively, experimenters can most easily observe interesting but unexpected occurrences. They can then test other subjects under identical conditions. If a relationship remains unchanged regardless of the age, gender, level of experience, and so forth of

**TABLE 11.1**   Fictitious Data on 27 Pairs of Identical Twins

| TWIN PAIR | RECEIVED MUSICAL TRAINING | CONTROL |
|:---:|:---:|:---:|
| 1 | + | |
| 2 | + | |
| 3 | + | |
| 4 | + | |
| 5 | | + |
| 6 | | + |
| 7 | + | |
| 8 | + | |
| 9 | + | |
| 10 | + | |
| 11 | | + |
| 12 | + | |
| 13 | + | |
| 14 | + | |
| 15 | | + |
| 16 | + | |
| 17 | + | |
| 18 | + | |
| 19 | | + |
| 20 | + | |
| 21 | + | |
| 22 | + | |
| 23 | + | |
| 24 | | + |
| 25 | + | |
| 26 | + | |
| 27 | + | |

*Note:* A "+" signifies the higher scorer on a test of creativity.

the new subjects, a strong argument can be made for population generality. If the new subjects respond differently, the experimenter may be led to testable speculations about the reasons. To quote Sidman again:

> Generality and variability are basically antithetical concepts. If there are major undiscovered sources of variability in a given set of data, any attempt to achieve subject or principle generality is likely to fail. Every time we discover and achieve control of a factor that contributes to variability, we increase the likelihood that our data will be reproducible with new subjects and in different situations. Experience has taught us that precision of control leads to more extensive generalization of data.

Arnold (1970) advocated the technique of dimensional sampling. The experimenter would select each subject according to some theoretically crucial dimension. For example, if her theory led to the prediction that both level of anxiety and gender were relevant, she might choose four people: an anxious man and woman and a nonanxious man and woman. Differences between them might point the way to rapid identification of the key variables and rapid tests for generality.

## Procedures for Conducting Single-Case Experimental Designs

**Collecting Baseline Data.** Single-case experimental research usually begins with evaluation of the subject's performance prior to treatment. Data are collected from this baseline phase until the behaviors of interest stabilize. No formula is available to tell when suitable stabilization has occurred. For further discussion of both practical and ethical considerations, see Sidman (1960) and Kazdin (1978).

The two most popular single-case experimental research designs are the ABAB and multiple-baseline designs (Kazdin, 1978).

*ABAB Designs.* ABAB is shorthand for baseline/treatment/baseline/treatment. Once the behavior of interest stabilizes at baseline, the researcher introduces a treatment (a positive or negative reinforcer whenever the behavior occurs). This continues until the behavior restabilizes at (it is hoped) a different level. The treatment is then withdrawn so the experimenter can see if the behavior is reversible, and it is reinstated when the behaviors have stabilized again. ABAB designs come in many variations. Instead of withdrawing reinforcers after the first B phase, the researcher may administer them randomly, that is, independently of the subject's behavior. In clinical work, some patients have baseline problems so severe that they are dangerous to others. For them, the treatment phase may be given first (BABA). The number of phases may be extended indefinitely (ABABABAB...). If the treatment has long-lasting effects, the start of the second B phase may require a lengthy wait. Experimenters must also concern themselves with the ethical implications of withdrawing treatments that have been effective in reducing harmful behaviors.

*Multiple-Baseline Designs.* In the multiple-baseline design, a researcher obtains baseline data on at least two behaviors and applies an intervention at different times to each. For example, Kazdin (1978) described a treatment program for a young boy with several behavioral problems. Training was first focused on his poor eye contact and inappropriate body position when in the company of others. Those two behaviors improved while his poor speech and bland affect remained unchanged. When treatment was extended to them, they improved as well. Thus, control was demonstrated over all four problem behaviors. Multiple-baseline designs, like ABAB designs, come in several variations. Baseline performance can be

obtained for several subjects on the same behavior, then an intervention applied to only one subject at a time. The goal is to show that the behavior of
each subject changes only when the intervention is applied. Baselines can be
obtained for a subject in each of several settings, and an intervention can be
applied to only one setting at a time.

## Experimenter as Subject

Two experiments that helped establish the legitimacy of single-subject studies (Ebbinghaus, 1885 on learning and Stratton, 1897, on perception) were
additionally noteworthy in that the experimenter was also the subject. Experimenter as subject (E/S) studies played a major role in the advancement
of medicine (Altman, 1987) and offer several advantages over other research
designs:

■ Human subjects are affected by factors other than the independent variable.
They are usually curious about the nature of the research and have expectations, called *demand characteristics,* which are influenced by the research setting
and influence behavior. For example, in early sensory deprivation experiments, most subjects reported extreme stress. Orne (1962) manipulated demand characteristics by asking some subjects to sign a frightening release
form and showing them a panic button they could press if the stress became
too great. He told others they were controls in a sensory deprivation experiment and did not show them the button. Although all subjects were then
taken to a well-lit room, the experimentals reported stress and the controls
did not.

Experimenter/subjects know the research hypothesis so they have no
need to guess about it. They face demand characteristics that are not like
those of the other subjects. If their performance differs from the others, they
have a clue about the role of demand characteristics:

■ The experimenter need not worry about misinterpretation of instructions or
about failure of subjects to do their best because of lack of interest.
■ Feedback is immediate, so the experimenter can adjust the values of important
variables until they are optimal.
■ Experimenters can use powerful yet inexpensive motivators that would be of
dubious value with unknown subjects. (Some people like pistachio nuts; some
like peanuts.) They have a particularly valuable source of feedback about the
effectiveness of the IV manipulation.
■ In many experiments, only the acute effects of a manipulation are measured
but with an implicit assumption that the chronic effects would be equivalent.
The assumption is often unwarranted, and the effects of chronic treatment
may have greater theoretical and practical implications. For example, first-
time heroin users typically become euphoric, whereas chronic users feel little
more than lethargy. The frequent users are of greater concern to society.

Chronic preparations and longitudinal studies that require careful tracking of subjects are much easier with small samples, especially with E/S studies.

■ Certain questions can be answered only through intensive study of individuals, as in biorhythm research. The study of biorhythms requires that subjects be monitored continuously over long time periods. It seems unlikely that many people would volunteer for a project that required daily visits to a laboratory for several months; but the inconvenience would be minimal, the commitment maximal, for experimenters who normally work every day in their laboratories or whose laboratories travel with them.

■ E/S studies maximize the likelihood that interesting and unexpected effects will be noticed. Once stable baseline responding is established, any disruption will become apparent and can be followed up inexpensively. Thus, hunches can be indulged and many variables tested at a time. Unlike the group situation, in which variability is regarded as a nuisance factor, variability in single-subject data increases the possibility that previously unrecognized determinants of behavior will be discovered. All single-subject studies are valuable in this respect, E/S studies especially so since the variables of interest can be isolated more rapidly from the enormous number of potentially relevant ones. In addition, natural experiments (the experimenter is sick, dieting, euphoric, despondent, sleepy, etc.) can be exploited as they occur. Interactions between variables can be studied easily.

## QUESTIONS FOR CONSIDERATION

Each of the four studies that follow is limited in a major way. What would you do next if you came across such a study? My answers are given after the studies.

1. MacMahon, Yen, and Trichopaulou et al. (1981) reported a direct relationship between the amount of coffee people drank and their risk of getting pancreatic cancer. Their conclusion, given much press coverage, was that heavy coffee drinking causes pancreatic cancer. But correlational studies never prove causal relationships.

2. Weiss et al. (1980) tested the idea that ingestion of food dyes causes problem behaviors in normal children. Over a 77-day period, they gave children drinks that contained food dyes on eight of the days and placebos on the others. On each of the eight food dye days one child had a small increase in problem behaviors and one child a dramatic increase. The other 20 children were unaffected.

3. To find out if the death penalty deters violent crime, researchers compared the incidence of violent crime in countries with and without the death penalty and changes in incidence of violent crime in countries that changed their death penalty policies. But correlational studies do not prove causes.

4. Schuster and Schuster (1969) tested the idea, which they believed followed from evolutionary theory, that the parent under less stress at the time of conception is more likely to have offspring of its gender. They immobilized either male or female rats in bandages for 24 hours prior to mating, and they asked people to estimate how stressed they were when their children were conceived. The data supported the predictions: When the father was more stressed at the time of conception, the majority of offspring were female; and when the mother was more stressed, they were male. But the underlying idea is wrong. From an evolutionary perspective, a parent is probably more successful when it has offspring of the opposite gender. Success is measured in terms of the number of genes contributed to the next generation. Female mammals contribute an X chromosome to both their daughters and sons; males contribute an X to their daughters and a Y to their sons. The X chromosome contains more genes than the Y, so daughters inherit relatively more genes from their fathers than sons do.

## ANSWERS

My answers are disputable but might provoke discussion. Researchers should strive to conduct flawless studies that allow only a single, unambiguous interpretation, but chance factors or unusual values of extraneous variables may bedevil even the most carefully controlled experiments. Although readers must distinguish between well-designed and poorly designed studies, they should reserve some doubt about the former and extract what useful information they can from the latter. Of course, some studies are so poorly done that the researcher's conclusions are no more plausible than various alternatives. Those studies should be ignored.

1. The coffee/pancreatic cancer study was correlational. Some third factor such as stress might have caused both heavy coffee drinking and pancreatic cancer. A 1981 study (Nomura, Stemmermann, & Heilbrun) failed to replicate the MacMahon et al. study; and a 1984 study (Kinlen, Goldblatt, Fox, & Yudkin) suggested the intriguing possibility that pancreatic cancer may cause excessive coffee drinking. Pancreatic cancer is usually associated with high levels of blood sugar and often with overt diabetes; these conditions are likely to increase thirst and intake of all beverages. Nevertheless, a correlation between two variables should alert one to the possibility of a causal relationship.

2. Science deals with universals, not individual events. Results that cannot be reproduced are not part of science, which is a major reason for the reluctance of most psychologists to accept ESP research. But the require-

ment that results be reproducible from one laboratory to another differs from the requirement that results found with one subject should also hold for others. In the food dye study, only one child had severe behavioral problems on food dye days, but the problems occurred reliably in that one child. The results are meaningful and lead to interesting questions about the unique characteristics of that child.

3. Psychologists trying to solve important problems do not always have the luxury of controlled experiments. They must do their best. See pp. 141–142 on quasi-experimentation.

4. Data should not be discarded because the theory that inspired the data collection is incorrect. Wynne-Edwards (1962) theorized that many animals act altruistically for the good of their species. Most modern biologists believe that Wynne-Edwards was wrong, but his book was a progenitor of the important field of sociobiology. His data were reinterpreted to fit with current beliefs. The Schusters' data, if replicable, are fascinating and need explanation.

# 12 Observing

*By the time you finish reading this chapter, you should be able to answer the following questions:*

What are the different reasons for doing observational studies?
Can observational studies test hypotheses?
What are the three basic forms of observational data?
What are illusory correlations?
How does a researcher decide how many observations to make?
Should observation sessions be scheduled at any special times of
    day?
Can observational skills be taught?
Can the reliability of observations be measured?
How many observations should be made?
Why should medical students always observe their instructors
    closely?

■　■　■　■　■

*"Most of the knowledge and much of the genius of the research worker lie behind his selection of what is worth observing. It is a crucial choice, often determining the success or failure of months of work, often differentiating the brilliant discoverer from the plodder."* Alan Gregg, Rockefeller Foundation

Careful, systematic observing has distinguished many eminent scientists. Charles Darwin spent decades collecting and observing specimens. Sigmund Freud took copious notes on his patients, and Jean Piaget meticulously observed and recorded the behaviors of his children. Physiologist Claude Bernard wrote that "experimental reasoning always and necessarily deals with two facts at a time: observation, used as a starting point; experiment, used as conclusion or control."

## ■ REASONS FOR DOING OBSERVATIONAL STUDIES

### To Describe Nature

Astronomers use star charts, chemists refer to handbooks on the properties of chemicals, biologists classify flora and fauna, geologists consult tables on the hardness of minerals, and meteorologists describe cloud formations. Psychologists should also attend to naturally occurring behaviors. Naturalistic observations leave variables uncontrolled and so are of limited use for testing causal hypotheses. But the description of nature is a legitimate end and, as noted later, can provide evidence to support or discredit hypotheses.

### To Generate and Test Hypotheses

Darwin did not observe passively; he selected, organized, and tried to make sense of what he saw. His observations led to hypotheses that were tested by additional observations and experiments. Some research questions and hypotheses can be tested directly with observational data. Several observational studies supported the hypothesis that boys are more active than girls.

### To Assess Behavior

Assessment of behavior through direct observation is essential to progress in psychotherapy, since changes in behavior cannot be measured or evaluated if the starting point is unknown. Deviance is meaningful only by contrast with normality, so normal behavior should be studied. Tinbergen and

Tinbergen's (1972) observation that certain characteristic behaviors of autistic children also occur in normal children when they are afraid was the starting point for a productive research program on autism. Direct observation should be used routinely when testing drugs on laboratory animals, because exclusive focus on a few preselected dependent variables may miss important behavioral changes.

## Because Other Methods Are Impractical

Experiments cannot answer questions about the social organization of animals or their reactions to naturally occurring stimuli, or the effects on human children of loss of a parent. Ethical considerations limit experiments that would cause great pain or stress. People may be unwilling to participate in research on sensitive social issues or may respond in biased ways. For questions about such topics, systematic observation may be the best route to knowledge.

## ■ BECOMING A GOOD OBSERVER

The first step in becoming a good observer is to clarify the reason for the research. Darwin wrote: "How odd it is that anyone should not see that all observation must be for or against some view if it is to be of any service." How could it be otherwise? Imagine being asked, with no further instructions, to record your observations of a group of young men and women at a party. Wouldn't the results depend on whether you are man or woman, single or married, minister, college recruiter, or salesperson? Wouldn't different strategies be required for the questions "Are there any eligible men present?" and "Who is the most likely prospect to buy a motorcycle?" So, before doing any actual observing, clarify the research question.

## Decide on Type of Observation

**Narratives.** Narratives are running accounts of behavior that require little preparation. With tape recorder or journal, try to record all relevant occurrences. Although narrative data may be useful during the early stages of a research project, observers may focus on different aspects of a situation or give different interpretations to the same aspect. When the 8-year-old English boy peeped into a darkened house, he reported that the couple within were fighting. His American friend said, knowingly, "They are making love." To which the French boy sadly nodded his head and said, "Oui, they are making love. Badly."

**Ratings.** Ratings require observers to evaluate what they see, and reliability is often low. Some raters give consistently high evaluations, some consistently low, and some consistently in the middle. Some raters tend to see others as like themselves; some tend to see others as different. Raters who score a person high on one trait tend to score that person high on others. More generally, certain traits are rated as going together even when the data do not show any association between them. They are called *illusory correlations.*

Chapman and Chapman (1967) asked subjects to sit in a chair and watch pairs of words projected on a screen. Four words appeared randomly on the left side and were paired with three words that appeared randomly on the right. Each word on the left (bacon, lion, blossoms, boat) appeared equally often, as did each word on the right (eggs, tiger, notebook). But when the subjects were asked, "When bacon was on the left, what percentage of the time were eggs, tiger, and notebook on the right?" the average of their estimates for eggs was 47%. A similar illusory correlation held for estimates of lion-tiger pairings.

Sadker and Sadker (1985) showed a videotaped classroom discussion to teachers and asked whether boys or girls had talked more. The teachers overwhelmingly said girls, even though the boys in the film outtalked the girls by a 3:1 ratio. The stereotype that girls talk more caused even educators active in feminist issues to observe incorrectly. The only corrective was to have them count and code.

**Checklists.** Checklists are sheets of paper listing all the behaviors likely to be observed, with space for indicating frequency and duration. Some checklists list only the behaviors of interest and others list all likely behaviors. The two types may yield different results. Levine (1977) supervised observers of patients hospitalized with spinal cord injuries. Those given a checklist of 45 preselected behaviors recorded a frequency of occurrence of the behaviors approximately four times greater than that recorded by observers without such a list.

Observe enough beforehand so you can include all the behaviors likely to occur, and define them unambiguously. Have a miscellaneous category and room for notes. If several "miscellaneous" behaviors are checked, add to the list. If certain behaviors always occur together, and records of the separate occurrences are not crucial to the research question, assign a single behavioral label to the entire sequence. Ignore intensity and speed of the behaviors unless they are important to the research question. The categories need not be mutually exclusive. In fact, the observer might be interested in seeing which behaviors co-occur. For example, he might test for associations between specific movements and specific vocalizations. Each combination of movement and vocalization could be put in a separate category, but the complexity of the checklist would be increased accordingly.

## Decide on the Number of Observations

Early in the planning of any research project, the investigator should estimate the amount of data that must be collected. Box 12.1 tells how to calculate the required number of observations.

## Decide on the Recording Procedures

Behaviors can be classified according to their purpose or by specific movements. If by purpose, then calling for a nurse and pressing a button to get a nurse would be classified in the same way. If by specific movements, then talking with a nurse, doctor, or family member would be classified the same. Whichever system is chosen should be applied consistently.

Molecular behaviors are finer, for example, muscle twitches, whereas molar behaviors involve large movements. There are generally many levels between the extremes of molecular and molar. Code behaviors at a level somewhat more molecular than the level at which the research question has been formulated. Whichever level is chosen should be applied consistently to all behaviors.

Many journals contain observational systems for use with humans and animals. Use these published taxonomic lists if the coding system is suited to the research question. However, be aware that a system adopted from someone else might not be sufficiently sensitive to the question.

Scoring can be based on events (behaviors of interest are recorded as they occur) or time intervals (behaviors are recorded only if they occur during set times, for instance, at the onset of each 20-second interval). Event recording is preferred.

Important observations can be made with nothing more than pencil and paper—see Darwin, Charles. But several attractive alternatives, such as tiny cameras and directional microphones, are available.

## Sampling of Observation Sessions

**Timing of Observations.** Observation sessions can be scheduled to begin at specific times or whenever a particular behavior occurs. They can end at specific times, after a fixed number of behaviors have occurred, or when the subjects are no longer in view. Alternatively, sessions can begin and end at the observer's convenience, as is probably true of most observational studies in which no mention is made of sampling method. The choice is important. For example, data from Altmann and Altmann (1970) seem to indicate that the social behavior of baboons peaks at mid-day. But Altmann (1974) noted that the observers were more likely to take a mid-day break if

## BOX

### Decide on Number of Observations

When the goal of an observational study is to estimate the mean value of an event in a population, for example, the mean number of conflicts per hour in a nursery school, an important early step (after operationally defining crucial terms such as *conflict*) is to decide how many observations will be necessary. The procedure is simple:

1. From either previous work or a pilot study, estimate the standard deviation (SD).
2. Pick a confidence level (C). (Other things being equal, the more confidence you demand, the more subjects you will need.)
3. Decide on the maximum error (E) you are willing to make, that is, the maximum acceptable difference between the mean you calculate and the true population mean. (Other things being equal, the smaller the tolerable error, the more subjects you'll need.)

Use the formula

$$N = (SD^2 \times C)/E^2$$

Example: Suppose you observe 10, 8, 12, 11, 12, and 7 conflicts during six 1-hour observation periods. How many additional periods should you observe to be 95% sure that your final sample mean is within two conflicts per hour of the true mean?

The formula for the standard deviation is

$$SD = \sqrt{\frac{\Sigma x^2 - \frac{(\Sigma x)^2}{N}}{N-1}}$$

$$= \sqrt{\frac{100 + 64 + 144 + 121 + 144 + 49 - (3600/6)}{5}}$$

$$= \sqrt{22/5}$$

$$= 2.1$$

E = 2. For confidence levels of 80%, 90%, 95%, and 99%, use C = 1.64, 2.70, 3.84, and 6.61, respectively. So, for the 95% confidence level,

$$N = (2.1^2 \times 3.84)/4 = 4.2 = \text{five additional subjects (always round upward)}$$

nothing of great interest was happening, so the observations were a biased sample of mid-day periods. Many researchers always observe at the same time even though the nature of individual and group behaviors changes throughout the day (cf. Harcourt, 1978). It is better to observe continuously throughout the day or spread several sessions across each 24-hour period; or to observe two or three times each day, for example, morning, noon, and evening; or to observe at a different time each day so that each hour is equally represented in the final sample. (Behaviors vary seasonally as well, so similar cautions apply.)

**Setting.** Clinicians may observe clients in the clinician's office, the laboratory, or settings where the client is having difficulties, such as home, workplace, or classroom. Animals can be studied in the wild, in zoos, and in labs. Settings influence behaviors. If observations are confined to boxing rings, the conclusion will be that subjects are aggressive. Kortlandt (1962) wrote: "Zoo observations have led most writers to assume that wild chimpanzees live in small closed harem groups of 5-15 members. I saw nothing of the kind." Caged baboons frequently fight and males may literally tear apart a sexually receptive female, but free-ranging baboons rarely fight.

Observations made in other than a natural setting should be preceded by an adaptation period. Sleep researchers let subjects adapt for at least one night to sleeping in a laboratory, because dreams during the first few nights are different from later dreams. Some rats, mice, and fruit flies have been bred in laboratories for many generations and may not need an adaptation period, but the laboratory is unnatural for most species. Explanations of laboratory behaviors may miss the mark unless compared with what occurs naturally. Consider this story cited by Willems (1973). An ornithologist added small, rare birds called bearded tits to a zoo's collection. He designed an environment that seemed ideal and put a male and female inside. They mated, built a nest, laid eggs, and hatched and fed babies. But shortly after their birth, the babies were found dead. The ornithologist assumed there had been an accident or illness, as the parents continued to eat, drink, and mate. In fact, they soon reproduced again. But again he found dead babies soon afterward. The cycle repeated itself several times, until one day he observed the parents push the babies out of the nest and onto the ground. He realized that something was seriously wrong with the environment he had created, so he went out to observe bearded tits in the wild. He noted three clear behavioral patterns. First, parents spent much of the day finding and bringing food to their nestlings. Second, the infants cried for food incessantly throughout the daylight hours. Third, parents meticulously cleaned their nests, shoving out inanimate objects such as leaves and beetle shells. These observations brought quick understanding of the problem of his captive birds. The parents had been supplied so abundantly that they fed their infants to satiety; so the infants fell asleep and were shoved out of the nest like other inanimate objects. The ornithologist remedied the situation by making food harder to get, and the birds then produced many families.

## Choose Between Natural and Contrived Conditions

Even researchers who observe in natural environments may arrange conditions, with or without the subject's knowledge, to provoke interesting behaviors. Jane Goodall merely observed wild chimpanzees most of the time, but she occasionally hid bananas. Jones et al. (1981) constructed a simulated bedroom at a school to assess how children at home in bed at night could learn to escape from emergency fire situations. To see whether a man treated for deficiency in verbal skills had improved, observers posing as shoppers went to the store where he worked and interacted with him in standardized ways.

## Obtrusive and Unobtrusive Observations May Give Different Results

Pedersen (1986) observed women in a public restroom. When an observer was visible, 18 of 20 women washed their hands after using the toilet. When the observer hid in a stall with her feet up, three of 19 washed. Some observers try to minimize the effects of their presence by concealing themselves in blinds or with one-way mirrors. Others sit quietly for long periods to let subjects habituate before they make their important observations. Still, different activities and individuals are affected unequally by the presence of observers. Also, even if the subjects under study habituate, others with whom they come into contact may not.

## Practice

Naturalist Louis Agassiz required that his students spend long hours learning how to observe. One student, Scudder (1874), described Agassiz's teaching methods. Agassiz gave Scudder a preserved fish called a haemulon and asked him to study it. Scudder returned in 10 minutes to report that he was done. But Agassiz was gone, so he went back to the fish. "Half an hour passed—an hour—another hour; the fish began to look loathsome. I turned it over and around; looked it in the face—ghastly; from behind, beneath, above, sideways, at 3/4 view—just as ghastly." Scudder had been told to use only his hands and eyes, no instruments, so he drew the fish. Agassiz, during a brief return, expressed approval and urged Scudder to keep observing. This continued for 3 days. On the fourth day a second fish of the same group was placed beside the first, and Scudder was told to find resemblances and differences between the two. More fish followed until the entire family was represented. Scudder was interested in insects, not fish, but he made continual, surprising discoveries throughout his ordeal and called it the best lesson he had ever had for the study of insects, "a lesson whose influence has extended to the details of every subsequent study."

Practice also helps with subjects who are alive and moving about. Argyle, Bryant, and Trower (1974) had trainees observe films of children sitting through a classroom lesson and being questioned about it. The trainees were asked to judge which children had understood, and they were then given the correct answers. When they were shown a new film of a second lesson, they showed marked improvement in their judgments.

## Measure the Reliability of Observations

Unreliable measures are useless (see chapter 5), but investigators do not agree on the best way to compute the reliability of observational data. Berk (1979) listed 16 different computational formulas. Note: Observer agreement is different from reliability, which refers to stability over time and to accuracy in comparison with an acceptable standard. Two observers who agree perfectly may nevertheless be unreliable. However, it is common practice to apply the term *reliability* to measures of agreement.

Estimates of agreement are often spuriously high. Observers who knew they were being checked had reliabilities considerably higher than when they were unaware. When aware, they tended to adjust their scoring to match that of the person with whom they were being compared, and their computational errors consistently inflated reliability scores (O'Leary, Kent, & Kanowitz, 1975). A partial solution is to monitor observers without telling them; this would not directly improve observer accuracy but would give better estimates of reliability.

Estimates of reliability are sensitive to the number of behaviors in a scoring system and the number of categories actually scored in a given session. The more categories, the lower the reliability. Fewer categories were scored when reliability was being checked than when it was not, probably because the observers became more conservative (Jones, Reid, & Patterson, 1975). Observers tend to "drift" in their scoring tendencies, that is, over time they change their criteria for scoring. Observers who work together over a long period of time may drift in the same way, thereby earning high reliability scores; but the scores will not be accurate.

To control drift:

■ Have observers meet periodically as a group, score behaviors, and receive immediate feedback on the accuracy of their scoring.

■ If possible, videotape the behaviors to be observed and score the tapes in random order at the end of the study.
■ Periodically bring in newly trained observers and compare their scores with those of old hands.

One additional strategy for improving the reliability of observations (and of all other research procedures) is to pick suitable behaviors. If the behavior of interest is not easily scored, search for a related one that is. For example, a researcher interested in people's postures during an interview situation might measure the height of their eyes as they sit. With closed-circuit television, this is a highly reliable indicator of posture.

# ■ SOME PROBLEMS

## Confounding

A *confound* is a variable not manipulated by an investigator that systematically biases results. To compare frequencies of various responses in different individuals or groups, an investigator might observe them on separate occasions. But if one group is observed in the morning and the other at night, the time of testing is a confound and may be a major cause of differences. Place and context of observations may also exert large effects. The best solution is to observe subjects more than once, and at different times, with the order of observation chosen randomly. Be aware that conditions of observation may profoundly affect results.

## Computing Relative Frequencies

Some behaviors are easier than others to observe. A report that young children cry more than they smile may rest on the tenuous assumption that crying and smiling are equally likely to be detected; a report that juvenile monkeys fight more than do adults, on the assumption that fighting is equally likely to be recorded in juveniles and adults.

## Feedback May Lead to Bias

O'Leary et al. (1975) told observers that they would see how an experimental intervention had modified the behaviors of children in a classroom. The children were shown on videotape, apparently before and after the intervention. Actually, however, the tapes were matched so that the crucial behaviors occurred with equal frequency. After the initial observation sessions, feedback was provided: positive if an observer scored behavior as changing in the right direction and negative if he reported no change or a change in the wrong direction. The combined effects of expectancies and feedback led to biases in the second round of observing, so that most behaviors were reported as changing in the right direction. A solution is to give observers feedback only about the accuracy of their observations, not whether they support the research hypothesis.

## Sloppy Observing Can Be Dangerous

Beveridge (1950) told the following story: A physician, while teaching a class of students, took a sample of diabetic urine and dipped a finger in to taste it. He then asked all the students to repeat his action. This they reluctantly did, making grimaces, but agreeing that it tasted sweet. "I did this," said the physician with a smile, "to teach you the importance of observing detail. If you had watched me carefully you would have noticed that I put my first finger in the urine but licked my second finger."

# Surveys

*By the time you finish reading this chapter, you should be able to answer the following questions:*

What are the different reasons for doing survey research?
How do survey results influence our daily lives?
How do surveyors decide how many subjects to use?
How should subjects be picked to be in surveys?
What is sampling error? Can it be avoided?
What, if anything, should be done about people who are asked to participate in a survey but refuse?
Do different survey formats (mailed questionnaires, personal interviews, telephone interviews, computer-assisted interviews) give essentially the same results?
Why does the unique nature of survey interviews (compared with ordinary conversation) often lead to untrustworthy answers?
Why are discrepant results between surveyors commonplace?
Are there any alternatives to surveys for finding out about people's attitudes or future behaviors?

■  ■  ■  ■  ■

*"The modern poll can become a bright and devastating light on the gap which too often exists between the will of the people and the translation of this will into law by legislators."* George Gallup

Surveys are inexpensive, require no elaborate equipment, and seem easy to design and interpret. No wonder they are the most widely used method of data collection in the social sciences. The U.S. government used surveys to explore the effects of projected reforms such as a negative income tax and universal health insurance:

> These joined such important government surveys as the Current Population Survey carried out monthly to estimate the nation's unemployment rate, the National Crime Survey collecting data on victimizations to supplement the police-report-based *Uniform Crime Reports,* and the National Health Interview Survey providing data on prevalence of illnesses and their effects. This proliferation of surveys has made them part of the very fabric of our lives, providing data for academic research and for crucial government policy. (Tanur, 1992, p. 4)

Surveys answer questions about the members of a population and differences between subgroups. Many have political implications; their results affect the actions of candidates (Lau, 1994), size of voter turnout (Ifill, 1988), and support for third-party candidates (Black & Black, 1993). Some surveys are part of scientific programs, helping to classify, unearth interesting relationships, and identify the key issues about a topic. Survey results can be treated as a dependent variable, as when subjects are assigned to one of two treatments and then given a questionnaire to measure posttreatment attitudes. Repeated surveys on the same topic measure changes over time, and surveys have themselves been subjects of study.

Surveys can influence subsequent behavior. Randomly selected married couples received either frequent, intense interviews over a 4-year period or only occasional interviews. The intensely studied couples reported lower marital satisfaction after 2 years and greater satisfaction by the fourth year (Veroff, Hatchett, & Douvan, 1992). As part of a large survey, only some households were asked the question, "When will the next new car be purchased by someone in your household?" Compared with households not asked, 37% more bought a car within 6 months. The question, "Do you or does anyone in your household plan to acquire a (another) personal computer in the future for use at home?" was followed by an 18% increase compared with households not asked (Morwitz, Johnson, & Schmittlein, 1993).

The prospective surveyor has four important tasks: writing questions, assembling the questionnaire, selecting the sample, and administering the questions.

# ■ WRITING QUESTIONS

Surveyors should formulate each question with explicit objectives in mind. Specificity is crucial. Rather than measuring "attitudes" of potential voters toward a particular candidate, indicate specific attitudes, such as attitudes toward the candidate's personality or platform. Review the literature to see what is available and then, since repetition of questions is encouraged, plagiarize. Sources for questions include the Gallup Poll, the CBS–*New York Times* Poll, and the polls section of the journal *Public Opinion Quarterly*. Many universities keep archives of survey research data, and other archives can be found on the Internet.

Questions must be written so that they fully prepare respondents to provide the answer, mean the same thing to all respondents, and communicate to respondents the kinds of answers that constitute an appropriate response. Pretesting questions safeguards against later misunderstanding. Sudman and Bradburn (1982) told of a respondent who was asked about the item "Is it better not to try to plan when to have children, but just to accept them when they come?" She said, "Of course you accept them when they come—you can't just leave them in the hospital." For a comparison of four pretesting approaches, see Presser and Blair (1994).

# ■ ASSEMBLING THE QUESTIONNAIRE

Questions should be ordered to make the respondents' task as pleasant as possible, minimize the time needed to complete the task, and maximize response accuracy. With those goals in mind, the following suggestions are offered:

- Start with nonthreatening, interesting questions that can be answered with little effort.
- Introduce topics with general questions, then move to specifics.
- Keep all questions on a single topic together, and introduce new topics with transitional phrases.
- Use several kinds of questions and vary their lengths. Let a "Yes" be the conservative answer to some questions and the liberal answer to others. (Some people have response biases; they tend to answer most questions with "Yes" or most with "No." Some people tend to agree, others to disagree, regardless of statement content.)
- When appropriate, ask screening questions. For example, instead of asking a series of questions on whether the respondent has recently read any of a long list of magazines, ask first, "Did you happen to read any magazines in the past

2 weeks, or not?" (Do not overuse screening questions, because respondents may learn to say "No," to save themselves from the follow-ups.)

■ Ask as few questions as possible to achieve the research objectives.

Make the questionnaire neat and easy to read. Number all questions and leave spaces between them. Write a cover letter that gives the name of the organization conducting the study and describes its purpose. Provide guidelines for answering and, for mail questionnaires, give the return deadline. End with a thank-you.

## ■ SELECTING THE SAMPLE

Surveyors must choose subjects according to carefully prescribed procedures and make inferences about nonrespondents. They should decide on the number of subjects before collecting data.

### Size of Sample

To find the average height of women in a classroom, a researcher could measure the height of each woman; the procedure would be simple. But if she wanted to know the average height of all women in the United States, she would have to sample and then generalize. It might seem amazing that data from samples of only 1,500 people permit accurate estimates, yet 1,500 is the standard sample size from which Gallup and other surveyors predict voting patterns. Since 1944, almost all of the Gallup Poll's predictions on U.S. presidential elections have come within 4 percentage points of the actual popular vote.

Unless a sample reflects the population from which it comes, generalizing is pointless. But because of chance factors, sample and population are rarely identical. The extent to which a properly chosen sample can be expected to deviate from the population from which it comes is called sampling error. Imagine trying to estimate the percentage of spades in a stack of playing cards. If you randomly pulled out 10 cards (your sample) and two were spades, your best estimate would be that spades comprise 20% of the entire stack (the population). But another sample of 10 might produce zero, six, or eight spades. A 52-card poker deck has 13 spades (25%), so no estimate based on a 10-card sample could ever be exactly right. This unavoidable error is the sampling error. As the number of cards (subjects) increases, sampling error is reduced. So, the first step in figuring out sample size is to decide how much error is acceptable. Only by sampling the entire population will sampling error equal zero. (Other errors, as discussed later, would still be likely.)

Once a surveyor decides how much sampling error (*SE*) she will tolerate, she can figure out the necessary number of subjects (*N*). See Box 13.1.

---

**BOX**

## Calculating Necessary Sample Size

To determine the sample size needed for estimating what proportion of a population has a certain characteristic, first decide on the tolerable sampling error.
Then use the formula

$N = .96/SE^2$, where *SE* is the sampling error.

If random samples of *N* subjects are surveyed repeatedly, and if there are
no other sources of error, then 95% of the sampled proportions should fall
within one *SE* of the true population proportion. Surveyors typically use the
95% confidence level. For other levels, see a good statistics book.

**Example 1.** Suppose a surveyor wishes to estimate the proportion of voters
who support a particular proposition. She is willing to accept a sampling error
of 0.05. Then $N = .96/.0025 = 384$. Suppose that 53% of her sample say they
favor the proposition. In 95% of cases, an observed proportion of .53 means
that the true proportion is between .48 and .58.

**Example 2.** For national surveys, the typical sample size is 1,500. For $N =
1500$, $SE^2 = .96/(1500) = .00064$. Then $SE = .0253 = 2.53\%$. Sampling error
equals 2.53%.
  Surveys can be used to estimate means instead of proportions. The formula
for sample size is $N = 3.84s^2/SE^2$, where *s* is the standard deviation of the population.

**Example 3.** Suppose that either from previous experience or a small study, a
researcher determines that the time to learn a particular task has a standard
deviation of 30 seconds. If he wishes to estimate time to learn the task and is
willing to accept a sampling error of 5 seconds, he would compute $N = (3.84 \times
30^2)/5^2 = 138$. The result indicates that repeated measures of learning times on
random samples of 36 subjects would, in 95% of cases, yield means within 5
seconds of the population mean.
  Intuitively, it seems that sample size should depend on population size, but
these formulas do not take population size into account. Intuition is right, and
there is a correction factor for population size, but it does not make much of a

difference. If $N$ is the initially calculated sample size and $P$ is the population size, then the more accurate sample size is given by $NP/(N + P)$. In example 3, $N = 138$. If the population were 1,000, the corrected value would be $NP/(N + P) = 138,000/1,138 = 122$.

Note that small sample surveys are not very helpful for estimating characteristics of populations. The sampling error is too large. Suppose that 50 subjects are used. Then, $SE^2 = (.96/50) = .0192$.

Sampling error would be .139. If 53% of respondents said they would vote yes, the true percentage would be anywhere between 39.1 and 66.9, but only if there were no errors but sampling error. Even with an $N$ of 100, $SE^2 = (.96/100) = .0096$. So $SE = .098$ and the true percentage would be between 43.4 and 62.6.

For many traits, individual scores distribute symmetrically about the mean for the trait. The distribution is called normal. The previously given method for computing sample size entails the assumption that the characteristic being measured is normally distributed, but even fairly large departures from normality can be tolerated. Alternative statistics are available if the normality condition is not met, but the required sample size is then much greater.

## Choosing Individual Subjects

Unless subjects have been properly chosen, inferences to populations are not justified. Even if all students in my large psychology class were to answer questions about their political preferences, generalizations to all U.S. citizens would be inappropriate. My sample would be students, mostly in the 18–25-year age range, at a single college, Cal State University. However brilliant, good-looking, and noble they might be, they are not representative of all U.S. citizens. I could not properly generalize to all college students, because expensive, small, private colleges in the East attract different students from those at large public institutions in the West. I could not generalize to all Cal State students, because psychology, art, and business majors differ. I could not generalize to all psychology students; freshmen and seniors differ, as do students who intend to specialize in clinical psychology, work in industry, pursue careers in research, and stay in school until they can draw on the family trust fund. I could not even generalize to the other classes I teach. Classes taught at different times of day attract different types of students. In short, the characteristics of any self-selected group are likely to differ from the characteristics of the population, often in subtle but important ways. Therefore, a sample is proper only if drawn randomly, that is, "selected by a process which gives every possible sample (of that size from that population) the same chance of selection" (Stuart, 1984, p. 4).

## Simple Random Sampling

To get a random sample, first define the population. If I wanted to generalize to the student population at Cal State, I would have to decide whether to include all or only full-time currently enrolled students taking courses on the Hayward campus. (We teach extension courses in other cities.) Then I would ask the registrar for a printout of all students, write each name on a slip, put the slips in an urn, and pull out as many as needed. More practically, I would assign a number to each student and use a table of random numbers to get my sample. That would be relatively easy. Randomly sampling the population of a city is much harder, and national surveys are harder still. The population, and hence the criteria for inclusion in the sample, must always be carefully specified beforehand. Surveyors must decide if there will be age limitations; if, in a city survey, everybody in the city at a specified time will be eligible or if the population will be restricted to permanent residents; if it will include people confined to mental hospitals and prisons; if the surveyors will try to reach residents traveling abroad; if a national survey will include Alaska or Hawaii.

Few cities have inclusive lists of residents comparable to the registrar's list of students. Telephone directories do not list everybody, and some people have more than one listed number. Many directory numbers belong to commercial and government establishments. (Random dialing techniques let interviewers reach people with unlisted numbers; still, some households are inaccessible by phone.) Lists of voters and property owners exclude many people. All methods typically exclude prisoners, soldiers, hospital patients, and children, even from surveys concerned with prison and military reform and hospital and child care. So random sampling, although crucial for making accurate generalizations, is almost never accomplished.

## Stratified Sampling

If subgroups within a population differ greatly with respect to the trait being measured, $s^2$ (see Box 13.1) will be large. It can be reduced by sampling subgroups in proportion to their population ratios. Thus, to estimate the mean weight of fruit from a crate containing 500 grapes, 400 apples, and 100 watermelons, the researcher could randomly pick 50 grapes from the grape bunches, then 40 apples and 10 watermelons. This strategy would decrease $s^2$ and hence both standard error and necessary sample size. An additional benefit of stratification is that it allows for collection of data on the separate subgroups.

## ■ NONRESPONSE

Selecting subjects is one matter, getting adequate data from them another. In any large-scale survey, some subjects will not be located; some will refuse or be unable to participate; and some will misunderstand instructions or otherwise give data that cannot be used. The proportion of people selected for a survey who give usable data is called the *response rate*. Surveyors disagree about how to calculate response rates and even who should count as a nonrespondent. For mailed questionnaires, nonrespondents are those who do not return usable answers; but the typical method for telephone and personal interviews is to count as nonrespondents only those who are located and contacted and then do not provide usable data.

Respondents and nonrespondents differ, often in ways that are relevant to a study's purpose. For example, blacks, older people, city-dwellers, and westerners were less willing than others to grant telephone interviews (Aneshensel, Frerich, Clark, & Yokopenic, 1982; DeMaio, 1980). Both the proportion of nonrespondents and the reason for their exclusion (unavailability, refusal, or unusable data) affect the degree of bias. If the proportion is small, their absence will not matter. But the return rate with mail surveys is often less than 50%, and nonresponse rates for both telephone and personal interviews have increased in recent years.

Sending an introductory letter before calling for an interview increases response rate (Dillman, 1978); and small rewards, follow-up telephone calls, and special delivery letters also help (Schewe & Cournoyer, 1976). But people who respond only after several follow-ups may differ in crucial ways from immediate respondents. In a telephone survey during the 1984 U.S. presidential campaign, Reagan edged Mondale by 3% among those interviewed at one call. After including results from people who responded to a callback, the lead increased to 6%, and the final results, which included people who were reached after as many as 30 callbacks, gave Reagan a 13% lead (Traugott, 1987). Cochran (1963) mailed three waves of questionnaires to fruit growers. One question ("How many fruit trees do you own?") asked for information also available from other sources. Growers who responded to the first wave averaged 456 trees. The mean number of trees owned by the second and third waves of respondents were 408 and 385, respectively. The mean of those who never responded was 290.

## ■ ADMINISTERING THE QUESTIONS

Surveyors choose between mailed questionnaires, personal interviews, telephone interviews, and several forms of computer-assisted self-administered interviews. Mailed questionnaires enable coverage of a wide geographic area. Because no interviewers are used, there are no interviewer effects, and training, payroll, and data processing costs are low. Respondents can take time to think about difficult questions. On the negative side, response rates are lower than with telephone and personal interviews. Mailed questionnaires are unsuited to the poorly educated, the aged, and others who have trouble reading or filling out answers. Questions must be kept simple, and investigators cannot follow up interesting answers with additional questions. Later questions may suggest answers to earlier ones, and respondents may then change their answers. Someone other than the intended respondent may fill out the questionnaire.

Telephone interviews share most of the advantages and few of the disadvantages of the other survey methods. More than 90% of U.S. households have phones, and the others are unlikely to be located by any other strategy. Although interviewers must be trained, they typically work in a centralized location under close supervision; with no travel expenses, overall costs are low. A wide geographic area can be sampled, and results are obtained rapidly. (On the other hand, as one who has often received calls at inopportune times, I urge telephone surveyors to consider whether their projects warrant such obtrusive behavior.)

Personal interviews allow for longer and more probing questions, with the potential for visual aids and follow-up of interesting answers. But interviewers are often part-timers with no serious stake in the integrity of the research. Yet they are expected to travel long distances and occasionally to dangerous places. They may be tempted to make up data and do not always resist temptation. Hyman and colleagues (Hyman et al., 1954) planted one or more respondents and secretly taped a series of interviews. Four of 15 interviewers made up much of their data.

Computer-assisted self-interviewing (CASI) gives respondents more privacy than the other methods. Respondents read questions from the computer screen and enter answers with the keyboard. Adding an audio component lets respondents hear questions through headphones as they appear on screen, which helps those who cannot read well.

The various formats give different results. Self-administration, compared with less private forms of interviewing, leads to higher reports of drug use, abortion, degree of fault in automobile accidents, suicidal ideation, risk behaviors for HIV, and medical symptoms (Lessler & O'Reilly, 1997). However, underreporting of socially stigmatized behaviors occurs even with formats that permit privacy. Harrell (1997) interviewed former drug treatment clients in their own homes and promised that no one would ever know how they responded. The procedures were modeled on the National Household Survey on Drug Abuse, which costs the federal government millions of dollars annually (General Accounting Office, 1993). Although all the respondents had undergone treatment, fewer than 40% reported that fact.

Subtle changes in format can make a difference. King (1994) had subjects complete two questionnaires, one specifically about alcohol consumption and the other, either 3 days earlier or 3 days later, on dietary intake over the previous year that included the identical questions about alcohol. Both men and women gave substantially higher estimates of their consumption of beer, white wine, red wine, and liquor on the dietary intake questionnaire. People who were called on sunny days and asked how they felt about their lives gave more positive answers than people who were called on rainy days (Schwarz & Clore, 1983).

# ■ RESEARCH ON SURVEY VALIDITY

Given this information, can survey data be trusted? Early researchers said yes and pointed to consistency between reports of drug use and reports of other deviant behaviors. But people who underreport both drug use and the other behaviors would show strong correspondence between the two. Concordance between self-reported use and older biological measures such as urinalysis also misleads, because the measures greatly underdetect drug use; thus, drug users who deny using appear to be telling the truth (Wish, Hoffman, & Nemes, 1997).

## Social Desirability

Survey measurement is reactive (see p. 72), especially when questions are asked about sensitive matters. Crowne and Marlowe (1964) developed a scale that distinguishes between people according to their need to respond in culturally sanctioned ways. High and low scorers answered differently to questions about number of close friends, marital happiness, general happiness, and other topics. The differences probably depended less on actual status with respect to the topics than on attempts to answer in ways that bring social approval.

Survey respondents have little incentive to acknowledge illicit drug use, politically incorrect attitudes, or other undesirable behaviors, and they often overreport desirable behaviors such as charitable giving. Teenagers give more socially desirable answers to questions asked at home than at school (Rootman & Smart, 1985). The reported use of illicit drugs is approximately 50% lower when evaluated by group-administered questionnaires than individual interviews (Cook, Bernstein, & Andrews, 1997), and men consistently report higher numbers of opposite-sex partners than do women (T. Smith, 1992).

# ■ UNIQUE QUALITIES OF SURVEYS

Clark and Schober (1992) pointed out several important differences between survey interviews and ordinary conversations. In the former:

- The person asking the questions is rarely the one who wrote them and may have no interest in the answers.
- The respondent has no say in the direction of the talk: The written survey schedule controls the topics raised, questions asked, and answers recorded.
- A respondent who does not understand a question can do little other than ask that it be repeated.

Clark and Schober believe that the unique quality of interviews explains why subtle changes in wording of questions can substantially affect responses. Respondents know that vague questions cannot be clarified, so they assume that the surveyor believes them capable of figuring out the meanings. They also believe that vague, ambiguous, or strange-seeming questions must not really be so. This has consequences.

## Pressure to Know

Because respondents believe that questions are about things they should know, they overstate their familiarity on issues. About 15% reported having heard of a fictitious civil rights leader (Sudman & Bradburn, 1982), and 5% of high school students described using a fictitious drug (Petzel, Johnson, & McKillip, 1973). People under time pressure, which is greatest with telephone interviews and least with mailed questionnaires, estimate factual answers that would take too long to figure out precisely.

Unless they are well-informed about a topic, respondents given the "don't know" option assume they should use it. If not given the option, they may assume they should answer from what they do know. So, when asked, "In general, do you think the courts in this area deal too harshly or not harshly enough with criminals?," 5.6% said too harshly, 77.8% not harshly enough, and 16.5% either "about right" or "don't know." When the option "not enough information to say" was included with a similar group, 4.6% said too harshly, 60.3% not harshly enough, and 35.1% either "about right" or "not enough information to say" (reported in Schuman & Presser, 1981).

## Perspectives

Questions are asked in contexts that imply perspectives. Loftus and Palmer (1974) had subjects view brief films of car accidents and then asked, "How fast were the cars going when they hit each other?" Others got the same question with "hit" changed to either "smashed," "contacted," "bumped," or "collided." Estimates of speed varied with the verb, ranging from 31.8 mph (contacted) to 40.8 mph (bumped). Clark and Schober (1992) wrote that each verb provided a different perspective. Respondents must answer from some perspective and are almost forced to accept the one given.

Compare the following two questions:

1. How frequently were you angry last week?
2. How frequently were you angry last year?

Respondents inferred that the researcher was interested in more frequent and less severe episodes of anger when the question asked about one week rather than one year. Schwarz (1999) noted an important implication, as illustrated by the next two questions:

1. How severe has your typical marital disagreement been during the past week?
   a. trivial        b. moderately serious        c. very severe
2. How severe has your typical marital disagreement been during the past 5 years?
   a. trivial        b. moderately serious        c. very severe

Question 1 suggests that the researcher is interested in more frequent events, so respondents are likely to report on relatively trivial ones. Respondents to question 2 will probably focus on more serious disagreements.

Other frequency issues affect perspectives (Schwarz, 1999). When respondents must choose among several response alternatives, they assume that the middle range of the scale reflects the usual behavioral frequency. Scales that present high- rather than low-frequency response alternatives result in higher estimates for behaviors as diverse as sexual activity, consumer behaviors, and physical symptoms. When people were asked how much time they spent watching television each day (up to ½ hour, ½ hour to 1 hour, 1 hour to 1½ hours, 1½ hours to 2 hours, 2 hours to 2½ hours, more than 2½ hours), 16.2% reported watching for more than 2½ hours. When they were asked the same question with the choices "up to 2½ hours, 2½ hours to 3 hours, 3 hours to 3½ hours, 3½ hours to 4 hours, 4 hours to 4½ hours, more than 4½ hours," 37.5% reported watching for more than 2½ hours. Moreover, the estimates affected later judgments. Those in the first group who checked "more than 2½ hours" were likely to infer that their TV watching was above average; they subsequently expressed less satisfaction with their other leisure-time activities than people in the second group who checked "more than 2½ hours."

Contexts establish perspectives. If a question about Richard Nixon and his role in the Watergate scandal is followed by a question about the trustworthiness of American politicians, politicians are likely to receive a low rating—respondents having just been reminded of a vivid example of the untrustworthiness of a politician. But if the Nixon question is followed by one on a particular politician, Nixon will be a standard of comparison and the second person will be judged more favorably than otherwise (Schwarz, 1999).

Loaded terms influence perspectives, and surveyors with political agendas choose carefully between "pro-choice" and "pro-abortion," "pro-life" and "anti-abortion," "peacekeeping forces" and "occupation army," and "taxes" and "revenues." All questions carry presuppositions—neutral questions do not exist.

## Vague Terms

Respondents presume that vague words mean something specific, namely, whatever occurs to them at that moment; and they interpret the words idiosyncratically. Belson (1981) received confident answers to a series of questions that included words such as "few." But 7 of 59 respondents interpreted "over the last few years" to mean "no more than 2 years," 22 to mean "between 2 and 7 years," 19 to mean "7 years or more," and 11 to mean "10 years or more."

## Desire to Appear Consistent

Many order effects are understandable in light of people's attempts to be consistent. Hyman and Sheatsley (1950) asked two questions:

1. Do you think the United States should let communist newspaper reporters from other countries come in here and send back to their papers the news as they see it?
2. Do you think a communist country such as Russia should let American newspaper reporters come in and send back to America the news as they see it?

When question 1 came first, 36% said yes. When question 1 followed question 2, 73% said yes to question 1. When question 2 came first, 90% said yes, when it came second, 66%. Clark and Schober concluded that the respondents tried to be consistent; if they had agreed that U.S. reporters should be allowed into communist countries, they had to let communist reporters into the United States.

## Desire to Be Helpful

Respondents generally omit answers that seem irrelevant to the researcher's needs. If asked to indicate their activities during the previous day, few would say "I brushed my teeth." But they would probably check "brushing teeth" if it were part of a checklist of activities. Checklists indicate the kinds of answers expected and remind respondents of material that might otherwise not be considered. Schwarz (1999) suggested that these effects explain many differences between open- and closed-question formats. For example, 61.5% of respondents asked to pick from a list about the most important thing to prepare children for life picked "To think for themselves." Yet only 4.6% in an open-response format gave an answer consistent with that view.

# ■ RETROSPECTIVE RECALL AND CONSISTENCY

Recall of the past (retrospective recall) is unreliable. In 1964, Powers, Goudy, and Keith (1978) interviewed a sample of 1,870 men on various aspects of their lives. In 1974, 1,332 were located again and asked to recall their situations and attitudes of 1964. Their memories were strikingly different from what they had reported a decade earlier. For example, to a question about whether recreation, comfort, friends, or work was their most important value, only 42% gave the same answer both times. Only 40% gave the same answer when asked to identify their 1964 yearly family income from a set of broad categories. Only 75% answered consistently to a question about the number of persons in the household. In most cases, the 1974 answers presented respondents in a more favorable light than did those of the initial interview.

Dasanayake (1995) compared mothers' recall of their children's antibiotic use with information from the children's health records. The mothers underestimated considerably.

Responses to questions about the past are influenced by attempts (possibly unconscious) to link past and present coherently. For example, Pearson et al. (1992) had high school students fill out a questionnaire asking for their opinions on several controversial issues. Several days later the students had a group discussion on one of the issues. One discussant, a respected senior, was a confederate of the researcher armed with persuasive arguments for one side, and he dominated the conversation. Afterward, the students were asked in private about both their current opinion and the opinion they had expressed at the first session. Not only had their opinions shifted dramatically, but they recalled their previous opinions as being very similar to their current ones (Goethals & Reckman, 1973).

U.S. respondents in 1976 were asked to recall their 1972 political party affiliation. The researchers had already obtained the information from another source. Of the 22% who had changed parties between 1972 and 1976, 91% incorrectly reported not changing (Niemi, Katz, & Newman, 1980).

Pearson, Ross, and Dawes (1992) suggested several strategies for reducing errors from retrospective reports. Then they proposed a radical solution: Surveyors should not use retrospective reports.

# ■ WHY SURVEY HOUSES DISAGREE

Commercial survey houses frequently report widely different results even when they have asked virtually identically worded questions at virtually the same times. Converse and Traugott (1986), Lau (1994), and Voss, Gelman, and King (1995) offered many reasons for discrepancies. Their analyses can help people to both plan and evaluate surveys.

## Sampling Error

Unless everybody in a population is surveyed, sampling error is unavoidable. The media typically report sampling error when describing survey results, but it probably accounts for less than half of the magnitude of discrepancies (Buchanan, 1986). Furthermore, sampling error calculations presume simple random sampling, which is too expensive to implement for large surveys. The normal procedure is cluster sampling, in which population units are divided into clusters such as city blocks or telephone numbers with a particular exchange, and the clusters are randomly sampled. Sampling error increases with the degree of homogeneity within clusters.

## Variability in Sample Composition

Voss et al. (1995) interviewed representatives from six large organizations. The Roper organization does not use telephone interviews for presidential election surveys, and the others differ in how they choose phone numbers and in answers to four types of questions: (a) How many callbacks should be made to a number that initially provides no answer, a busy signal, or a mechanical answering mechanism? (b) What if all adults at a phone number refuse to answer? (c) Should respondents be selected randomly or by a systematic system? (d) What should be done if a respondent claims not to be a registered voter? After sampling is completed, pollsters adjust in various ways to make up for differences between the sample and target populations. Suppose that only 200 women have been chosen for a 1,000 person sample although the population is comprised of 60% women. One adjustment would be to weight each woman's response so that it counts six times as much as each man's. (My daughters believe that the 6:1 ratio is reasonable under all circumstances.)

Many factors affect sample compositions. Most people who work during the week are Democrats, so weekday-only polls have a Republican bias. A Democratic bias is found among respondents reached on the first call, so apparent support for Republicans increases with the number of days a pollster spends in the field (Traugott, 1987, 1992). In most elections, a higher proportion of registered Republicans vote than registered Democrats or Independents. So, Lau reasoned, samples of likely voters have a Republican bias compared with samples of registered voters. The polls he analyzed showed the predicted bias.

## Interviewer Effects

Each survey house has unique criteria for hiring, training, and posttraining supervision of interviewers. Interviewer characteristics make a difference. When people were asked questions about race, blacks were more militant and whites gave more pro-black answers to black than to white interviewers (Hatchett & Schuman, 1975; Sudman & Bradburn, 1974). Similarly, both Hispanics and whites answered questions on bilingualism differently depending on whether the interviewer was Hispanic or white (Reese et al., 1986). Both men and women expressed more egalitarian attitudes about gender to women interviewers (Kane & Macaulay, 1993).

Interviewers who received half a day of lectures and demonstrations plus a professional manual to read, a practice interview, and weekly posttraining supervision were noticeably less effective than those who received more training (Fowler & Mangione, 1990). The skills of the interviewers who had only half a day's training did not improve much during the 6-week study. Fowler and Mangione urged surveyors to train interviewers for at least 2 days, consistently monitor them afterward, and give frequent feedback.

Interviewers were required to find out if respondents had been hospitalized during the preceding year, and their supervisors checked the data against hospital records. There was a strong negative correlation between accuracy and size of interviewers' case loads (National Center for Health Statistics, 1977).

## Wording, Sequence, and Context of Questions

Surveyors from different houses rarely ask questions in exactly the same way. As discussed earlier, slight changes may yield quite different results. Incumbents are better known than challengers who, especially in the early stages of a campaign, are less likely to have strong supporters. Questions framed to identify only strong supporters will have a bias toward the incumbent (Lau, 1994).

## Other Sources of Inaccuracy

The ability of surveyors to predict voting behavior should not give undue optimism about the accuracy of other types of surveys. Answers to questions about intentions often bear little resemblance to subsequent behaviors. For example, Schwarz (1972) reported that only 33 of 72 people who said they planned to buy a car within the next 6 months actually did so. At least four differences between voting surveys and surveys on other matters contribute to error in the latter:

1. Questions about voting have been refined over many decades. Few other types of survey questions have received such scrutiny.
2. Most citizens probably feel comfortable about their political preferences, but they may find some questions threatening.
3. The shorter the time interval between voting surveys and elections, the more accurate the predictions. Time intervals are long between some surveys and the behaviors they predict.
4. The question "Which candidate do you intend to vote for?" places no burden on respondents' memories. Answers to other types of questions are often distorted because of faulty memory.

## Illogicality

As part of a larger study, Dawes and Mulford (1993) asked 288 randomly assigned subjects about one of two events:

1. How often has this happened to you: Waking up paralyzed with a sense of a strange person or presence or something else in the room?
2. How often has this happened to you: Waking up paralyzed?

Forty percent of those asked the first question, but only 14% of those asked the second, answered that the event had happened at least once. The results demonstrate a common illogicality in memory recall. Waking up paralyzed without sensing a strange person in the room is possible; but anyone who wakes up paralyzed with a sense of a strange person, wakes up paralyzed. So, the frequency of event 2 should be at least as great as that of event 1. Additional question pairs yielded similar results (Mulford & Dawes, 1993). This has implications. Surveyors who ask people to estimate the frequency of things they have experienced or done, could ask:

1a. How many times in the last month have you seen a political ad with which you agreed?
1b. How many times in the last month have you seen a political ad with which you disagreed?

or

2. How many times in the last month have you seen a political ad?

The findings of Mulford and Dawes suggest that the sum of 1a and 1b would be greater than 2.

# ■ ALTERNATIVES TO SURVEYS

## Recent Advances in Measuring Attitudes

Most people try to appear tolerant, so traditional methods for measuring attitudes reveal little prejudice (cf. Dovidio & Gaertner, 1991). But traditional methods are misleading. White subjects answered in a more unprejudiced way with black than with white interviewers (McConahay, Hardee, & Batts, 1981). And, when hooked up to a machine they thought was measuring physiological responses and could detect lies, whites gave more negative evaluations of blacks than did white control subjects (Sigall & Page, 1971).

Various indirect methods of assessing attitudes, all variants of the one following, have in common that they do not directly ask a respondent to express an attitude. But they predict prejudiced behavior more accurately than do traditional surveys. For example, Dovidio and Fazio (1992) showed subjects the name of an object and then an adjective, then asked the subjects to press a key as quickly as possible to indicate whether the adjective was positive or negative. Subjects pressed quicker when object and adjective both aroused negative feelings or both aroused positive ones—quicker, for example, to the adjective "disgusting" when primed by "cockroach" rather than "teddy bear." So, the rapidity of pressing to the adjective is an indirect measure of attitude toward the object. On nonsensitive issues, self-reports and indirect measures gave similar profiles. But substantial discrepancies arose on sensitive issues such as race, abortion, pornography, and homosexuality. Predictions to behaviors not influenced by social norms were more accurate from indirect measures than from self-reports.

## Recent Advances in Predicting Voting Behavior

Most surveys conducted early in U.S. presidential campaigns forecast election outcomes inaccurately. Survey results change enormously from the start of each campaign until election day, at which time all pollsters tend to make virtually identical predictions. Mainstream journalists interpret the variations as reflecting the performances of the candidates. The journalists believe that campaign strategies and tricks play a central role in influencing survey results and voting behavior. Gelman and King (1993) offered the alternative hypothesis that people vote on the basis of the candidates' ideologies and positions on major issues. At the start of a presidential campaign, voters do not have the information necessary to make enlightened decisions. When questioned, they answer based on the information at their disposal. But they have more extensive information by election day. According to Gelman and King, the central role of election campaigns is to inform voters. The media provide the information, and voters pay attention, especially just before election day.

Gelman and King cited an extensive literature showing that political scientists, using models based on economic and political variables measured before the start of campaigns, have predicted outcomes of presidential elections much more accurately than national polls and media. Furthermore, information theoretically but not actually available before the election, such as late changes in real disposable income, would have improved the models significantly (cf. Lewis-Beck & Rice, 1992; Rosenstone, 1983).

# Other Types of Self-Report

By the time you finish reading this chapter, you should be able to answer the following questions:

What is introspection?
Why did the early behaviorists reject introspective data?
Can introspective reports ever be verified?
Can introspective reports suggest falsifiable hypotheses?
What are some reasons for collecting self-report data?
What are some methods for collecting self-report data?

■ ■ ■ ■ ■

*"Without introspective analysis of the mental elements of speech, the doctrine of Aphasia, for instance, which is the most brilliant jewel in Physiology, would have been utterly impossible."* William James (1892)

Answers to survey questions give insights into voting and other behaviors. That is, scientists infer from what people say to what they are feeling or will do. Does what people say also give insights into how their minds work? That question has been debated for almost a century.

Please complete the following statement: "Fingers are to hand as toes are to_____." Did any images form in your mind? In the early 1900s, psychologists called structuralists debated the possibility of imageless thought. With a goal of learning how mental processes are interrelated, the structuralists introspected. That is, they observed their own conscious processes as they solved problems, recalled experiences, and summoned up emotions. Another group of psychologists, the functionalists, studied the constant stream of consciousness. They also supported introspection.

Because introspection requires people to report on their own mental experiences, it excludes inarticulate observers—the mentally retarded and disturbed, children, and animals—and material inaccessible to consciousness. A second problem is that people cannot simultaneously experience emotions and observe them with detachment and objectivity. Third, because all the data come from within, introspection appears unverifiable. A person who claims to have imageless thought can maintain his position regardless of anybody else's observations. As it turned out, a German group reported imageless thought, an American group denied its existence, and the matter was unresolvable.

The first two problems limit the method and the third seemed to doom it. Watson (1913) realized that self-reports can be treated like other behaviors, with no assumption that they directly mirror inner mental activity, but he urged psychologists to restrict themselves to objective and publicly verifiable data, that is, to descriptions of overt behavioral acts. He said they should exorcise mentalistic concepts such as consciousness, imagery, and mind. Because of the great initial success of the behaviorist revolution, psychologists became reluctant to use self-reports. Nelson (1996) repeated a joke that epitomized the behaviorists' position: The first behaviorist says to the second after making love, "It was great for you, but how was it for me?"

Lieberman (1979) gave several examples of behaviorists' reluctance to acknowledge inner mental events:

■ Systematic desensitization is an effective technique for treating phobias. Patients are taught to relax, then to stay relaxed while imagining frightening scenes involving their phobias. Although systematic desensitization has been studied intensively, few researchers examined the nature of the images formed or the extent to which their content and vividness correlate with therapeutic outcome.

■ For many years, psychologists who studied hypothesis formation assigned problems to subjects and inferred their hypotheses from the solutions offered. Not until 1971 (Karpf & Levine) did anybody ask the subjects directly what their hypotheses were.

■ Mischel (1974) asked children to try different ways to imagine rewards, for example, to imagine marshmallows as either fluffy white clouds or as soft and chewy. The instructions affected the children's ability to tolerate delays in receiving the rewards, but Mischel never indicated in his publications that he interviewed the children to find out what images they had actually used.

Despite the history, today even some behaviorists study aspects of consciousness (cf. Hilgard, 1980). Still, the rare methodology books that discuss introspection typically do so to criticize. Introspection is distrusted because of its historical associations and because some current proponents have contented themselves with scientifically inadequate studies. Nevertheless, analysis of self-report data is a legitimate research method. Although we can never be sure if a subject's report of her thoughts, perceptions, or feelings are honest or accurate, some aspects of such reports are verifiable.

## ■ THE EXISTENCE OF SELF-REPORTS IS OBJECTIVE AND VERIFIABLE

Both the existence of self-reports about experiences and their precise wordings are verifiable. If people who take a hallucinogenic drug claim to be having inner conversations with God, competent scientists will agree that the claims were made. They can be skeptical about the truth of the claims and refuse to prostrate themselves or offer sacrifices. But by collecting objective, verifiable data on the frequency and nature of the claims, they can learn a great deal about the drug experience.

## ■ THE CORRESPONDENCE BETWEEN DESCRIPTIONS OF INNER EXPERIENCES AND OTHER DATA CAN OFTEN BE EVALUATED

Whether a self-report faithfully describes an inner experience can never be known. But, although we can only speculate about the true motives that underlie behavior, relevant, objective, and verifiable evidence may be available. A person claiming to have inner conversations with God might be persuaded to divulge some of her revelations about the future. If the information were highly specific and reliably came to pass, we might begin to accept the claim as true. Lieberman (1979) noted that the accuracy of any report is judged by its correspondence with other events. A person's claim to have witnessed a meteor passing overhead might be evaluated by tracing radar records at nearby airports, looking for impact craters, checking seismographic reports, and so forth. Reports of internal events can also be checked. For example, when subjects exposed to a uniform visual field for a lengthy period said they were unable to see, other observable events consistent with temporary blindness occurred at the same time: Brain wave activity changed, saccadic eye movements disappeared, and the subjects claimed not to detect anything when visual stimuli were presented (W. Cohen, 1960).

Facts can often be checked, as when hypnotized adults who have been regressed to earlier ages give detailed answers to questions about schools, friends, and so forth. Sources of information for validating the hypnotically induced memories include school records, newspaper clippings, and the testimony of parents and older siblings.

## ■ HYPOTHESES GENERATED FROM INTROSPECTIVE DATA CAN BE FALSIFIED

Introspective data may suggest falsifiable hypotheses. For example:

- The suicide rate is high among people who claim to be deeply depressed.
- Ninety-seven percent of people exposed to a uniform visual field for more than 5 minutes will claim to be unable to see.
- There is a positive correlation between claims of having inner conversations with God and voting Republican.

## ■ SOME USES OF SELF-REPORT METHODS

### Self-Report Methods May Provide Unique Insights into Mental Phenomena

Hayes (1982) asked subjects to think aloud as they sought solutions to several problems, and he learned enough to program a computer to solve problems the way people do. Nevertheless, although self-report data can be crucial, they should never be accepted uncritically. Rogers and Layton (1979) asked heroin addicts in treatment to judge their likelihood of using drugs in the near future, and they also collected information about the occurrence of certain events, such as being around drug users. The events predicted more accurately than the addicts' judgments.

## Self-Reports May Be the Only Possible DVs

Singer (1975) developed a variety of methods for investigating daydreaming. Most require some form of self-report, as does much current research on the meanings of experiences. Werth and Flaherty (1986) explored the phenomenon of deception by asking women to describe incidents in which they had been deceived or had deceived others. The investigators extracted five dominant themes: self-deception and collusion, ramification (the deception extended beyond one person), pervasiveness, feelings, and motivations (explanations of why people remained in relationships in which they were being deceived). They documented each with extensive quotes that, read collectively, give a vivid portrayal of how it feels to be deceived. But so does Shakespeare's *King Lear*. Scientific descriptions, although not necessarily better than literary ones, are held to different standards. From a scientific standpoint, the research on deception is unacceptable. However, the following shortcomings are not an inevitable part of the introspective method:

■ Subjects were not chosen randomly.

■ No indication was given of how something qualified as a dominant theme. The authors had no formal scoring system to guide them, so their biases almost certainly played a role. They themselves wrote that different investigators might have emphasized other aspects of the materials.

■ No numbers were used. Readers do not know how many words were collected from which the dominant themes were abstracted.

■ No precautions were taken to insulate the subjects from the researchers' views on deception. Perhaps the subjects spoke about deception in a certain way because the interviewers were especially attentive when they did.

■ There was no control group. People who have never been painfully deceived might give similar accounts (in which case the supposed benefit of introspection—providing access to direct experience—does not apply). And the subjects might have used the same themes in talking about experiences unrelated to deception.

■ The subjects reported from memory, and memories are often inaccurate.

## Self-Reports May Predict Behavior
## More Accurately Than Do Other
## Dependent Variables

Although the study on drug addicts cited earlier shows that introspective reports are not invariably reliable, they often are. Perhaps researchers will some day be able to accurately predict people's voting patterns from their brain waves. At present, however, it is better to ask them.

## Self-Reports May Have Heuristic Value

Barker (1971–1972) wrote, "It seems to me that in many areas, the only intelligent way to begin is to spend some time in observing life situations and in interviewing people about the topic under consideration from their own internal frame of reference." Barker told of a student who spent weeks having informal conversations and tape recording interviews on the topic of loneliness, asking people to describe and compare the experiences of being lonely, being alone, being with a group, being with a close friend, and so on. Then she collected essays on lonely and not-lonely experiences. She felt ready to begin formal procedures only after she had developed and informally tested several hypotheses.

## Self-Reports Provide a Distinct Kind of Measurement

Operational definitions are essential for measuring scientific concepts, but no single, concrete, operational definition can measure an abstract concept in all its richness. Single measures are sometimes misleading, which is why methodologists urge scientists to measure concepts in more than one way. For the same reason, the measures should be distinctive. Reports of inner states tap a different dimension from the behavioral and physiological measures used by traditional researchers, and this increases their value. More than that, many researchers collect data so they can make inferences about processes not directly observable, such as anxiety, self-esteem, love, and hostility. Self-reports about these inner processes can yield stronger inferences.

## Self-Reports May Reveal the Key Features of a Situation

Lieberman (1979) and Richardson (1984) gave several examples in which subjects' reports of their thoughts and strategies during an experiment helped researchers identify important features. At the end of a study, subjects' reports can help the experimenter evaluate whether manipulation of the independent variable induced the intended state.

# ■ METHODS OF COLLECTING SELF-REPORT DATA

Each method discussed is described in detail in Richardson's (1994) book.

## The Focused Interview Method

People who have had unusual experiences are asked for descriptions. The interviewers listen in a friendly manner without expressing opinions or arguing. They talk if necessary to relieve the subject's anxiety, to give approval when an experience has been described successfully, and to direct the subject's attention to possibly overlooked aspects of the experience. Interviewers may videotape and record physiological measures as subjects have an experience. Played back before the subjects introspect, the tapes may improve the specificity of memories. Less elaborate reconstructions of the original experiences may also help.

## The Association Methods

Spontaneous thoughts can be recorded and analyzed, as in a study on sadness by Cicchini (1976). The instructions make the subjects' task clear:

> Shortly, I'm going to ask you to do a bit of talking. Your task will be to tell me something about your thoughts—I'll explain what I mean. Soon I'm going to ask you to think out loud. Although this task may sound hard, it's not—all you have to do is say whatever comes into your head. So when I say "begin," I would like you to think out loud and say whatever comes into your head and I will tell you to stop in about five minutes. Now, if something comes into your head that you'd rather not report, you're quite free to withhold it. Just let me know by saying there was something in your head that you don't wish to report. Of course anything you say will be kept confidential and will not be identified with you, personally. Okay. So what you are to do is to think out loud, or report whatever comes into your head, and I will tell you when to stop. Do you have any questions now, before we begin, because I'd rather not answer any questions during your talking period? (Pause) Okay. Just relax, close your eyes, if you want, and say whatever comes into your head. Begin.

Another association method requires subjects to speak or write down all the ideas that occur to them as they free-associate to an experience. Then they analyze reports from others who have done the same thing, trying to extract common themes. They free-associate again, followed by another period of analysis, and repeat the cycle several times.

## The Phenomenological Method

The goal of the phenomenological method is to describe the essence of an experience in as few words as possible. Fischer (1975) tried to describe the essence of "being in privacy." She made detailed notes of each instance she could remember when in that state and used the notes to identify core features. Then she asked other people to provide instances of their own experiences of privacy, and she discussed all the submissions with colleagues. Her definition follows:

> The watching self and world fade away, along with geometric space, clock time, and other contingencies, leaving an intensified relationship with the subject of consciousness lived in a flowing Now. The relationship is toned by a sense of at-homeness or familiarity, and its style is one of relative openness to or wonder at the object's variable nature.

Science needs descriptive studies, and Fischer described how her subjects defined the experience of "being in private." But whatever feelings her summary statement may evoke, it is unreliable: Other investigators, even if they used identical procedures, would probably find other core features. Fischer's words are not operational, cannot be tested, and do not seem to lead to any falsifiable hypotheses.

Imagine a subject who reported that "being in private" means having a sharp pain in the stomach. Fischer might have argued that having a sharp pain in the stomach means the same as "an intensified relationship with the subject of consciousness lived in a flowing Now." That implies a method for deciding if the subject's words can be translated to mean the same as Fischer's, but there is none. More probably, Fischer would have concluded that the subject did not understand what being in private means. That is, her criterion for deciding whether a subject understood would be that the subject's report corresponded to her own. Neither of the two alternatives would lead to an agreed-upon method, based on empirical evidence, for resolving the controversy. Thus, her view is protected from falsification.

Imagine a bit further. Suppose that a dictionary reader reported that being in private means being "secluded from the sight, presence, or intrusion of others." Fischer would probably have responded with one of the two strategies presented earlier. The first implies a criterion for deciding if the subject's words can be translated to mean the same as Fischer's, and there is none. The second strategy might result in arguments about who "really" understands what "being in private" means. In neither case would there be a method based on empirical evidence for resolving the controversy. Thus, Fischer's approach is not part of science.

## The Critical Incident Method

The researcher describes an experience, such as a particular emotional state, in enough detail so that subjects have no doubt what it is. Then he asks subjects questions about times when they felt the same emotion. McKellar (1949) recorded and analyzed instances over a 47-day period in which he became angry, then formulated tentative hypotheses about anger behavior. He asked 120 subjects the following questions:

1. Describe in your own words the most annoying thing that has happened to you in the last day (or two days).
2. How did you feel when this occurred?
3. Did you blame anybody? If so, whom?
4. What did you actually do as a result of the situation?
5. Describe in your own words one other annoying thing that has happened to you recently.
6. State whether this was more, less, or equally annoying in comparison with the previous situation described.

Questions 2, 3, and 4 were repeated for the second situation. McKellar had falsifiable hypotheses, such as the hypothesis that about half of all incidents involving the experience of anger would be unaccompanied by any expression of verbal or physical aggression, and they were confirmed.

# Using Existing Data

*By the time you finish reading this chapter, you should be able to answer the following questions:*

What are the advantages and weaknesses of archival research?

What are the different types of archival research?

How can material be located?

If many studies with different sample sizes and results have been done on a single topic, how can the results be combined to reach an overall conclusion?

Is there any reason to be concerned about using existing records as a source of information?

■　■　■　■　■

*"Although clothed in elaborate rationalizations, the process [of meta-analysis] is dangerously vulnerable to the injection of prejudice and bias."* Smith, Glass, and Miller (1980)

Suppose a researcher wishes to learn how U.S. attitudes about the size of the ideal family change over a 30-year period. The question seems best answered with a survey, so he might dutifully plan his life's work. He would make up a questionnaire, administer it to a pilot group, revise it, distribute it across the country for 30 years, and collect and analyze the data. In the process, he might spend hundreds of thousands of dollars and build a small empire of students and other staff. Alternatively, he might do what Judith Blake (1966, 1967a, 1967b) did.

Blake searched through archives until she found 13 national surveys, spanning a period of 30 years, that had asked an appropriate question about ideal family size. Then she combined the data and published a series of papers. She had a small budget and collected no original data, yet she answered her question creatively. Her approach, using raw data for other than their original purposes, is called *archival research*.

## ■ REASONS FOR USING EXISTING DATA SOURCES

Archival research offers several advantages over other research designs:

- ■ It is economical. Solving a problem by analyzing existing materials saves money, time, and personnel. Scientists with limited resources cannot conduct large-scale primary studies, but they can do archival research.
- ■ It is nonreactive. Collecting data on sensitive issues may heighten community tensions, either directly or by providing ammunition for political partisans. Archival research uses no new subjects.
- ■ It is the best way to answer certain questions. White (1966) developed a theory about factors that promote war. Instead of waiting for a new war to break out, he supported his argument by citing already available materials. A single research team trying to compare national attitudes by collecting worldwide survey data would face overwhelming difficulties, but it might find the information in archives. Scientists who study long-term trends in attitudes have no choice but to rely on old records.
- ■ Even if an investigator uses an adequate sample, his subgroups may be too small to support generalizations about them. With archival research, he can increase sample size. Also, he may be able to locate the original subjects of a research project and persuade them to participate in a longitudinal study.
- ■ Data collectors generally measure their concepts with narrow focuses. Archival researchers must make do with what is available, so they examine a variety of measures. This forces them to think of the concepts in odd ways and through the minds of people often far removed in time and place. That is a

good prescription for creativity, and researchers may gain special insights about the concepts.

■ Playing with data facilitates scientific discovery, and secondary sources provide a rich playground. Even investigators who intend to conduct primary research can get ideas from preliminary analyses about how to define concepts and design studies efficiently.

■ Activists use archives to raise public awareness of social issues. They demonstrated patterns of race and gender bias in the judicial, lending, and health care systems (cf. Dieter, 1998; Goff, Muntz, & Cain, 1997; Munnell, 1992; Zito, Safer, dos Reis, & Riddle, 1998). In 1987, 35,000 people were interviewed about various medical issues. Willcox et al. (1994) subsequently analyzed the data on the 6,171 individuals aged 65 years or older. They counted the number of prescriptions for 20 drugs that an expert panel in geriatrics and pharmacology had previously listed to be entirely avoided in the elderly. During 1987, 23.5% of the elderly had received at least one of the 20 drugs; and 28.7% of those prescribed any drug had received at least one of the 20.

# ■ LOCATING THE APPROPRIATE MATERIALS

Government documents are an excellent source for demographers and other researchers who need vital statistics. Stewart and Kamin (1993) told where to find statistical information on births, deaths, marriage, divorce, education, labor, delinquency, crime, and many additional topics. Brown and Semradek (1992) wrote about sources for health-related subjects and pointed out that Florence Nightingale used archival research to persuade British politicians to institute health reforms. The Internet has an enormous amount of archival material. Try http://www.fedstats.gov for government documents and statistics.

Archival researchers are an eclectic lot. They study books, newspapers, magazines, suicide notes, television shows and commercials, tape recordings, diaries, bathroom graffiti, speeches, photographs, letters, and any other written or oral materials that bear on their research questions. If dogs conducted the analyses, they would study odor trails. In short, all data sources are fair game.

# ■ TYPES OF ARCHIVAL RESEARCH

At least five types of archival research can be distinguished: directly using statistical material, using documents that develop and support a position, reanalyzing experimental and survey data, doing meta-analysis, and analyzing content of messages. The different procedures can be combined, as in Sulloway's (1996) analysis of birth order effects (see Box 15.1).

---

**BOX**

### Birth Order

Frank Sulloway (1996) developed a provocative theory of personality based on archival research. He incorporated information from more than 10,000 biographies of 6,566 participants in 121 radical revolutions and reform movements. He also used personality measures that had been reviewed and summarized in an earlier book. (His conclusions differed from those of the authors.)

Sulloway argued that the most crucial determinant of personality is the order of being born into a family, although age gaps between siblings, innate temperament, illness, isolation, gender, and parental conflict all play a role. Firstborns are stronger than their siblings and have more advanced skills, higher social status, and greater responsibilities. Therefore, in the struggle for parental approval and resources, they tend to identify with parental values and reject new ideas. They become ambitious, conscientious, achievement oriented, conventional, and conservative. (Sulloway treated only children like firstborns.) Laterborns, and especially the youngest child, must find their own niches. They become open to experience, take greater risks, and are more easygoing, cooperative, socially active, and willing to revise what they have been taught. They oppose the status quo and are sympathetic to underdogs. Middle children become mediators and compromisers.

The distinctive character differences due to birth order are independent of social class, family size, and culture, and they have evidenced themselves throughout history. After analyzing 121 historical events, Sulloway reported that far more laterborns than firstborns developed and supported radical scientific theories and political movements such as the theory of evolution, the Protestant Reformation, the French Revolution, and the struggle to abolish slavery. Firstborns were much more likely to oppose radical ideas and defend the status quo.

Sulloway's book received lavish praise, but many critics accused him of picking data and making arbitrary decisions to support his thesis. His explanations for the many firstborn revolutionaries—scientists such as Galileo, Newton, and Einstein; politicians like Marat, Robespierre, and Hitler—seemed glib to them. Similar concerns apply to much archival research.

---

## Direct Use of Statistical Material

Data from public or private documents are searched for possible relationships. Two studies on mortality show possible approaches:

1. In 1921, Lewis Terman recruited 1,528 boys and girls who had scored well on IQ tests and followed them into adulthood. About half of them had died by 1995. Friedman et al. (1995) hunted down and coded their death certificates to identify factors correlated with longevity. The original subjects had been carefully selected, so the results might not generalize to other groups. Still, the data suggest exciting areas for future researchers. Some of the major findings follow:

- Children of divorced parents did not live as long as people whose parents had remained married at least until they reached age 21. Death of a parent, however, had little effect. This suggests that the key factor was parental strife.
- Widowed, divorced, and currently separated people had the highest risk for premature death. People who had remained in their first marriage and those who had never married had the lowest risk. Married people not in their first marriage were intermediate. This latter finding suggests that divorce increases mortality rather than that marriage protects against it.
- Children whose parents had divorced were more likely to get divorced themselves.
- Childhood cheerfulness, optimism, and sense of humor were related inversely to longevity. The cheerful children grew up to be more likely to smoke, drink, and take risks.

2. Phillips (1972) speculated that people sometimes postpone their deaths until after some special event such as their birthday. From various sources of biographical information, he found both birth and death dates of more than 1,200 people. As predicted, fewer deaths occurred in the month prior to the birth month than would be expected under the hypothesis that month of death is independent of month of birth. He also found fewer deaths than would be expected in the United States before presidential elections.

## Documents Used to Develop and Support a Position

Material extracted from letters, diaries, newspaper accounts, and so forth can be used to support arguments about causes and sequences of events and to develop personality profiles of historic characters. Phillips used a document to strengthen his claim that people often postpone their deaths until an important event has occurred. He noted that both Jefferson and Adams died on July 4th, 50 years after the Declaration of Independence was signed. He cited Jefferson's last words, quoted by his physician:

> About seven o'clock of the evening of that day, he [Jefferson] awoke, and seeing me staying at his bedside exclaimed, "Oh Doctor, are you still there?" in a voice however, that was husky and indistinct. He then asked, "Is it the

Fourth?" to which I replied, "It soon will be." These were the last words I heard him utter.

But documents must be used cautiously. Disraeli wrote that "all great events have been distorted, most of the important causes concealed, some of the principal characters never appear, and all who figure are so misunderstood and misrepresented that the result is a complete mystification." Voltaire, more succinctly, called histories "fables that have been agreed upon."

Christopher Columbus is typically portrayed to U.S. schoolchildren as a brave and skillful hero. Zinn (1980) illustrated Voltaire's point by examining Columbus's journal. Columbus wrote exuberantly about Native Americans:

> They are very simple and honest and exceedingly liberal with all they have, none of them refusing anything he may possess when he is asked for it. They exhibit great love toward all others in preference to themselves.

Then he added, "They would make fine servants. With fifty men we could subjugate them all and make them do whatever we want."

## Experiments and Surveys

The re-analysis of original data allows investigators to assess the credibility of research findings. Wolins (1962) requested the raw data from 37 authors of published studies. Only seven sent the data, and he found serious arithmetic and conceptual errors in three of them. Dar et al. (1994) examined the use of statistical tests in psychotherapy research published in the *Journal of Consulting and Clinical Psychology*. They documented many serious errors and concluded that much current research that uses statistical tests is flawed. See Box 17.1 (p. 215).

## Meta-Analysis

One of the myths about science is that a single study is usually enough to justify important and far-reaching conclusions. But series of studies on the same problem frequently yield dissimilar and even conflicting results. So, prior to designing their own projects, scientists read the literature. They learn what has already been done, find out about pitfalls and useful techniques, and clarify their research questions. Sometimes they write review articles that evaluate and organize previous work; such articles may contribute more than additional empirical studies. Pflaum, Walberg, Kareglanes, and Rasher (1980) reviewed 97 studies of methods for teaching children to read, and DerSimonian and Laird (1983) reviewed 36 studies on the benefits of receiving coaching for the Scholastic Aptitude Test (SAT). Despite presenting no new data, both sets of authors resolved apparently conflicting findings.

Meta-analysis, a group of techniques for combining the results of studies, can improve the quality of reviews. By increasing the number of subjects on which data have been collected, meta-analysis increases statistical power. Because each study is conducted with a single set of subjects in a particular setting, comparisons may isolate key features that make treatments effective, identify particularly sensitive and insensitive subgroups, indicate how robust the treatments are, relate results to research designs, explain conflicting results, and test generalizations. Cooper and Rosenthal (1980) had university faculty and graduate students review seven studies that collectively showed a strong relationship between gender and task persistence. Reviewers taught meta-analysis were much more likely to detect the effect than those who used their normal criteria for literature reviews. Light (1984) suggested a systematic procedure for doing meta-analyses.

**Organize a Reviewing Strategy.**  Decide what question you want to answer and formulate it precisely. Three examples follow:

1. What is the average effect of a treatment? Although an answer to this question is important, reviewers will generally want to know if the treatment works better with some groups than others. When findings conflict, astute reviewers seek out reasons. This entails going beyond average effects.
2. Under what conditions is a treatment particularly effective or ineffective? Effectiveness may depend on many factors. A heart transplant that saves a patient with a defective heart will not increase the life expectancy of a healthy 20-year-old. In the social sciences, interactions between variables occur routinely and are often subtle. Systematic reviews are more likely than individual studies to uncover them.
3. Will it work here? Reviewers interested in improving therapeutic practices should watch for studies conducted under circumstances similar to their own.

**Decide Whether the Review Will Test a Specific Hypothesis or Is Exploratory.**  Whereas reviewers testing a specific hypothesis focus on obviously relevant studies, exploratory researchers cast their nets wider. This creates a problem: As more and more potential relationships are examined, chance alone is likely to make some relationships seem strong. To minimize error, reviewers should randomly divide the full collection of studies into two groups. They should use the first group to explore relationships among variables and generate hypotheses, and the remaining studies as though new, to test the hypotheses.

**Decide How Studies Should Be Selected.** Try to locate every available study, both published and unpublished. This will probably require a computer retrieval service. Rosenthal (1985) explained how reference librarians can help, and she constructed an extensive table of databases. Searching the databases thoroughly will yield nearly every published and unpublished study in any area of the social and behavioral sciences. Rosenthal (1991) gave several methods for weighting studies according to quality or other criteria.

**Evaluate the Findings.** Determine the population to which results can be generalized. Suppose a review of job training programs showed an inverse relationship between hours of training and subsequent trainee income. This would seem to imply that the programs are harmful. But suppose further that, in each study, increased training was associated with higher salaries. The conflict would be resolved with the realization that programs providing the most training are based in the poorest neighborhoods, where job prospects are dimmest.

Meta-analyses can help counter misleading impressions gained from individual studies. A small successful training program might fail if implemented more widely, because the market would be unable to accommodate more workers in the particular field. Nothing in the single study's research design would suggest the saturation problem; only by reviewing many job training studies might the issue be identified.

**Relate Outcomes to Study Characteristics.** Reviewers can see if outcomes vary systematically with specific attributes of studies. Instead of mechanically averaging effect sizes, they can compute the average effect size for subgroups of studies based on criteria such as date of publication, type of subject, duration of treatment, and so forth. Reviewers should look for studies with extreme outcomes and develop hypotheses that account for differences between the best and worst studies. These can be tested either by using data from the less extreme studies or by additional research.

Light and Pillemer (1984) suggested several attributes that should be considered routinely when examining human service programs. Adapted slightly, they apply to any body of research:

- *Program characteristics.* Even programs with similar labels may differ in times of availability or types of services or numbers of participants.
- *Setting characteristics.* Where a program is located and who administers it may affect outcomes.
- *Participant characteristics.* Only certain types of people may benefit from a program.

- *Research design.* Some researchers measure short-term, others long-term outcomes. New and old studies may differ because of advances in instrumentation and data analysis.
- *Analysis techniques.* There are at least two ways to correlate SAT scores with grade point averages (GPAs): (a) Compute overall grade point averages for each of several schools, average the SAT scores of students at the schools, and find the correlation between school GPA and student SAT scores. (b) Analyze data from a single school to see if students with high GPAs also score high on the SAT. Conclusions from the two analyses might differ, perhaps obviously, under the circumstances. But when subtle differences in research design are embedded in lengthy reports, they may be missed. Meta-analysts deliberately investigate relationships between analytic procedures and conclusions.

Not all scientists approve of meta-analysis. Eysenck (1984, p. 47) argued that subjective factors—what scientists know, suspect, or intuit from the literature—determine the quality of their judgments: "To try and reduce this complex and important aspect of a scientist's work to a simple additive statistical procedure, which even a young and inexperienced student can easily follow, is to make a laughing stock of the whole business of science." In a widely cited meta-analysis, Smith, Glass, and Miller (1980) concluded that psychotherapy is effective. Eysenck (1984) showed that Smith et al. made subjective judgments about which studies to include, what were the appropriate controls, what constituted improvement, and how the results should be interpreted. Still, Eysenck acknowledged that under the right conditions, meta-analyses can improve the quality of reviews. Box 15.2 is an example of a meta-analytic study.

## Content Analysis

Content analysis is a group of techniques for making inferences from messages. Qualitative data are systematically analyzed to yield quantitative findings. For example, a task force of the National Organization for Women (NOW) systematically analyzed 2,760 stories from 134 textbooks for young children (Women on Words and Images, 1972). The task force counted each occurrence of male and female characters, what the characters did, and whether the stories were male centered or female centered. They found that males outnumbered females and were more frequently portrayed as smart, brave, strong, independent, and ambitious. The study, evidence that our schools foster stereotyped gender roles, led to discussions about the harm caused by such stereotypes and to increased sensitivity on the part of writers, publishers, parents, and teachers.

Tannen (1990) integrated findings from studies that analyzed tapes of male/female conversations. She concluded that many misunderstandings between men and women stem from their profoundly different ways of communicating. Her book is a fascinating read.

**BOX**

## Reductionist versus Integrative Approaches

*Reductionism* is the view that complex phenomena can best be understood by understanding their component parts. According to this view, sociology will ultimately be explained by psychology, which will be cannibalized by the neurosciences, which in turn will be reduced to physics and chemistry. Sapolsky and Balt (1996) wrote that most scientists as well as laypeople probably believe that we can learn more about causes of schizophrenia by studying dopamine receptors than the responses of schizophrenics to Rorschach inkblot patterns. But chaos theorists emphasize that a minuscule change in one part of a complex system can have large and unpredictable consequences. In the 1960s, meteorologist Ed Lorenz described computer simulations showing that a butterfly, flapping its wings in Brazil, could change the weather system sufficiently so as to cause a snowstorm in Alaska the following day.

Reductionists believe that reductionist approaches result in decreased variability of data. Chaos theorists predict that average variability will be about the same in reductive and integrative disciplines. Sapolsky and Balt (1996) did a meta-analysis to test the competing hypotheses. They examined papers published in respected journals in 1987 from several disciplines that were relevant in some way to the role played by testosterone in aggressive behavior. At the integrative end were studies such as the correlation between testosterone profiles and human adolescent aggression. An example at the reductive end was a study on the effects of androgens on expression patterns of a secretory protease inhibitor. For each paper, Sapolsky and Balt calculated a coefficient of variation (standard error divided by the mean). The main finding supported the chaos theorists: The average coefficient of variation was similar across the various levels, with no tendency to decrease with more reductive approaches.

**Sampling of Sources.** Content analysts frequently select small samples from large populations, as when the NOW task force sampled from the enormous population of textbooks. The proper procedure, as in surveying, is to use random sampling. But whereas all voters are essentially equal, because each has one vote, newspapers, television shows, and other sources for content analysis vary in important features, such as size, geographical location, and political orientation of their audiences. So, stratified sampling of sources may be necessary. The sources themselves are often sampled rather than studied in their entirety. Thus, an investigator interested in newspaper coverage of a political campaign might choose an appropriate cross-section of papers, then study selected editions and pages from each one. Sampling decisions, including what to do if selected sources are unavailable, must be made before collecting data and must be adhered to strictly.

**Scoring.** Units of any type are acceptable if they can be reliably scored, including the number of articles in a newspaper, the amount of column space in inches, the time in minutes of radio programming, and specific words. The NOW task force had little difficulty counting frequency of occurrence of male and female characters. Sometimes, though, the same object is referred to in several ways and judgments must be made. Richard Nixon was called, among other things, "Tricky Dick," "the 37th President of the United States," "the first president to visit China," "the occupant of the White House between 1969 and 1974," and "he" (Krippendorff, 1980). Therefore, careful guidelines for counting and making judgments should be drawn up in advance.

The task force also judged whether males and females were being portrayed as smart, brave, and so forth. Reliabilities of complex judgments are usually lower than those of counts but can be high if units are carefully defined and raters are trained.

## ■ WEAKNESSES OF ARCHIVAL RESEARCH

Many research questions cannot be answered by archival research, because the appropriate data are unavailable. And, as is true of all nonexperimental forms of research, the methods do not answer causal questions unambiguously. (But they often provide support for the position that one event has caused another. The view that the media influence behavior received support from Phillips, 1982, 1983). He documented an increase in suicides following television episodes depicting suicides, and in homicides after extensive media coverage of championship heavyweight boxing matches.)

Because archival researchers do not participate in the process of data collection, they do not know how adequate it was. Because they use materials housed by others, they cannot control for the possibility of selective retention. Some archival researchers are probably discomfited by a situation in which quality control standards have been implemented by unknown predecessors.

Aaronson and Burman (1994) disagreed with the popular view that records are more probably correct than other sources of information. They cited a study in which differences were found between health records and mothers' recall of such events as whether the child had been breastfed. The authors concluded that the mothers' memories were faulty. Aaronson and Burman argued that the discrepancy is more plausibly attributed to faulty records. They cited Marrie, Durant, and Sealy (1987), who compared standard medical records with data collected as part of a systematic study. Only 57% of patients identified in the medical records as having pneumonia actually did.

Jacobson, Koehler, and Jones (1987) showed that sensitive information is frequently not documented in health records—91% of physical and sexual assaults detected in an independent research project were not recorded. Alcohol abuse is also infrequently documented (Leckman, Umland, & Blay 1984). Even when the original data are correct, errors may occur in interpreting them. Aaronson (1990) found that one coder identified maternal and fetal problems in 25% of the cases; the other two coders detected such problems in 37% and 38% of the cases.

Data may be destroyed or altered for political reasons, as in the erasure of the Watergate tapes. A state mental institution reported a drop in the number of patients with suicidal tendencies. Jacob (1984) attributed it to budgetary cuts that required a reduction in staff. Physicians were concerned that if a patient who was documented as suicidal but not closely supervised actually committed suicide, a malpractice suit would follow. So they did not document.

Archival research of surveys poses two problems that can usually be remedied. First, different surveys are rarely worded identically, so concepts must be modified and questions lumped in meaningful ways. Second, although surveys with methodological weaknesses should be excluded, selective exclusions may be done in a biased way. To increase the likelihood that decisions about comparability of questions and exclusion of studies are not influenced by the research hypothesis, they should be assigned to a scientist unaware of the hypothesis.

Although the steps given earlier are important, the possibility of bias is a major problem for most archival research. Whereas double-blind experiments limit bias, archival researchers work in relative privacy with an enormous quantity of data. They have considerable discretion in choosing and interpreting. Overt cheating, though probably rare, is easy. The reason is that archival researchers can sample and resample, combining data in infinite ways and discarding anything that does not support the research hypothesis, before submitting their results to public scrutiny. As a result, archival research may be more effective as a tool for convincing the researcher herself rather than for convincing others. Some archival researchers, such as Barnes and Bero (1998; see p. 34) attempt to locate all the relevant work in an area. Such comprehensive reviews are much less vulnerable to sampling bias.

# 16 Using Animals in Research

*By the time you finish reading this chapter, you should be able to answer the following questions:*

What are the advantages of using animals in research?
How do scientists evaluate animal models of human behaviors?
Does it make sense to generalize from animals such as rats to humans?
What value is there in studying animals that have unique properties?
What are the advantages of concentrating on a single species such as the Norway rat?

You will also be able to liven up dull conversations with extraordinary tales of giant squids, armadillo quadruplets, and rotating eyeballs of frogs.

■   ■   ■   ■   ■

*"Ants are so much like human beings as to be an embarrassment. They farm fungi, raise aphids as livestock, launch armies into wars, use chemical sprays to alarm and confuse enemies, capture slaves....They exchange information ceaselessly. They do everything but watch television."* Lewis Thomas, American Medical Educator

*"I think animal testing is a terrible idea; they get all nervous and give the wrong answers."* From the television show *A Bit of Fry and Laurie*

The principles of research apply whether the subjects are human or nonhuman animals (except that some nonhumans are notoriously uncooperative when it comes to filling out questionnaires about their personal lives). The use of nonhuman animals (called "animals" throughout the chapter) confers many advantages. The most important is control. Researchers can control the administration and measurement of independent, dependent, and extraneous variables much more fully than they can in work with humans and can test the variables over a greater range. In addition, animals such as Norway rats fit conveniently into small cages yet are large enough for most surgical techniques. They breed readily in captivity and have short generation spans, which is valuable for developmental and behavioral genetic research. They are resistant to infections and easily handled.

U.S. researchers use between 18 and 22 million animals per year (Mukerjee, 1997). The number would be greater except that many people question the relevance of animal research to humans and others discredit the research on ethical grounds. On the other side of the debate, Botting and Morrison (1997) detailed the many important advances in virtually every area of medicine that owe their success to animal experiments. Their examples include new vaccines for treating infectious disease; drugs for hypertension, ulcers, and bacterial and microbial invasions; insulin for diabetes; and techniques for open-heart surgery, replacement heart valves, and organ transplants. They speculated that genetic research on the roles of proteins in disease will play a major role in advancing medicine; and they noted that research on nerve regeneration in animals has caused physicians to rethink the dogma that damaged nerve cells in the mammalian spinal cord cannot have their function restored.

Animal research helped psychologists identify the factors underlying addictive behaviors, guided the development of humane strategies for modifying the self-injurious behaviors of autistic children and teaching mentally retarded people self-reliance, and demonstrated the effects of stress on health. Animal research deepened understanding of motivation, sensory and cognitive processes, and the neurobiological bases of pleasure and pain.

# ■ WHY USE ANIMALS IN RESEARCH

Several overlapping purposes for studying animals follow and are expanded on in the next sections. Each of the first four purposes is often achieved efficiently even when a single species is studied. Achievement of the last purpose requires at least two and often several species.

1. To estimate how an independent variable affects or would affect humans
2. To create an animal model of a particular condition
3. To study naturally occurring systems in animals in order to learn about comparable systems in humans
4. To study a species that has an interesting property
5. To gain a better understanding of how our evolutionary past and current environments shape our behaviors

## Using Animals to Test How Independent Variables Affect or Are Likely to Affect Humans

Researchers use animals to test the beneficial and hazardous effects of drugs, cosmetics, surgical techniques, safety helmets, and environmental conditions with potentially important health consequences, such as pollution, crowding, noise, and nutritional deficiencies. But the assumption that results will improve predictability about human responses and lead to more effective treatments and wiser decisions must constantly be tested.

Recall the research of Zucker and of Falk, discussed in chapter 4. Zucker studied biorhythms in rats. He kept his animals in temperature-controlled, light-controlled, largely soundproof environments and monitored their eating and wheel-running behaviors 24 hours per day. Falk deprived rats of food and then fed them at 1-minute intervals for 3 hours per day. He measured their food and water intakes during feeding sessions and when the rats were in their home cages. Both lines of research, which have important implications for humans, required continuous, precise control and so could not have been conducted on human subjects.

The species must be chosen carefully. For drug research, generalizations to humans are better from cats than from most other animals, but the two species react quite differently to morphine and a few other drugs. Bustad (1966) encouraged the use of miniature pigs for anatomical and physiological studies, because the hearts, circulatory systems, diets, digestive systems, and teeth of pigs and humans are strikingly similar. For many years, the Norway rat was such an essential part of psychology experiments that one person defined psychology as the behavior of the white rat and college freshman taking introductory psychology. Rats are similar to humans in dietary needs; physiology of nerves, muscles, and glands; geographic distribution; world population; and colony formation (Richter, 1954). Bruce Alberts, president of the U.S. National Academy of Science, wrote:

> It has become increasingly clear over the past two decades that knowledge from one organism, even one so simple as a worm, can provide tremendous power when connected with knowledge from other organisms. And because of the experimental accessibility of nematodes, knowledge about worms can come more quickly and cheaply than knowledge about higher organisms. (1997, p. xii)

Even bacterial responses can be relevant to humans. Certain bacteria mutate when exposed to substances that cause human cancers. Thus, bacterial response provides an inexpensive method for screening potential human carcinogens. When the goal of an animal study is to improve predictions about how an independent variable will affect humans, focus on that goal. The reason for the bacterial mutations is irrelevant when screening for carcinogens.

## Creating Animal Models of Human Conditions

Many of the greatest medical success stories, including those about polio, scarlet fever, strep throat, and malaria, begin with the development of an animal model. Animals were infected with the diseases and then exposed to various test drugs until cures were found. But behavioral models, though they have a long history, are rarely so simple. Pavlov (1928) required hungry dogs to distinguish between a circle and an ellipse. When successful, they were fed. Then he made the figures more and more similar to each other until the dogs could no longer discriminate. Previously normal dogs soon began to struggle and howl constantly, and Pavlov claimed to have created an animal model of neurosis. Such claims may be made too easily, because animal models of schizophrenia, depression, neurosis, and ulcers have different causes, symptoms, neurobiological mechanisms, and responses to treatments from their supposed human analogues (Reines, 1982). On the other hand, a model's usefulness does not necessarily depend on how closely it mimics a human syndrome. For example, Zucker (1988) acknowledged that models of seasonal affective disorder (SAD, a depression that occurs in wintertime) differ in many ways from the expression of SAD in people. Still, he argued, they have considerable practical value. They have suggested ways to measure, classify, and manipulate the disorder in humans and to get at its physiological basis. Several principles relevant to humans emerged from research on biological rhythms of animals, and specific treatments have been developed as a result. The development of a model is a beginning, not an end. Scientists must assess their models for relevance to humans and try to improve them.

**Alcoholism.** Physical dependence can be produced by injecting ethanol or mixing it with an animal's food rations. The procedure is compatible with some research goals, such as testing whether a new drug reverses liver damage in alcoholics. But if the goal is to understand human alcoholism, a model that involves voluntary drinking is essential. Animals of some species drink voluntarily, and some scientists seek genetic and metabolic differences between alcohol-preferring and non-preferring species and individuals. The important point to keep in mind is that models should always reflect the purposes of the scientist.

## Using Animals to Learn About Human Systems

Our understanding of many human behavioral and physiological systems has been increased by studies of corresponding systems in animals. The strategy is to pick an appropriate species, study the system of interest thoroughly, and see how the results might apply to humans. Dolphins are master communicators and highly social, and research on dolphins has yielded important insights into human communication and social behavior. Observations of lions, hyenas, wolves, and African hunting dogs, all cooperative hunters, may help scientists understand how primitive human hunters lived. Pigeons and other birds are ideal subjects for research on color vision. Many useful generalizations have been made from fruit fly genetics to human genetics. Chimpanzees, our closest relatives, are used in studies on learning, motivation, and mother/infant attachments. Norway rats are inexpensive and convenient, so more experiments have been done with rats than with any other animal.

The simplicity of the rat brain may make it a more rather than less appropriate species than the chimpanzee for some research. Simple preparations are often better than complex ones for revealing how things work. That is why many researchers interested in human aging study aging in single-celled animals. Similarly, experiments with domesticated laboratory rats have helped illuminate human psychological processes. Richter (1954) extolled their virtues but also detailed a host of anatomical, physiological, and behavioral differences between laboratory and wild rats. Laboratory rats have larger gonads and a greater reproductive capacity than wild ones, but they have smaller adrenal glands and a less efficient response to stressful situations.

Lockard (1968) concluded that domesticated rats, having evolved under less challenging conditions than wild ones, are inferior and should not be used by behavioral scientists. But laboratory rats may not be inferior (cf. Pavlov, 1928; Price, 1972). In any event, the laws of physics and evolution apply to all species; whether or not behavioral principles also generalize is an empirical question.

Henshel (1980) urged sociologists to study phenomena even if they occur only inside laboratories. He wrote: "Sociologists have consistently overlooked a fundamental feature of the experiment in natural science, something we shall call unnatural experimentation. Unnatural experimentation is the deliberate exposure of phenomena to conditions or circumstances not found anywhere else." Scientists learned about normal brain functioning by studying brain-damaged people and people exposed to radiation. They learned about the nervous system by studying the effects of sensory deprivation and the after-effects of limb amputation and resulting phantom sensations. Henshel's argument is relevant to discussions about the "artificiality" of experiments with domesticated rats.

If the purpose of an animal research project is to make discoveries that apply to human systems, applicability to humans should be the criterion of success. According to Lowe (1983), the most extensive studies in animal behavior have been on schedules of reinforcement. Early proponents claimed great generality for their results, but later reviews have been less enthusiastic. Lowe (1983, p. 73) wrote:

> The behavior of humans with respect to scheduled reinforcement differs in fundamental respects from that of other animal species. The differences appear so extensive, applying as they do to all the basic schedules of reinforcement, that they throw into doubt much of the theorizing about human learning which is based upon animal experimentation. And if the animal model does not hold good for human operant behavior under controlled experimental conditions why should it do so in the hospital, school, or stock exchange?

But, Lowe's pessimism notwithstanding, behavior modifiers have successfully applied principles learned from rat experiments to treatments of human behavior problems.

Failed generalizations do not necessarily mean failure. On the contrary, they may generate research into why organisms that are similar in some ways differ in others; this in turn may lead to more profound generalizations. For example, early behaviorists believed that animals of all species respond similarly to all reinforcing events. When this proved false, the deeper generalization emerged that the responses of animals to stimuli are shaped by the environments in which they evolve. Exceptions to the generalization that animal species respond essentially the same to drugs stimulated research into species differences in rates of absorption, metabolism, and excretion. This led to the generalization that drug effects are better predicted from knowledge of how a drug concentrates at its site of action than by administered dose, which has important consequences for human pharmacology. It helps explain differences in responsiveness to drugs due to gender, race, age, and many other factors.

## Studying a Species Because It Has an Interesting Property

The animal kingdom is breathtaking in its diversity, and many animals have properties that seem bizarre from the human perspective. Scientists welcome the bizarre and organize research projects around it. One reason is that an unusual property may provide a window to an important but otherwise inaccessible phenomenon. Second, unusual properties pose puzzles, which scientists love. Scientists who were motivated solely by the opportunity to solve puzzles have changed our perceptions of the world and enriched our culture.

All species have evolved intricate and intermeshing adaptations for surviving in their particular ecological niche, so all animals are potential puzzles to be solved. (Only one reference is listed for most of the examples below, but none is based on a single study. Solving puzzles about behavior, like solving jigsaw and crossword puzzles, requires fitting many pieces together.)

**Studying a Species Because It Offers Special Access to a Phenomenon.** Because of squids, we know a lot about nerve cells. Each nerve cell has an axon that carries the nerve impulse away from the cell body to adjacent cells. Most axons are about one millionth of a meter in diameter, but squids have several giant nerve cells with axons about one thousand times as large. The axons can be dissected out of the squid and kept alive for many hours in a special water bath. Hodgkin and Keynes (1956) and Hodgkin and Huxley (1952) took advantage of these properties to study the sequence of events leading to the firing of nerve cells. Their work, which generalizes to all nerve cells, earned a Nobel Prize. (The squids left the awards ceremony in disgust, feeling they should have been at least co-winners.)

Marsupials (pouched animals like kangaroos and opossums) are born prematurely compared with other mammals. The red kangaroo reaches more than 6 feet in height but is only about three-quarters of an inch long at birth. So, marsupials are valuable subjects for embryological and developmental research. See Sharman (1973).

Nine-banded armadillos typically give birth to genetically identical quadruplets, and Storrs and Williams (1968) took advantage of this unique property. They measured weights of various anatomical organs and activity of several neurotransmitters in newborn quadruplets. They found many large differences between the highest- and lowest-scoring newborns of each set. The results indicate that the intrauterine environment plays an important role in development. Behavior geneticists might profit from armadillo research.

Frogs and toads regenerate body parts, so research on them may provide clues to the healing process. Sperry (1943) removed the eyes of mature frogs and rotated them 180 degrees. The nerve endings regenerated and soon the frogs could see again, but their visual worlds were displaced 180 degrees. When a fly was offered above and to the left of them, their tongues flicked down and to the right. Sperry's work is of interest to scientists concerned with behavioral plasticity and nerve growth.

Some species have an artificially unique property: They have been studied a great deal. Scientists who work with such species can compare, combine, and correlate their findings, which helps ensure accuracy and accelerates the acquisition of data. The popularity of rats stems in part from the accumulation of information about them and techniques for using them. Similarly, the early focus on mice of behavior genetics researchers promoted the breeding of inbred mouse strains with special properties. Suppliers list more than 200 inbred strains. Do you want a mouse strain susceptible to auditory convulsions? With a low level of spontaneous activity? Likely to experience retinal degeneration? Go through a Sears-like catalog and place your order. The availability of so many strains ensures continued use of mice.

**Studying a Species Because It Poses a Puzzle.** Some behavioral and anatomical properties of animals puzzled scientists so much that they launched research projects to find answers. Many projects had important practical consequences: new techniques, later used in applied research; inventions, patterned after sophisticated feats of biological engineering; increased understanding of how all animals adapt to their environments; and generation of ideas for additional research and theory, often with relevance to humans. The Griffin and von Frisch references that follow are highly readable accounts that show excellent scientists at work, observing, correlating, and experimenting according to the problems at hand. The scientists continually considered explanations that conflicted with their own and designed studies to test the alternatives. Serious students of methodology should read the original accounts.

Bats fly in the dark, avoiding obstacles and capturing prey with marvelous efficiency. To learn how they do it, Griffin and his colleagues (1950) observed them hunting under natural conditions, then brought them into the laboratory. The scientists measured the rates at which bats capture insects and the minimum distances at which the prey are detected. In one experiment, the bats had to fly around a big screen, then through a series of narrowly spaced bars, to enter an area where they successfully caught small, moving insects. In another, they were placed in a room with a swarm of mosquitos and caught an average of 14 per minute. Selective masking experiments with low and high frequency noise conclusively demonstrated that bats intercept at least some of their prey by echolocation. That is, bats emit sounds and then orient to the sounds as they are reflected off objects.

In the early 1900s, scientists had concluded that insects, including honeybees, are color blind. Karl von Frisch (1950) thought that inconceivable. "Why," he asked, "would flowers have evolved so many colors except to attract bees to pollinate them?" The puzzle started von Frisch on a career studying honeybees. He used no elaborate equipment, but he solved the puzzle and was awarded a Nobel Prize. His book communicates the joy of research, and it is a wonderful model of sound methodology.

## Studying Animals from an Evolutionary Perspective

The studies described so far can be carried out with a single species such as rats, though investigators often use two or more species to (a) improve the accuracy of generalizations to humans, (b) create better models, and (c) make sense of unusual properties of closely related species. Researchers in such cases rarely concern themselves with the ecological niches of the species or their biological relatedness. By contrast, those factors are preeminent for biologists and psychologists interested in the evolutionary histories and functions of behaviors. See p. 124 for further discussion.

# Data Analysis

*By the time you finish reading this chapter, you should be able to answer the following questions:*

Why have critics argued against null hypothesis significance testing?

One critic wrote, "If rejection of the null hypothesis were the real intention in psychological experiments, there usually would be no need to gather data." How can that be?

What are Type I and Type II errors?

Why do critics contend that much more than 5% of published articles contain Type I errors?

How does reliance on significance testing affect public policy?

Increased experimental sophistication has opposite effects on theory testing in physics and psychology. Why?

Are there any alternatives to significance testing?

What is exploratory data analysis?

*"If an experiment requires statistical analysis to establish a result, then one should do a better experiment."* Nobel Prize–winning physicist Ernest Rutherford

If a coin is tossed once and comes up heads, that does not mean the coin is biased toward heads. If subjects who receive an experimental treatment score higher than controls, that does not mean the treatment worked. Pure luck may explain both results. Scientists use statistics to help them evaluate the likelihood that their results are reliable or due to luck. Other forms of data analysis, such as visual inspection, are useful for detecting patterns.

## ■ NULL HYPOTHESIS SIGNIFICANCE TESTING

For many decades, the preferred statistical strategy in medical and social science has been null hypothesis significance testing. The null hypothesis is the hypothesis that no relationship exists between variables. For example, if classical music is played to one group and hard rock to another, the null hypothesis is that music type has no effect on the dependent variable. Of course, even before they hear the music the groups are likely to differ some-what—even identical twins are not 100% identical. So the real question is whether the differences are large enough to rule out chance factors as a plausible explanation. If so, the results are said to be statistically significant and the null hypothesis is refuted. The convention among scientists is this: Only if the probability is .05 or less (5 times in 100 or less) that luck has caused a result will the result be assumed true.

Many methodologists disagree with conventional strategy; in fact, they argue that null hypothesis significance testing is scientific malpractice. Gigerenzer (1993) wrote that the works of such scientific luminaries as Piaget, Kohler, Bartlett, Pavlov, and Skinner would have been rejected under editorial policies that demand statistically significant results. Whereas exploratory data analysts (see following) are open to whatever the data show, null hypothesis testers limit their possible conclusions to two—that results (differences between experimental and control groups, interactions, correlations) probably are or probably are not due to chance. That limitation is relatively trivial. Consider these comments by eminent methodologists:

> Paul Meehl, upon receiving an American Psychological Association Distinguished Scientist Award: "I believe that the almost universal reliance on merely refuting the null hypothesis as the standard method for corroborating substantive theories…is a terrible mistake, is basically unsound, poor scientific strategy, and one of the worst things that ever happened in the history of psychology."

W. Deming: "Small wonder that students have trouble with statistical hypothesis testing. They may be trying to think."

B. F. Skinner: "They [statisticians] have taught statistics in lieu of scientific method."

J. Nunnally: "If rejection of the null hypothesis were the real intention in psychological experiments, there usually would be no need to gather data."

J. Cohen: "What's wrong with [null hypothesis significance testing]? Well, among many other things, it does not tell us what we want to know, and we so much want to know what we want to know that, out of desperation, we nevertheless believe that it does!"

P. Meehl: "Scholars who are pardonably devoted to making more money and keeping their jobs...are unlikely to contemplate with equanimity a criticism that says that their whole procedure is scientifically feckless and that they should quit doing it and do something else...that might...mean that they should quit the academy and make an honest living selling shoes."

F. Schmidt: "Teachers must revamp their courses to bring students to understand that (a) reliance on significance testing retards the growth of cumulative research knowledge; (b) benefits widely believed to flow from significance testing do not in fact exist; and (c) significance testing methods must be replaced with point estimates and confidence intervals in individual studies and with meta-analyses in the integration of multiple studies."

However cogent and impassioned the criticisms, they have had insufficient impact on publication policies of psychology journals and minimal impact on the teaching of psychology students. Meehl (personal communication, 1996) wrote, "Psychologists continue to honor me and ignore what I say." Kendall (cited in Gigerenzer, 1991, p. 258) wrote that statisticians "have already overrun every branch of science with a rapidity of conquest rivaled only by Attila, Mohammed, and the Colorado beetle."

Although it is generally better to focus on how to do things right rather than what not to do, methodology textbooks continue to teach significance testing. So, before discussing alternative methods of testing reliability of results, I hope to persuade readers that the traditional approach does a great deal of harm.

## ■ TYPES OF ERRORS

Scientists distinguish between Type I and Type II errors. A Type I error occurs when a researcher concludes that a statistically significant relationship exists between variables that are actually unrelated. A Type II error occurs when variables are related but the researcher concludes they are not. Scientists who use the conventional .05 level of significance should make Type I errors 5% of the time. But the standard statistical techniques have their stated accuracy only if the data are of a certain form. Wilcox (1998) gave examples, using both hypothetical and real data with just small deviations from the appropriate form, to show that a test at the .05 level may have a probability of a Type I error substantially greater than .05. McNemar (1960) reported that the error rate in published articles is much higher, because published articles are a biased sample of the research that has actually been done. The reasons are that (a) journal editors reject papers without significant results, (b) scientists, knowing editorial policies, do not submit papers with nonsignificant results, (c) scientists select out their significant findings for inclusion in reports, and (d) theorists discard data that do not fit their theories (see pp. 22–23 on publication bias).

Many investigators use small samples because of budgetary constraints. Others, despite sufficient resources, cannot recruit enough subjects who meet the diagnostic criteria and agree to participate. Their small samples result in a substantial probability of committing a Type II error. Freiman, Chalmers, Smith, and Kuebler (1992) examined 71 "negative" experiments published in the *New England Journal of Medicine* in 1978 to 1979. Only 30% had used enough subjects to have a 90% chance of detecting a difference as great as 50% in the effectiveness of the treatments being compared. A 1988 replication yielded similar results. Moher, Dulberg, and Wells (1994) reviewed all two-group experiments with randomized controlled trials published in leading medical journals in 1975, 1980, 1985, and 1990. Twenty-seven percent had negative results, and only 16% of those had enough power to detect a 25% difference 80% of the time. Only 36% had enough power to detect a 50% difference 80% of the time. In other words, if the mortality rate was 20% among patients given a new medical treatment and twice that for patients treated in the conventional way, 64% of investigators would have reported negative results at least 20% of the time.

Suppose a coin is biased so that on a given flip the probability that it will land with the head side up is .60. Some of the problems of null hypothesis significance testing can be appreciated by considering Table 17.1. The first column lists varying numbers of flips, the second lists the minimum number of heads needed to reach statistical significance, the third converts

**TABLE 17.1**

| Number of Flips (N) | Minimum Number of Heads (H) Needed for Statistical Significance | Percent H | Probability of at Least H Heads in N Flips With an Unbiased Coin | Probability of Getting Statistically Significant Results With a Coin Biased .6 Toward Heads |
|---|---|---|---|---|
| 4 | impossible | | | impossible |
| 5 | 5 | 100 | .03 | .08 |
| 75 | 46 | 61 | .03 | .46 |
| 100 | 59 | 59 | .04 | .62 |
| 1000 | 527 | 52.7 | <.05 | 1 |
| 32000 | 16150 | 50.5 | <.05 | 1 |

to percentages, and the fourth gives the probabilities of getting those percentages. With only four flips, statistical significance cannot be reached. The probability of getting four out of four heads with a fair coin is .06, which is greater than the magic .05 level. So, if your coin were biased .60 or .999 toward heads and you flipped it only four times, you would make a Type II error. When researchers testing more complex hypotheses use too few subjects, they also ensure that Type II errors will be extremely likely or even inevitable. Now, note the following:

1. As the number of flips is increased, the percentage of heads needed for statistical significance becomes smaller and smaller. With five flips, it is 100%; with 32,000 flips, it is 50.5%. In other words, even tiny and trivial effects will reach statistical significance if enough subjects are used.
2. If you flipped the coin 75 times and 45 were heads (which is 60%, the exact bias of the coin), the results would not be significant.
3. With five flips, 100% heads is needed. So you would either get fewer than five heads and fail to demonstrate bias or get five heads and conclude that the most likely degree of bias is 100%.
4. Column 5 indicates the probability of reaching statistical significance with exact replications and a coin biased .6 toward heads. Despite what some researchers believe (see following), successful replications are far from certain, and the probability of a successful replication varies with the number of trials.

## ■ MISINTERPRETATIONS BY PROFESSIONALS

Suppose the null hypothesis is rejected at the .05 level. Gigerenzer (1993) asked, "In what percentage of exact replications will the result again turn out significant?" The answer cannot be known unless the effects of the variables are known in advance (which would eliminate the need to do the research). Gigerenzer then cited widely used statistics textbooks that give an answer; for example, "If the statistical significance is at the .05 level…the investigator can be confident with odds of 95 out of 100 that the observed difference will hold up in future investigations" (Nunnally, 1975, p. 195). Oakes (1986) asked 70 research psychologists and advanced graduate students to mark six statements true or false concerning a study in which experimental and control groups differed significantly ($p = .01$). The percentage of psychologists who answered each statement true is noted in parentheses:

1. You have absolutely disproved the null hypothesis (that there is no difference between the population means). (1.4%)
2. You have found the probability of the null hypothesis being true. (35.7%)
3. You have absolutely proved your experimental hypothesis (that there is a difference between the population means). (5.7%)

4. You can deduce the probability of the experimental hypothesis being true. (65.7%)

5. You know, if you decided to reject the null hypothesis, the probability that you are making the wrong decision. (85.7%)

6. You have a reliable experimental finding in the sense that if, hypothetically, the experiment were repeated a great number of times, you would obtain a significant result on 99% of occasions. (60.0%)

Only three subjects marked all six statements as false. They are all false. The correct answer to question six is 43%.

Rosenthal and Gaito (1963) asked 19 academic psychologists to rate their degree of confidence in hypothetical experiments with either 10 or 100 subjects. The respondents incorrectly indicated that results from the larger sample size were more trustworthy, even though probability levels were the same.

Most statisticians interpret probability statements in this way: "A probability of $p = .05$ means that data at least this extreme would be observed 5% of the time if the null hypothesis were true. So, over the course of many studies, experimenters should incorrectly reject the null hypothesis 5% of the time." Yet many presumed experts use a definitely unacceptable interpretation: "A probability of $p = .05$ is the probability that the null hypothesis is true." Not surprisingly, perfectly compatible results seem to conflict.

Sedlmeier and Gigerenzer (1989) reviewed 440 studies in the *Journal of Abnormal Psychology* and found that many scientists interpreted a failure to reject the null hypothesis as confirmation of its truth. That is incorrect (just as a jury's verdict of not guilty does not mean they believe that the defendant is innocent). For additional proof that professionals misinterpret, see Box 17.1.

---

**BOX**

### Archival Research on Null Hypothesis Significance Testing

The logic of null hypothesis significance testing requires that the criterion for making a Type I error (the alpha level) be set in advance, and unless there are compelling reasons to the contrary the same alpha level should be used for each statistical analysis within a study. The only appropriate conclusion for each analysis is that the criterion has (or has not) been reached (as a pregnancy test reveals that a woman is or is not pregnant—there are no gradations). However, Dar et al.'s (1992) archival research showed that authors frequently add interpretive comments to their analyses: "These results are highly significant; extremely significant; almost significant." Dar et al. reviewed all regular research articles on psychotherapy (163 of them) that appeared in the *Journal of Consulting and Clinical Psychology* in the years 1967 to 1968, 1977 to 1978, and

1987 to 1988. The studies used as many as 20 different alpha levels, and only one 1980s study used a single alpha level. Almost half the studies in each time period discussed effects that were nonsignificant but close to the .05 alpha level.

Authors enamored of probability levels ignored more meaningful information. Dar et al. cited a study on weight loss in which the treated group was reported to be significantly different from the control group ($p < .001$), but without any measure given of amount of weight lost. In most cases authors did not report effect sizes, and in none of the 163 articles did they report confidence intervals (see pp. 224–225).

Although the null hypothesis cannot be proved true, in 53.3% of studies in the 1980s, nonsignificant differences between groups prior to treatment were interpreted to mean that the groups were statistically equivalent—which is a claim that the null hypothesis is true.

The probability that a fair coin will come up heads five times in a row is .03; but if 50 fair coins are flipped five times each, the probability is almost .80 that at least one will come up heads five times in a row. Similarly, if multiple statistical tests are used within a single study, the probability of a Type I error increases unless a compensation procedure is used. Yet 76.6% of the studies with multiple tests did not use a compensation procedure. Dar et al. cited other errors that inflated the Type I error rate in a sizable number of studies.

## ■ IMPLICATIONS FOR PUBLIC POLICY

Schmidt (1996) noted that significance testing sabotages the usefulness of psychological research for solving practical problems. Researchers have repeatedly and enthusiastically tackled social problems and expended time and taxpayer money amassing vast amounts of data. But more often than not the accumulated data seemed to conflict, as data must seem to conflict if significance tests guide their interpretation, and the researchers eventually gave up in despair. The reason that data interpreted by significance tests inevitably seem to conflict is that unless large numbers of subjects are used, significance will be reached only by results that make interventions seem more effective than they really are. The remaining interventions will be discontinued because of nonsignificant results.

As knowledge accumulates in a given area, the types of questions tend to change. Initial questions such as, "Does this treatment have an effect?" are replaced by questions about subtle differences such as, "Is this treatment better than the alternatives?" Because the expected effect sizes are small, inquiries with statistical significance as the criterion may require 1,000 or more subjects. Most researchers do not have the resources to use such large numbers of subjects.

# ■ THEORY TESTING

The formulation of a useful theory probably stands at the pinnacle of scientific achievements. Popper (1963) urged scientists to propose theories boldly but then to test them as ruthlessly as possible. Because theories play a central role in the well-developed sciences, research to test them can have enduring value. But partly as a result of the popular statistical models, social science theories are poorly developed and theory-testing research is often trivial. Meehl (1970b) noted that improvements in technology increase the likelihood that incorrect physics theories will be rejected, but improvements have the reverse effect in the social sciences. In his words:

> In the physical sciences, the usual result of an improvement in experimental design, instrumentation, or numerical mass of data, is to increase the difficulty of the "observational hurdle" which the physical theory of interest must successfully surmount; whereas, in psychology and some of the allied behavioral sciences, the usual effect of such an improvement in experimental precision is to provide an easier hurdle for the theory to surmount.

The reason is that physical scientists test mathematical relationships between variables, so that specification of the independent variable leads to a narrow range of acceptable values for the dependent variable. As experimental precision increases, the range of DV values that support the theory is reduced. In most psychology experiments, however, predictions are of the sort that a group treated one way will differ from a group treated otherwise; that is, the null hypothesis is false. But, as Cohen (1990) noted: "The null hypothesis is always false in the real world." So increased precision increases the likelihood that a real though trivial difference will be detected. With sensitive enough measuring devices, theories that predict differences in a particular direction will be confirmed 50% of the time even if they have no foundation. To quote Meehl again: "The whole business is so radically defective as to be scientifically almost pointless."

Showing differences between two groups does little to increase confidence in a theory because many plausible alternatives can explain differences (Dar, 1987). Yet failure to find a predicted difference does not mean that a theory is incorrect; many factors can obscure small differences. But if both successful and unsuccessful predictions can be easily explained away, why should anyone take the theory seriously? Dar wrote that statistical significance testing has replaced good theory building in psychology. He gave three reasons:

1. Graduate students in psychology receive considerable training in statistics, little in philosophy of science or principles of scientific methodology. So when they start research on their own, they feel satisfied with results significant at

the .05 level. They feel no pressure to develop theories with high internal consistency or explanatory power.

2. Many psychologists act as though statistically significant results provide strong proof that the research hypothesis tested is true. All they actually show is that the results were probably not due to chance.

3. "High-tech" statistical tests create the illusion of scientific respectability and are used as substitutes for strong theories.

Table 17.1 gives the number of heads needed to reach statistical significance after different numbers of coin tosses. The likelihood that a study will reach statistical significance varies directly with the number of subjects used, and researchers with the most money can use the most subjects to test their theories. If the perceived value of social science theories depends on their reaching statistical significance, then perceived value varies directly with the amount of money available to the theorists.

## ■ INCENTIVE TO CHEAT

As indicated in chapter 3, some scientists cheat. One reason is that professional advancement depends on publishing, and statistically significant results make publication much easier. Suppose a scientist predicts that a coin will be biased toward heads. If he flips the coin 1,000 times, 527 heads is a statistically significant result ($p = .046$), but 526 heads is not ($p = .053$). If publication depended on showing statistically significant bias, he would be sorely tempted in the second case to mis-score one flip.

## ■ A FEW USEFUL STATISTICAL PROCEDURES

Data analysis requires data, but wise researchers plan for analysis before the first subject has been run.

Before collecting data:

■ A procedure should be instituted for measuring the reliability of observations. See p. 158 for discussion.

■ For experiments, a choice must be made between independent and matched sample designs. The latter requires that subjects be paired according to their performance on a variable that correlates satisfactorily with the dependent variable. The potential savings increases as the correlation increases. As a practical matter, if the correlation is .30 or higher, matching will generally save enough subjects to be worth the effort. Negative correlations increase the number of subjects needed but can be turned into positive correlations by redefining variables.

■ Researchers must determine how many subjects to use. If there are too few, results will be untrustworthy. Using too many subjects wastes time and money and, when painful or injurious procedures are involved, should be resisted for humane reasons. A method for choosing sample size for surveys can be found on p. 165; and for observational studies, on p. 155. For experiments, first decide how large a difference between means you must detect for the experiment to be a success. The choice is subjective and depends on the research goal. The larger the difference required, the more subjects you will need. Then select the power, that is, the likelihood that you will see a difference at least as large as the one specified if the difference really is at least that large. Common choices for power are 80%, 90%, and 95%. The higher the power, the more subjects needed. For further discussion, see Cohen (1988) or Kraemer and Thiemann (1987).

Some research designs do not require a predetermined sample size. In sequential experiments, researchers analyze data as they go along and decide after each pair of subjects whether more information is needed. This generally results in a considerable saving of subjects compared with nonsequential designs. Consider a fictitious example: A conventional researcher tests a potentially valuable drug that may, however, produce serious side effects. She injects the drug into 100 monkeys and a placebo into 100 others and intends to follow up the study only if the drug-injected group shows less than 10% excess sickness. Suppose that 75 of the drug-injected and none of the controls get sick. Had she tested one pair at a time, she could have saved a lot of money—and monkeys. For sequential designs to be most useful, subjects' responses should be available shortly after treatments are administered. The method would be impractical, for example, for studying the effects of diet on longevity. Interested readers should consult Armitage (1960), whose short book gives procedures for graphically analyzing results from sequential designs. The mathematics is rigorous and the steps are simple. Leavitt (1991) summarized Armitage's work.

## ■ EXPLORATORY DATA ANALYSIS

Although data analysis almost always involves manipulation of numbers, the two terms are not synonymous. Hartwig and Dearing (1979) wrote:

> Data analysis should be a confrontation *between* theory and data, but for this to be effective, the researcher needs to be as familiar with the data as with the theory. Unfortunately, much data analysis in the social sciences relies so heavily on numerical summaries of the data that these summaries intervene between the researcher and the data, often shielding the researcher *from* the data.

Numeric summaries of data may conceal or even misrepresent important information. Therefore, data analysis should begin with visual inspection of the complete dataset. Exploratory data analysis (EDA) is a set of techniques that emphasizes flexible probing of data. Exploratory data analysts seek patterns that can stimulate hypotheses (which should be tested with a second phase of data collection and analysis). Of the many ways of describing a dataset, they emphasize six characteristics:

*Shape:* The shape of a distribution, largely ignored by traditional statistical procedures, is commonly categorized as symmetric, left skewed or right skewed; and unimodal, bimodal, or multimodal.

*Location:* Location is roughly synonymous with measure of central tendency and refers to the point at which a distribution is anchored. Common measures are the mean, median, and mode. For bimodal distributions, the mean or median of each section can be calculated independently.

*Spread:* Spread measures the amount of variation in a distribution. Two useful measures are the standard deviation and the interquartile range (the range that covers the middle 50% of the scores).

*Outliers:* An outlier is a case that lies well above or well below most of the other cases in a distribution. Outliers should be analyzed carefully, as they are likely to be either the result of error or an indication of something significant. A 1985 field study showed that ozone levels had dropped to 10% below normal January levels for the South Pole. The ozone hole had been detected by a satellite years before, but NASA computers discarded sudden, large drops in ozone concentrations as "errors." When the data were rerun without the filter program, evidence of the ozone hole was seen as far back as 1976. Boxplots (see later) are useful for detecting outliers.

*Clustering:* Clustering implies that the data tend to bunch up around certain values. For example, annual wages in a university may cluster around $40,000 for office workers, $60,000 for professors, and $120,000 for administrators.

*Granularity:* Granularity implies that only certain discrete values are allowed. For example, a company may pay salaries only in multiples of $1,000. Discrete data are always granular, and continuous data may be granular if rounded.

The original scale on which a variable is expressed may not be best. Re-expression involves finding a scale for simplifying data analysis, as when temperature data are converted from Fahrenheit to Celsius or vice versa, or pounds are converted to kilograms or vice versa. The various types of re-expression have specific uses. For example, when data have been generated by a growth process or when the ratio of the largest to the smallest measurement in a group is greater than 10, converting data values to logs may reveal otherwise hidden patterns (Ramsey & Schafer, 1997).

## Stem-and-Leaf Displays

Stem-and-leaf displays are easy to construct by hand, use all the data, and show the shape of distributions pictorially. They can be used to show the shape of a single distribution or to compare two or more distributions. Table 17.2 presents fictitious data from 30 experimental (E) and 30 control (C) subjects. The scores within each group are ranked from low to high.

The scores of the experimental subjects have five different first digits (1, 2, 3, 4, and 5) and the scores of the controls also have five (1, 2, 3, 4, and 6). To con-

**TABLE 17.2**

| E | C |
|-----|-----|
| 116 | 118 |
| 129 | 125 |
| 158 | 133 |
| 168 | 174 |
| 174 | 185 |
| 184 | 210 |
| 186 | 255 |
| 199 | 274 |
| 226 | 281 |
| 256 | 288 |
| 281 | 295 |
| 314 | 297 |
| 319 | 299 |
| 355 | 315 |
| 410 | 335 |
| 416 | 344 |
| 421 | 367 |
| 429 | 386 |
| 438 | 389 |
| 452 | 392 |
| 462 | 395 |
| 466 | 420 |
| 469 | 430 |
| 473 | 445 |
| 481 | 451 |
| 489 | 459 |
| 489 | 466 |
| 493 | 478 |
| 497 | 541 |
| 501 | 615 |

struct a stem-and-leaf display, put the first digit of each number to the left of a vertical line. That digit is called the stem. The next digit(s), the leaves, are put to the right of the line (see Figure 17.1). Note that two experimental subjects scored 489 and both of them are listed. Every score must be recorded.

Traditional statistical analysis of the data would yield nonsignificant results, yet the stem-and-leaf displays show that the two distributions are dissimilar. The distribution of experimental subjects is bimodal; that is, it has two peaks. Bimodal distributions suggest the possibility that two groups that should be analyzed separately have been combined, for example, women and men. The distribution is skewed (one end has many more cases than the other). The control distribution includes an outlier, the 615 score. Outliers indicate either intriguing legitimate cases or errors. Further investigation would be strongly advised.

Stem-and-leaf displays can be modified in various ways to simplify analysis and clarify relationships. The number of digits in each observed value can be reduced by rounding. For example, each three-digit number of the experimental group could be rounded to a two-digit number, producing a simplified stem-and-leaf display. Each row could be subdivided, for example, by having one row containing all second digits from 0 to 4 and another row containing all second digits from 5 to 9.

## Boxplots

Boxplots are useful for comparing two or more sets of sample data. They display location and spread of the distributions and identify outliers. To construct one of the several varieties of boxplots, first order scores from low to high. Then divide the distribution into quarters. The first quartile (Q1) divides the lower 25% of scores from the upper 75%, the second quartile (the median) divides the distribution into two halves, and the third quartile (Q3) divides the lower 75% of scores from the upper 25%. The difference between Q1 and Q3 is called the interquartile range (IQR).

If a distribution consists of an odd number of scores, the median is the middle score. If there is an even number of scores, the median is the midpoint between the two middle scores (for the experimental group from which the stem-and-leaf display was constructed, 413; and for the controls, 339.5). Q1 is the median for the lower 50% of the scores (199 and 274, respectively), and Q3 is the median for the upper 50% of the scores (469 and 430). The IQRs are 270 and 156.

The boxplot is a rectangle with its left and right boundaries drawn at the location of Q1 and Q3, respectively, and a vertical line inside the rectangle at the location of the median. So, half the cases in the distribution lie within the box. Dashed lines called whiskers are extended horizontally on either side to the minimum and maximum scores, but they do not go beyond 1.5 times the IQR above Q3 or more than 1.5 times the IQR below Q1. Such scores are defined as outliers and specially noted. Figure 17.2 shows boxplots of the data from which the stem-and-leaf displays were drawn. The control scores include an outlier and have a greater range than the experimentals, but the IQR is greater for the experimental distribution.

**FIGURE 17.1**

| E | C |
|---|---|
| 1\| 16 29 58 68 74 84 86 99 | 1\| 18 25 33 74 85 |
| 2\| 26 56 81 | 2\| 10 55 74 81 88 95 97 99 |
| 3\| 14 19 55 | 3\| 15 35 44 67 86 89 92 95 |
| 4\| 10 16 21 29 38 52 62 66 69 73 81 89 89 93 97 | 4\| 20 30 45 51 59 66 78 |
| 5\| 01 | 5\| 41 |
| | 6\| 15 |

**FIGURE 17.2a**

| Numerical Summary | |
|---|---|
| Minimum | 116 |
| First quartile | 199 |
| Median | 413 |
| Third quartile | 469 |
| Maximum | 501 |

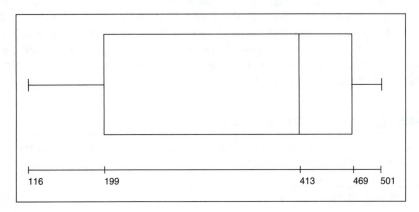

**FIGURE 17.2b**

| Numerical Summary | |
|---|---|
| Minimum | 118 |
| First quartile | 274 |
| Median | 339.5 |
| Third quartile | 430 |
| Maximum | 615 |

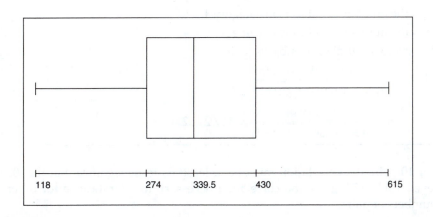

# ■ TWO ALTERNATIVES TO NULL-HYPOTHESIS TESTING

## Measure Effect Size With the Point-Biserial Correlation Coefficient

The size of effect of an IV on a DV conveys more useful information than does mere significance testing. Afer two-group experiments, the point-biserial correlation coefficient can be calculated to measure both statistical significance and effect size.

Table 17.3 gives the computational formula for the point-biserial, and Table 17.4 presents a hypothetical set of test scores of students in a small class. The point-biserial can be used to find the relationship between test scores and gender. First, assign all the females to category 1 and all the males to category 0. (One level of the variable must be assigned a 1, the other a 0, but the choice is arbitrary.)

**TABLE 17.3** The Point-Biserial Corrèlation

If the dependent variable (in this case, test scores) is called $Y$, the formula for the point-biserial correlation coefficient $r$ is

$$r = \frac{N\Sigma Y_1 - N_1\Sigma Y}{\sqrt{N_1 N_0 [N\Sigma Y^2 - (\Sigma Y)^2]}}$$

where $\Sigma Y$ = the sum of all the $Y$ values. So, using the data Table 17.3, $Y$ =
$21 + 20 + 20 + 20 + 18 + 15 + 13 + 12 + 10 + 9 = 158$
$\Sigma Y^2$ = the sum of the squares of each $Y$
$21^2 + 20^2 + 20^2 + 20^2 + 18^2 + 15^2 + 13^2 + 12^2 + 10^2 + 9^2 = 2{,}684$
$(\Sigma Y)^2$ = the square of the sum of each $Y$
$(21 + 20 + 20 + 20 + 18 + 15 + 13 + 12 + 10 + 9)^2 = 249{,}664$
$\Sigma Y_1$ = the sum of test scores of subjects in category 1
$21 + 20 + 20 + 18 + 15 + 9 = 103$
$N_1$ = the number of subjects in category 1 = 6
$N_0$ = the number of subjects in category 0 = 4
$N$ = the total number of subjects = 10

Then $r = \dfrac{(10 \times 103) - (6 \times 158)}{\sqrt{(6 \times 4)[(10 \times 2{,}684) - 158^2]}}$

$= \dfrac{1{,}030 - 948}{\sqrt{24 \times (26{,}840 - 24{,}964)}} = 82 / 212.2 = .39$

For 10 pairs the correlation must be at least .63 to be significant at the .05 level. Table 17.5 gives the correlation necessary for significance for other numbers of pairs.

**TABLE 17.4** Data for Computing the Point-Biserial Correlation Coefficient

| SUBJECT | SCORE | CATEGORY |
|---------|-------|----------|
| Donna | 21 | 1 |
| Erika | 20 | 1 |
| Anthony | 20 | 0 |
| Marianne | 20 | 1 |
| Gayle | 18 | 1 |
| Phyllis | 15 | 1 |
| Bob C. | 13 | 0 |
| Carlos | 12 | 0 |
| Bob M. | 10 | 0 |
| Corinne | 9 | 1 |

**TABLE 17.5** Critical Values for Significance at the .05 Level for the Point-Biserial Correlation Coefficient

| NUMBER OF PAIRS | CORRELATION COEFFICIENT MUST EXCEED |
|-----------------|-------------------------------------|
| 5 | .88 |
| 10 | .63 |
| 15 | .51 |
| 20 | .44 |
| 25 | .40 |
| 30 | .36 |
| 35 | .33 |
| 40 | .31 |
| 45 | .29 |
| 50 | .28 |
| 60 | .25 |
| 70 | .24 |
| 80 | .22 |
| 90 | .21 |
| 100 | .20 |

Q: Correlation does not prove causation (see p. 86), so does not use of the point-biserial correlation coefficient defeat the purpose of doing experiments? See p. 226 for answer.

■ ■ ■

## Find Confidence Intervals

Suppose that 200 out of 1,000 randomly selected people are left handed. Thus, p (proportion of left-handers in the sample) = .2 and *q* (proportion of right-handers) = .8. To calculate 95% confidence limits for the true proportion of left-handers in the population, use the formula

$$\text{true proportion} = p \pm 1.96\sqrt{pq / N} + 1 / 2N$$

$$= .2 \pm 1.96\sqrt{(.2)(.8) / 1000} + 1 / 2000$$

$$= .2 \pm 1.96\sqrt{.00016} + .0005$$

$$= .2 \pm .025$$

So the investigator could be 95% sure that the proportion of left-handers in the population is between 0.175 and 0.225. (For 99% limits, replace 1.96 with 2.58.)The example shows how to calculate confidence limits for proportions. Different formulas are used for calculating confidence limits for experiments and correlational studies. Consult a statistics test.

## ANSWER

In most correlational studies, subjects are not randomly assigned to groups. As long as they are randomly assigned, the results can be interpreted causally.

# 18 Philosophical Challenges

Even after you finish reading this chapter, you won't be able to answer some of the following questions:

What is Hempel's paradox?

On what grounds can we be confident in assuming that the future will resemble the past?

Given a body of data, say the number series 2 4 6 8 10, how do we justify any particular inductive inference?

What is the next number in the series 1 2 3 4 5?

Which if either of the following syllogisms is valid?

    1. If T, then O.
       O.
      ———————
      Therefore, T.

    2. If T, then O.
      Not O.
      ———————
      Therefore, not T.

■　■　■　■　■

*"It is characteristic that all three (Einstein, Laue, and Planck) had the greatest admiration for Kant's work, agreeing with his view that philosophy should be the basis of all sciences."* Ilse Rosenthal-Schneider, *Reality and Scientific Truth*

*"Philosophy of science is as useful to scientists as ornithology is to birds."* (I think Nobel Prize winner Richard Feynman said it.)

When interpreting data, laypeople are susceptible to a variety of errors, such as failure to recognize the importance of control groups, attributing causality to correlational data, and ignoring placebo and experimenter effects. Methodology textbooks give examples of such errors to illustrate the value of scientific training. But the texts, and most practicing scientists, are oblivious to or ignore philosophical challenges to scientific methodology. I describe four of the challenges here. They are interrelated, and only the first can be considered resolved.

## ■ HEMPEL'S PARADOX

Many scientific laws and theories are of the form "All A is B." Two examples are "Water at sea level boils at 100 degrees centigrade" and "Schizophrenia is associated with an excess of dopamine in the limbic system." Philosopher and logician Carl Hempel (Hempel, 1945) pointed out a seeming paradox in the way scientists test such theories. The propositions "All ravens are black" and "All nonblack things are nonravens" are logically equivalent. To test the former, a scientist would look for ravens, and each black one would provide supporting evidence. To test the latter, she would look for nonblack things, and each nonraven would provide supporting evidence. A white handkerchief would support the proposition "All nonblack things are nonravens."

But if a white handkerchief supports the proposition "All nonblack things are nonravens," it must also support the proposition "All ravens are black" (since the two propositions are equivalent). The paradox has two aspects: first, that a white handkerchief should be as informative as a black raven; second, that a white handkerchief should have any bearing at all on the proposition "All ravens are black" (or green or red). The paradox seems to have important implications for testing scientific theories. See pp. 233–234 for my resolution.

## ■ INDUCTION: HUME, RUSSELL, GOODMAN

Science would be of little value without generalizations, which require the assumption that what has not been observed is similar to what has been observed, for example, that the future will resemble the past. David Hume showed that this principle of induction is not justified, and Bertrand Russell made Hume's concern vivid. Russell invoked a chicken that was fed by a man every day of its life and eventually learned to expect the daily feedings. Yet in the end its neck was wrung by the same man. Russell concluded that there is no rational basis for induction:

> The general principles of science, such as the belief in the reign of law, and the belief that every event must have a cause, are as completely dependent upon the inductive principle as are the beliefs of daily life. All such general principles are believed because mankind have found innumerable instances of their truth and no instances of their falsehood. But this affords no evidence for their truth in the future, unless the inductive principle is assumed. (Cited in Copi & Gould, 1964, p. 310)

## Inductive Inferences Are Ambiguous

If Hume and Russell destroyed the illusion that induction can be rationally justified, Nelson Goodman (1973) put a stake through the dead. For Hume, inductive inferences were straightforward: The sun will rise in the east tomorrow because that is what it has always done. But Goodman showed that an infinite number of wildly incompatible inductive inferences can be drawn from any body of data. For example, in a world in which all emeralds ever observed have been green, the obvious inductive inference is that all are green. So Goodman coined a word, "grue," which refers to objects that are green before January 1, 2000, and blue from that date on. He observed that all evidence supporting the induction "All emeralds are green" equally supports "All emeralds are grue." Nobody has formulated an acceptable reason for inferring to the first rather than the second. Or to "All emeralds are grack, grellow, or gravender."

## ■ THE FUNDAMENTAL UNCERTAINTY

Stripped to the bone, science is a search for relationships between variables. Scientists observe and experiment to determine how one variable changes with another. Then they try to find equations that relate the variables mathematically and they create theories to explain the equations. For example, an industrial psychologist might vary the number of motivational lectures given to different groups of salespeople, then record their average number of sales per week. She might then record her data in a table such as Table 18.1. The equation $Y = X + 1$ fits the data, but so do other equations such as:

$$Y = \frac{X^5 - 17X^4 + 107X^3 - 307X^2 + 576X}{180}$$

**TABLE 18.1**

| X (number of motivational lectures) | Y (number of sales per week) |
|---|---|
| 1 | 2.0000 |
| 2 | 3.0000 |
| 3 | 4.0000 |
| 4 | ? |
| 5 | 6.0000 |
| 6 | 7.0000 |

and

$$Y = \frac{X^7 - 1582X^4 + 14651X^3 - 49322X^2 + 101772X}{32760}$$

When X = 4, the three equations give Y values of 5.0000, 5.0667, and 5.0974, respectively. The differences may seem trivial, and in any case the data show that number of sales increases with increased frequency of motivational lectures. But now look at Table 18.2. Again, the obvious solution is that Y = X + 1 and thus that the missing Y = 4. But another equation that fits the data is:

$$Y = \frac{55X^4 - 382X^3 + 749X^2 - 374X}{24}$$

For the new equation, when X = 3, Y = − 10. In fact, an infinite number of equations yielding an infinite number of predictions can be found that perfectly fit the data of Tables 18.1 and 18.2. For *any* set of data, an infinite number of equations can be found that perfectly fit.

The data from Table 18.1 can be graphed as the straight line of Figure 18.1. The figure accurately summarizes the relationship between X and Y and gives clear predictions for new values. But so do Figures 18.2, 18.3, and an infinite number of others.

**TABLE 18.2**

| X | Y |
|---|---|
| 1 | 2 |
| 2 | 3 |
| 3 | ? |
| 4 | 5 |

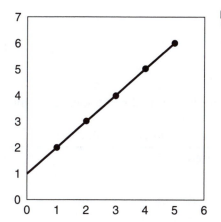

**FIGURE 18.1**
$Y = X + 1$ (or maybe not)

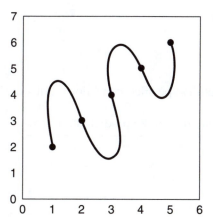

**FIGURE 18.2**
$Y = X + 1$ (or maybe not)

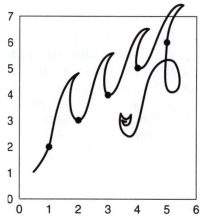

**FIGURE 18.3**
$Y = X + 1$ (or maybe not)

## ■ LOGIC

Consider two pairs of syllogisms:

Pair 1.

Theory T predicts that, under carefully specified conditions, outcome O will occur.
I arrange for the conditions and obtain the predicted outcome.

Therefore, theory T has been supported.

In symbols:

If T, then O.
O.

Therefore, T.

Pair 2.

Theory T predicts that, under carefully specified conditions, outcome O will occur.
I arrange for the conditions but fail to obtain the predicted outcome.

Therefore, theory T is false.

In symbols:

If T, then O.
Not O.

Therefore, not T.

People who have taken an introductory logic course will recognize the second pair of syllogisms as valid. As long as the premises (the statements above the line) are true, the conclusion must be true and there can be no counter-examples. Counter-examples for the first two syllogisms are easy to imagine, and that demonstrates their invalidity. For example, a prediction from the hypothesis "Unicorns run around at night in Golden Gate Park," (U) is that animal droppings will be found in the park (D).

In symbols:

If U, then D.
D.

Therefore, U.

Although animal droppings can be found, that does not prove that unicorns roam the park. A key feature that distinguishes science from other endeavors is that scientific hypotheses and theories can be tested. Karl Popper perceived an asymmetry between tests that confirm, as exemplified by the first pair of syllogisms, and tests that falsify, exemplified by the second pair. The asymmetry led to his proposal that falsifiability should be a key criterion for science (see pp. 2–3). Yet the invalid confirmatory syllogism form is the basis of virtually all scientific research and reasoning (and much of everyday reasoning).

Two points should be noted about the falsifiability model. One, it denies the possibility of ever proving the truth of a hypothesis. At best, scientists can expose a hypothesis to severe tests and consider it viable until falsifications occur. Two, many philosophers of science dispute the view that the second pair of syllogisms properly represents the falsifiability model. Theories are never tested in isolation; that is, additional premises are always taken for granted, and a falsification can mean that either the primary hypothesis or any of the other premises are in error. Therefore, falsifications can never be conclusive. See p. 4 for further discussion.

## ■ COMMENTS ON THE PHILOSOPHICAL CHALLENGES

Philosophers are better suited than psychologists for dealing with the implications of the limitations of science. But two points can be safely made. First, the limitations apply to all attempts to understand the world, not just to the scientific approach. Second, the limitations do not lessen the intellectual excitement and challenge of solving scientific problems. Although an infinite number of equations fit the data relating mass, energy, and the speed of light, it took the genius of Einstein to find even one.

### ANSWER TO THE RAVEN PARADOX

There are two propositions (P1 and P2) and two pieces of evidence (E1 and E2).

> P1: All ravens are black.
> P2: All nonblack things are nonravens.
> E1: This raven is black.
> E2: This white thing is not a raven.

P1 and P2 are logically equivalent; that is, any evidence that supports P1 supports P2 to the same extent. But E1 and E2 are not equivalent. E1 provides much stronger support for both propositions. To see why this is so, consider an aviary in which there are two ravens and 98 nonblack birds.

P3: All ravens in the aviary are black.
P4: All nonblack birds in the aviary are not ravens.
E3: This raven is black.
E4: This white bird is not a raven.

E3 represents 50% of the evidence needed to prove P3. It also represents 50% of the evidence needed to prove P4. (If the only other raven is found to be black, P4 must be true.) An investigator could prove P3 by checking all 98 nonblack birds and verifying that they are not ravens, and the proof would also apply to P4. But one nonblack nonraven would be less useful than one black raven, because the former would represent 1/98ᵗʰ of the necessary evidence and the latter 50%. E1 and E3 are more significant than E2 and E4 because they account for a greater proportion of the total number of cases under consideration. (If there were different proportions of ravens and other birds, the relative significances would differ.) Under the circumstances, E2 to a trivial extent and E4 to a much greater extent have evidentiary value; a nonblack nonraven eliminates one potential falsifier of the proposition "All ravens are black."

 # References

Aaronson, L. (1990). *Nursing factors in pregnancy health behavior and outcome: final report*. National Center for Nursing Research, PHS, DHHS.

Aaronson, L., & Burman, M. (1994). Use of health records in research: Reliability and validity issues. *Research in Nursing and Health, 17*, 67–73.

Alberts, B. (1997). Preface. In D. Riddle, T. Blumenthal, B. Meyer, & J. Priess (Eds.), *C. ELEGANS II*. Plainview, New York: Cold Spring Harbor Laboratory Press.

Allison, D., Faith, M., & Gorman, B. (1996). Publication bias in obesity treatment trials? *International Journal of Obesity and Related Metabolic Disorders, 20*, 931–937.

Altman, L. (1987). *Who goes first?* New York: Random House.

Altmann, J. (1974). Observational study of behavior: Sampling methods. *Behaviour, 49*, 227–267.

Altmann, S., & Altmann, J. (1970). *Baboon ecology*. Chicago: University of Chicago Press.

Americans for Nonsmokers' Rights. (1996, May 28). Front groups and allies of the tobacco industry.

Amir, Y., & Sharon, I. (1991). Replication research: A "must" for the scientific advancement of psychology. In J. Neuliep (Ed.), *Replication research in the social sciences*. Newbury Park, CA: Sage.

Anderson, H. (1985). The use and misuse of multivariate analysis of variance. *Southern Psychologist, 2*, 72–75.

Aneshensel, C., Frerichs, R., Clark, V., & Yokopenic, P. (1982). Measuring depression in the community: A comparison of telephone and personal interviews. *Public Opinion Quarterly, 46*, 110–121.

Antman E., Kupelnick, B., Mosteller, F., & Chalmers, T. (1992). A comparison of results of meta-analyses of randomised controlled trials and recommendations of clinical experts. *Journal of the American Medical Association, 268*, 240–248.

Argyle, M., Bryant, B., & Trower, P. (1974). Social skills training and psychotherapy: A comparative study. *Psychological Medicine, 4*, 435–443.

Armitage, P. (1960). *Sequential medical trials*. Springfield, IL: Charles C. Thomas.

Armitage, P. (1983). Exclusions, losses to follow-up, and withdrawals in clinical trials. In S. Shapiro & T. Louis (Eds.), *Clinical trials: Issues and approaches*. New York: Marcel Dekker.

Arnold, D. (1970). Dimensional sampling: An approach for studying a small number of cases. *American Sociologist, 5*, 147–150.

Auerbach, O., Stout, A., Hammond, E., & Garfinkel, L. (1962). Changes in bronchial epithelium in relation to sex, age, residence, smoking, and pneumonia. *New England Journal of Medicine, 267*, 111–119.

Baddeley, A., Thomson, N., & Buchanan, M. (1975). Word length and the structure of short-term memory. *Journal of Verbal Learning and Verbal Behavior, 14*, 575–589.

Bahrick, H. (1984). Semantic memory content in permastore: Fifty years of memory for Spanish learned in school. *Journal of Experimental Psychology: General, 113*, 1–29.

Bahrick, H. (1991). A speedy recovery from bankruptcy for ecological memory research. *American Psychologist, 46*, 76–77.

Banaji, M., & Crowder, R. (1989). The bankruptcy of everyday memory. *American Psychologist, 44*, 1185–1193.

Banaji, M., & Crowder, R. (1991). Some everyday thoughts on ecologically valid methods. *American Psychologist, 46*, 78–79.

Barker, E. (1971–1972). Humanistic psychology and scientific method. *Interpersonal Development, 2*, 137–172.

Barkow, J., Cosmides, L., & Tooby, J. (Eds.). (1992). *The adapted mind: Evolutionary psychology and the generation of culture.* New York: Oxford University Press.

Barnes, D., & Bero, L. (1996). Industry-funded research and conflict of interest: An analysis of research sponsored by the tobacco industry through the Center for Indoor Air Research. *Journal of Health, Politics, Policy and Law, 21*, no. 3, 515.

Barnes, D., & Bero, L. (1998). Why review articles on the health effects of passive smoking reach different conclusions. *Journal of the American Medical Association, 279*, 1566–1570.

Bauer, H. (1992). *Scientific literacy and the myth of the scientific method.* Urbana: University of Illinois Press.

Beldecos, A. et al. (1988). The importance of feminist critique for contemporary cell biology. *Hypatia, 3*, 172–185.

Belson, W. (1981). *The design and understanding of survey questions.* Aldershot, England: Gower.

Bergin, A. (1966). Some implications of psychotherapy research for therapeutic practice. *Journal of Abnormal Psychology, 71*, 235–246.

Bergin, A. (1971). The evaluation of therapeutic outcomes. In A. Bergin & S. Garfield (Eds.), *Handbook of psychotherapy and behavior change.* New York: Wiley.

Berk, R. (1979). Generalizability of behavioral observations: A clarification of interobserver agreement and interobserver reliability. *American Journal of Mental Deficiency, 83*, 460–472.

Berke, J. (1997) Book review: Living downstream: An ecologist looks at cancer and the environment. *New England Journal of Medicine, 337*, 1562.

Bettelheim, B. (1967). *The empty fortress: Infantile autism and the birth of the self.* New York: Free Press.

Beveridge, W. (1957). *The art of scientific investigation* (2nd ed.). New York: Vintage.

Binder, A., McConnell, D., & Sjoholm, N. (1957). Verbal conditioning as a function of experimenter characteristics. *Journal of Abnormal Social Psychology, 55*, 309–314.

Black, G., & Black, B. (1993). Perot wins! The election that could have been. *Public Perspective, 4*, 15–16.

Blake, J. (1966). Ideal family size among white Americans: A quarter of a century's evidence. *Demography, 3*, 154–173.

Blake, J. (1967a). Family size in the 1960's—A baffling fad? *Eugenics Quarterly, 14*, 60–74.

Blake, J. (1967b). Income and reproductive motivation. *Population Studies, 21*, 185–206.

Blanchard, D., Griebel, G., & Blanchard, R. (1995). Gender bias in the preclinical psychopharmacology of anxiety: Male models for (predominantly) female disorders. *Journal of Psychopharmacology, 9*, 79–82.

Bonjean, C., Hill, R., & McLemore, D. (1967). *Sociological measurement.* San Francisco: Chandler.

Bornstein, R. (1991). The predictive validity of peer review: A neglected issue. *Behavioral and Brain Sciences, 14*, 138–139.

Botting, J., & Morrison, A. (1997). Animal research is vital to medicine. *Scientific American, 276*, 83–85.

Brennan, T. (1994). Buying editorials. *The New England Journal of Medicine, 331*, 673–675.

Brewer, J., & Hunter, A. (1989). *Multimethod research.* Newbury Park, CA: Sage.

Broad, W., & Wade, N. (1982). *Betrayers of the truth.* New York: Simon & Schuster.

Bronowski, J. (1956). *Science and human values.* New York: Harper.

Brown, H. (1988). *Rationality.* London: Routledge.

Brown, J. (1996). Redefining smoking and the self as a nonsmoker. *Western Journal of Nursing Research, 18*, 414–428.

Brown, J., & Semradek, J. (1992). Secondary data on health-related subjects: Major sources, uses, and limitations. *Public Health Nursing, 9,* 162–171.

Brown, L. et al. (1992). Psychotherapist-patient sexual contact after termination of treatment. *American Journal of Psychiatry, 149,* 979–980.

Browne, M. (1989, October 17). Nobel fever: The price of rivalry. *New York Times,* pp. C1, 14.

Bruner, J. (1965). The growth of mind. *American Psychologist, 20,* 1007–1017.

Buchanan, W. (1986). Election predictions: An empirical assessment. *Public Opinion Quarterly, 40,* 222–227.

Budd, J., Sievert, M., & Schultz, T. (1998). Phenomena of retraction: Reasons for retraction and citations to the publications. *Journal of the American Medical Association, 280,* 296–297.

Burleson, B., Kunkel, A., Samter, W., & Werking, K. (1996). Men's and women's evaluations of communication skills in personal relationships: When sex differences make a difference—and when they don't. *Journal of Social Personal Relationships, 13,* 201–224.

Buss, D. (1995). Psychological sex differences: Origins through sexual selection. *American Psychologist, 50,* 164–168.

Bustad, L. (1966). Pigs in the laboratory. *Scientific American, 214,* 94–100.

Callaham, M., Baxt, W., Waeckerle, J., & Wears, R. (1998). Reliability of editors' subjective quality ratings of peer reviews of manuscripts. *Journal of the American Medical Association, 280,* 229–231.

Campbell, D., & Boruch, R. (1975). Making the case for randomized assignment to treatments by considering the alternatives: Six ways in which quasi-experimental evaluations in compensatory education tend to underestimate effects. In C. Bennett, & A. Lumsdaine (Eds.), *Evaluation and experiment.* New York: Academic Press.

Campbell, D., & Fiske, D. (1959). Convergent and discriminant validation by the multitrait-multimethod matrix. *Psychological Bulletin, 56,* 81–105.

Campbell, D., & Stanley, J. (1966). *Experimental and quasi-experimental designs for research.* Chicago: Rand McNally.

Carlson, R. (1971). Where is the person in personality research? *Psychological Bulletin, 75,* 203–219.

Casti, J. (1994). *Complexification.* New York: HarperCollins.

Ceci, S., & Bronfenbrenner, U. (1991). On the demise of everyday memory: "The rumors of my death are much exaggerated." (Mark Twain). *American Psychologist, 46,* 27–31.

Cederlof, R., Friberg, L., & Lundman, T. (1977). The interactions of smoking, environment and heredity and their implications for disease etiology. A report of epidemiological studies on the Swedish Twin Registries. *Acta Medica Scandanavia, 612,* 1–128.

Celermajer D. et al. (1993). Cigarette smoking is associated with dose-related and potentially reversible impairment of endothelium-dependent dilation in healthy young adults. *Circulation, 88,* 2149–2155.

Chalmers, A. (1976). *What is this thing called science?* Queensland, Australia: University of Queensland Press.

Chapman, L., & Chapman, J. (1967). The genesis of popular but erroneous psychodiagnostic observations. *Journal of Abnormal Psychology, 72,* 193–204.

Choldin, H. (1994). *Looking for the last percent.* New Brunswick, NJ: Rutgers University Press.

Chubin, D., & Hackett, E. (1990). *Peerless science: Peer review and U.S. science policy.* Albany: State University of New York Press.

Cicchetti, D. (1982). We have met the enemy and he is us. *Behavioral and Brain Sciences, 5,* 205.

Cicchetti, D. (1991). The reliability of peer review for manuscript and grant submissions: A cross-disciplinary investigation. *Behavioral and Brain Sciences, 14,* 119–135.

Cicchini, M. (1976). Thought content and psychopathology: Themes within the stream of consciousness of depressed and nondepressed subjects. Unpublished master's thesis, University of Western Australia, Nedlands, Australia.

Clark, H., & Schober, M. (1992). Asking questions and influencing answers. In J. Tanur (Ed.), *Questions about questions: Inquiries into the cognitive bases of surveys.* New York: Russell Sage Foundation.

Clark, L., & Watson, D. (1995). Constructing validity: Basic issues in objective scale development. *Psychological Assessment, 7,* 309–319.

Clearinghouse on Environmental Advocacy and Research (1997, July). Show me the science! Corporate polluters and the "junk science" strategy. www.ewg.org/pub/home/CLEAR/By_Clear/ShowMe.html.

Cobb, L. (1990). Top-down research design. Published by Aethling.com at www.Aethling .com/docs/TopDown.htm.

Cochran, W. (1963). *Sampling techniques* (2nd ed.). New York: Wiley.

Cohen, J. (1988). *Statistical power analysis for the behavioral sciences.* Hillsdale, NJ: Lawrence Erlbaum.

Cohen, J. (1990). Things I have learned so far. *American Psychologist, 45,* 1304–1312.

Cohen, W. (1960). Form recognition, spatial orientation, perception of movement in the uniform visual field. In A. Morris & E. Horne (Eds.), *Visual search techniques* (Publication No. 712). Washington, DC: National Academy of Sciences.

Comroe, J., & Dripps, R. (1976). Scientific basis for the support of biomedical science. *Science, 192,* 105–111.

Connors, E., Lundregan, T., Miller, N., & McEwen, T. (1996). *Convicted by juries, exonerated by science: Case studies in the use of DNA evidence to establish innocence after trial.* NIJ Research Report. U.S. Department of Justice Office of Justice Programs.

Converse, P., & Traugott, M. (1986). Assessing the accuracy of polls and surveys. *Science, 234,* 1094–1098.

Cook, R., Bernstein, A., & Andews, C. (1997). Assessing drug use in the workplace: A comparison of self-report, urinanalysis, and hair analysis. In NIDA Research Monograph 167. *The Validity of Self-Reported Drug Use: Improving the Accuracy of Survey Estimates.* U.S. Dept. of Health & Human Services, Rockville, MD.

Cook, T., & Campbell, D. (1979). *Quasi-experimentation.* Skokie, IL: Rand McNally.

Cooper, H., & Rosenthal, R. (1980). Statistical versus traditional procedures for summarizing research findings. *Psychological Bulletin, 87,* 442–449.

Copi, I., & Gould, J. (1964). *Readings on logic.* New York: Macmillan.

Cosmides, L., & Tooby, J. (1994). Beyond intuition and instinct blindness: Toward an evolutionarily rigorous cognitive science. *Cognition, 50,* 41–77.

Council, J. (1993). Context effects in personality research. *Current Directions in Psychological Science, 2,* 31–34.

Crawford, C. (1989). The theory of evolution: Of what value to psychology? *Journal of Comparative Psychology, 103,* 4–22.

Cronbach, L. (1975). Beyond the two disciplines in scientific psychology. *American Psychologist, 30,* 116–127.

Crook, J. (1964). The evolution of social organization and visual communication in the weaver birds (*Ploceinae*). *Behaviour (Supplement), 10,* 1–178.

Crowne, D., & Marlowe, D. (1964). *The approval motive.* New York: Wiley.

Cullen, E. (1957). Adaptations in the kittiwake to cliff-nesting. *Ibis, 99,* 275–302.

Dalbey, W., Nettesheim, P., Griesemer, R., Caton, J., & Guerin, M. (1980). Chronic inhalation of cigarette smoke by F344 rats. *Journal of the National Cancer Institute, 64,* 383–390.

Dalton, K. (1960). Menstruation and accidents. *British Medical Journal, 2,* 1425–1426.

Dar, R. (1987). Another look at Meehl, Lakatos, and the scientific practices of psychologists. *American Psychologist, 42,* 145–151.

Dar, R., Serlin, R., & Omer, H. (1994). Misuse of statistical tests in three decades of psychotherapy research. *Journal of Consulting Clinical Psychology, 62,* 75–82.

Dasanayake, A., Macaluso, M., Roseman, J., & Field, P. (1995). Validity of the mother's recall of her child's antibiotic use. *Journal of Dentistry for Children, 62,* 118–122.

Davidson, R. (1986). Source of funding and outcome of clinical trials. *Journal of General Internal Medicine, 1,*155–158.

Dawes, R., & Mulford, M. (1993). Diagnoses of alien kidnapping that result from conjunction effects in memory. *The Skeptical Inquirer, 18,* 50–51.

Deane, F., Spicer, J., & Todd, D. (1997). Validity of a simplified target complaints measure. *Assessment, 4,* 119–130.

Deary, I., Whiteman, M., & Fowkes, F. (1998). Medical research and the popular media. *Lancet, 351,* 1726–1727.

DeMaio, T. (1980). Refusals: Who, where and why. *Public Opinion Quarterly, 44,* 223–233.

Denenberg, V. (1982). Comparative psychology and single-subject research. In A. Kazdin & A. Tuma (Eds.), *Single-case research designs.* San Francisco: Jossey-Bass.

Derry, P. (1996). Buss and sexual selection: The issue of culture. *American Psychologist, 51,* 159–160.

Der Simonian, R., & Laird, N. (1983). Evaluating the effect of coaching on SAT scores: A meta-analysis. *Harvard Education Review, 53,* 1–15.

De Semir V., Ribas, C., & Revuelta, G. (1998). Press releases of science journal articles and subsequent newspaper stories on the same topic. *Journal of the American Medical Association, 280,* 294–295.

Diamond, M., Schiebel, A., Murphy, G., & Harvey, T. (1985). On the brain of a scientist: Albert Einstein. *Experimental Neurology, 88,* 198–204.

Dickersin, K. (1997). How important is publication bias? A synthesis of available data. *AIDS Education and Prevention, 9, Supplement A,* 15–21.

Dickersin K., Min, Y., & Meinert, C. (1992). Factors influencing publication of research results. Follow-up of applications submitted to two institutional review boards. *Journal of the American Medical Association, 267,* 374–378.

Dickersin K., Scherer, R., & Lefebvre, C. (1994). Identifying relevant studies for systematic reviews. *British Medical Journal, 309,* 1286–1291.

Dickersin, K., & Yuan, I. (1993). Publication bias: The problem that won't go away. *New York Academy of Science Annals, 703,* 135–148.

Dieter, R. (1998). The death penalty in black & white: Who lives, who dies, who decides. Washington, DC: Death Penalty Information Center.

Dillman, D. (1978). *Mail and telephone surveys: The total design method.* New York: Wiley-Interscience.

Doll, R. (1955). Etiology of lung cancer. *Advances in Cancer Research, 3,* 1–50.

Doll, R., & Hill, A. (1956). Lung cancer and other causes of death in relation to smoking. A second report on the mortality of British doctors. *British Medical Journal, 2,* 1071–1081.

Dontenwill, W., & Wiebecke, B. (1966). Tracheal and pulmonary alterations following the inhalation of cigarette smoke by golden hamsters. In L. Severi (Ed.), *Lung tumors in animals.* Perugia, Italy: University of Perugia, International Conference on Cancer.

Dovidio, J., & Fazio, R. (1992). New technologies for the direct and indirect assessment of attitudes. In J. Tanur (Ed.), *Questions about questions: Inquiries into the cognitive bases of surveys.* New York: Russell Sage Foundation.

Dovidio, J., & Gaertner, S. (1991). Changes in the nature and expression of racial prejudice. In H. Knopke et al. (Eds.), *Opening doors: An appraisal of race relations in contemporary America.* Tuscaloosa: University of Alabama Press.

Dovidio, J. et al. (1989). Resistance to affirmative action: The implications of aversive racism. In F. Blanchard & F. Crosby (Eds.), *Affirmative action in perspective.* New York: Springer-Verlag.

Dowie, M. (1998, July 6). What's wrong with the *New York Times'* science reporting? *The Nation.*

Duhem, P. (1954). *The aim and structure of physical theory.* Princeton, NJ: Princeton University Press.

Easterbrook P., Berlin, J., Gopalan, R., & Matthews, D. (1991). Publication bias in clinical research. *Lancet, 337,* 867–872.

Ebbinghaus, H. (1885). *Uber das gedachtnis.* Leipzig: Duncker & Humblot.

*eBMJ.* (1997). Editorial, 315.

*eBMJ.* (1998). News, 316, 1553.

*eBMJ.* (1998). News, 316, 1850.

Edgerton, R. (1965). "Cultural" vs. "ecological" factors in the expression of values, attitudes, and personality characteristics. *American Anthropologist, 67,* 442–447.

Editorials. (1997). Ethnic variation as a key to the biology of human disease. *Annals of Internal Medicine, 127,* 401–403.

Egger M., Zellweger, T., & Antes, G. (1996). Randomised trials in German-language journals. *Lancet, 347,* 1047–1048.

Egger M. et al. (1997). Language bias in randomized controlled trials published in English & German. *Lancet, 350,* 326–329.

Ellis, N., & Hennelley, R. (1980). A bilingual word-length effect: Implications for intelligence testing and the relative ease of mental calculation in Welsh and English. *British Journal of Psychology, 71,* 43–52.

Epstein, S. (1998). *The politics of cancer revisited.* Fremont Center, New York: East Ridge Press.

Ernst, J., & Resch, K. (1994). Reviewer bias: A blinded experimental study. *Journal of Laboratory and Clinical Medicine, 124,* 178–182.

Eysenck, H. (1952). The effects of psychotherapy: An evaluation. *Journal of Consulting Psychology, 16,* 319–324.

Eysenck, H. (1980). *The causes and effects of smoking.* Beverly Hills: Sage.

Eysenck, H. (1984). Meta-analysis: An abuse of research integration. *Journal of Special Education, 18,* 41–59.

Falk, J. (1969). Conditions producing psychogenic polydipsia in animals. *Annals of the New York Academy of Science, 157,* 569–593.

Falk, J. (1977). Animal model of alcoholism: Critique and progress. In M. Gross (Ed.), *Alcohol intoxication and withdrawal.* New York: Plenum.

Falk, J. (1984). Excessive behavior and drug-taking: Environmental generation and self-control. In P. Levison (Ed.), *Substance abuse, habitual behavior, and self-control.* Boulder: Westview Press.

Falk, J. (1985). Schedule-induced determinants of drug-taking. In L. Seiden & R. Balster (Eds.), *Behavioral pharmacology: The current status.* New York: Alan Liss, Inc.

Falk, J. (1986). The formation and function of ritual behavior. In T. Thompson & M. Zeiler (Eds.), *Analysis and integration of behavioral units.* Hillsdale, NJ: Erlbaum Associates.

Faust, D. (1984). *The limits of scientific reasoning.* Minneapolis: University of Minnesota Press.

Ferster, C., & Skinner, B. (1957). Schedules of reinforcement. New York: Appleton-Century-Crofts.

Feyerabend, P. (1975). *Against method.* London: NLB.

Fischer, C. (1975). Privacy as a profile of authentic consciousness. *Humanitas, 11,* 27–43.

Fisher, S. (1995). Hanky-panky in the pharmaceutical industry. http://www.psycom.net/fisher.html

Foltin R., Fischman, M., & Levin, F. (1995). Cardiovascular effects of cocaine in humans: Laboratory studies. *Drug and Alcohol Dependence, 37,* 193–210.

Fowler, F. & Mangione, T. (1990). *Standardized survey interviewing.* Thousand Oaks, CA: Sage.

Freedman, J. (1984). Effect of television violence on aggressiveness. *Psychological Bulletin, 96,* 227–246.

Freiman J., Chalmers, T., Smith, H., & Kuebler, R. (1992). The importance of beta, the type II error, and sample size in the design and interpretation of the randomized controlled trial: Survey of two sets of "negative" trials. In J. Bailar & F. Mosteller (Eds.), *Medical uses of statistics* (2nd ed.). Boston: NEJM Books.

Freud, A. (1948). *The ego and the mechanisms of defense.* New York: International Universities.

Friedman, H. et al. (1995). Psychosocial and behavioral predictors of longevity. *American Psychologist, 50,* 69–78.

Fulford, P. (1998). The COPE report. Fraud and plagiarism. http://www.bmj.com/misc/cope/ tex6.shtml

Fulton, J., & Jacobsen, C. (1935). The functions of the frontal lobes: A comparative study in monkeys, chimpanzees, and man. *Advances in Modern Biology, 4,* 113–123.

Gale, A. (Ed.). (1988). *The polygraph test: Lies, truth, and science.* London: Sage.

Garcia, J., Hankins, W., & Rusiniak, K. (1974). Behavioral regulation of the milieu interne in man and rat. *Science, 185,* 824–831.

Garfield, E. (1996). In truth, the "flood" of scientific literature is only a myth. *The Scientist, 10,* 13, 16.

Garmezy, N. (1982). The case for the single case in research. In A. Kazdin & A. Tuma (Eds.), *Single-case research designs.* San Francisco: Jossey-Bass.

Gelman, A., & King, G. (1993). Why are American presidential election campaign polls so variable when votes are so predictable? *British Journal of Political Science, 23,* 409–451.

George, P., & Robbins K. (1994). Reference accuracy in the dermatologic literature. *Journal of the American Academy of Dermatology, 31,* 61–64.

Gergen, K. (1978). Experimentation in social psychology: A reappraisal. *European Journal of Social Psychology, 8,* 507–527.

Gielen, U. (1994). American mainstream psychology and its relationship to international and cross-cultural psychology. In A. Comunian & U. Gielen (Eds.), Advancing psychology and its applications: International perspectives. Milan: FrancoAngeli.

Gigerenzer, G. (1991). From tools to theories: A heuristic of discovery in cognitive psychology. *Psychological Review, 98,* 254–267.

Gigerenzer, G. (1993). The superego, the ego, and the id in statistical reasoning. In G. Keren & C. Lewis (Eds.), *Methodological and quantitative issues in the analysis of psychological data.* Hillsdale, NJ: Erlbaum.

Gilbert, N. (1997). A simulation of the structure of academic science. *Sociological Research Online,* 2,(2). www.socresonline.org.uk/socresonline/2/2/3.html

Gilligan, C. (1982). *In a different voice.* Cambridge, MA: Harvard University Press.

Goethals, G., & Reckman, R. (1973). The perception of consistency in attitudes. *Journal of Experimental Social Psychology, 9,* 491–501.

Goff, B., Muntz, H., & Cain, J. (1997). Is Adam worth more than Eve? The financial impact of gender bias in the federal reimbursement of gynecological procedures. *Gynecologic Oncology, 64,* 372–377.

Goldman, L., Sia, S., Cook, E., Rutherford, J., & Weinstein, M. (1988). Costs and effectiveness of routine therapy and long-term beta-adrenergic antagonists after acute myocardial infarction. *New England Journal of Medicine, 319,* 152–156.

Goldstein, A. (1980). Thrills in response to music and other stimuli. *Physiological Psychology, 8,* 126–129.

Goldwater, B., & Collins, M. (1985). Psychologic effects of cardiovascular conditioning: A controlled experiment. *Psychosomatic Medicine. 47,* 174–181.

Goodman, N. (1973). *Fact, fiction, and forecast.* Indianapolis: Bobbs-Merrill.

Goodstein, D. (1991). Conduct and misconduct in science. *Engineering and Science* (Winter), 11.

Gorman, M. (1994). Male homosexual desire: Neurological investigations and scientific bias. *Perspectives in Biology and Medicine, 38,* 61–81.

Gould, S. (1981). *The mismeasure of man.* New York: W. W. Norton.

Graham, S. (1960). The influence of therapist character structure upon Rorschach changes in the course of psychotherapy. *American Psychologist, 15,* 415.

Greenwood, P. (1982). *Selective incapacitation.* Report R-2815-NIJ. Santa Monica, CA: Rand Corporation.

Gregoire , G., Derderian, F., & LeLorier, J. (1995). Selecting the language of the publications included in a meta-analysis: Is there a Tower of Babel bias? *Journal of Clinical  Epidemiology, 48,* 159–163.

Griffin, D., Webster, F., & Michael, C. (1960). The echolocation of flying insects by bats. *Animal Behavior, 8,* 141–154.

Gurwitz, J., Col, N., & Avorn, J. (1992). The exclusion of the elderly and women from clinical trials in acute myocardial infarction. *Journal of the American Medical Association, 268,* 1417–1422.

Haber, E. (1996). Industry and the university. *Nature Biotechnology, 14,* 441–442.

Halperin, S. (1989). Analysis of statistical procedures and designs commonly used in drug research studies. In S. Fisher & R. Greenberg (Eds.), *The limits of biological treatments for psychological distress.* Hillsdale, NJ: Lawrence Erlbaum.

Hanneman, R., and Patrick, S. (1997). On the uses of computer-assisted simulation modeling in the social sciences. *Sociological Research Online,* 2(2). www.socresonline.org.uk/socresonline/2/2/5.html

Hansen, M., & McIntire, D. (1994). Reference citations in radiology: Accuracy and appropriateness of use in two major journals. *American Journal of Roentgenology, 163,* 719–723.

Hanson, N. (1958). *Patterns of discovery.* London: Cambridge University Press.

Harcourt, A. (1978). Activity periods and patterns of social interaction: A neglected problem. *Behaviour, 66,* 121–135.

Harcum, E., & Rosen, E. (1993). *The gatekeepers of psychology.* Westport, CT: Praeger.

Harding, S. (1987). Is there a feminist method? In S. Harding (Ed.), *Feminism and methodology.* Indianapolis: Indiana University Press.

Harrell, A. (1997). The validity of self-reported drug use data: The accuracy of responses on confidential self-administered answer sheets. In *The validity of self-reported drug use: Improving the accuracy of survey estimates.* NIDA Research Monograph 167. Rockville, MD: U.S. Dept. of Health & Human Services.

Harris, B. (1979). Whatever happened to Little Albert? *American Psychologist, 34,* 151–160.

Hart, R., Turturro, A., Leakey, J., & Allaben, W. (1995). Diet and test animals. *Science, 270,* 1419–1420.

Hartwig, F., & Dearing, B. (1979). *Exploratory data analysis.* Newbury Park, CA: Sage Publications.

Hartz, J., & Chappell, R. (1997). *Worlds apart.* Nashville, TN: First Amendment Center.

Hatchett, S., & Schuman, H. (1975). White respondent and race-of-interviewer effects. *Public Opinion Quarterly, 39,* 523–528.

Hazan, C., & Shaver, P. (1987). Romantic love conceptualized as an attachment process. *Journal of Personality Social Psychology, 52,* 511–524.

Heitzmann, C., & Kaplan, R. (1988). Assessment of methods for measuring social support. *Health Psychology, 7,* 75–109.

Hempel, C. (1945). Studies in the logic of confirmation. *Mind, 54,* 1–26.

Hempel, C. (1966). *Philosophy of natural science.* Englewood Cliffs, NJ: Prentice Hall.

Hempel, C. (1992). The significance of the concept of truth for the critical appraisal of scientific theories. In W. Shea & A. Spadafora (Eds.), *Interpreting the world.* Canton, MA: Science History Publications.

Henrion, M., & Fischhoff, B. (1986). Assessing uncertainty in physical constants. *American Journal of Physics, 54,* 791–798.

Henshel, R. (1980). Seeking inoperative laws: Toward the deliberate use of unnatural experimentation. In L. Freese (Ed.), *Theoretical methods in sociology.* Pittsburgh: University of Pittsburgh Press.

Hersen, M., & Barlow, D. (1976). *Single case experimental designs: Strategies for studying behavior change.* New York: Pergamon.

Hilgard, E. (1980). Consciousness in contemporary psychology. *Annual Review of Psychology, 31,* 1–26.

Hodgkin, A., & Huxley, A. (1952). A quantitative description of membrane current and its application to conduction and excitation in nerve. *Journal of Physiology, 117,* 500–544.

Hodgkin, A., & Keynes, R. (1956). Experiments on the injection of substances into squid giant axons by means of a microsyringe. *Journal of Physiology, 131,* 592–616.

Hofman, M., & Swaab, D. (1991). Sexual dimorphism of the human brain: Myth and reality. *Experimental and Clinical Endocrinology, 98,* 161–170.

Holekamp, K., & Sherman, P. (1989). Why male ground squirrels disperse. *American Scientist, 77,* 232–239.

Hollandsworth, J., Glazeski, R., & Dressel, M. (1978). Use of social-skills training in the treatment of extreme anxiety and deficient verbal skills in the job-interview setting. *Journal of Applied Behavior Analysis, 11,* 259–269.

Hopkins, B., & Hermann, J. (1977). Evaluating interobserver reliability of interval data. *Journal of Applied Behavioral Analysis, 10,* 121–126.

Horan, J. (1995, August 11). *Paradigms for establishing experimental construct validity in counseling and psychotherapy.* Paper presented at the annual meeting of the American Psychological Association, New York.

Horgan, J. (1990, March). Test negative: Science & the citizen. *Scientific American, 18,* 22.

Horton, R. (1998). The COPE Report. http://www.bmj.com/misc/cope/tex8.shtml

Huffman, R. (1996). Cs₃Te₂₂, the one we know now. *American Scientist, 84,* 327–329.

Hughes, J., Casal, D., & Leon, A. (1986). Psychological effects of exercise: A randomized crossover trial. *Journal of Psychosomatic Research, 30,* 355–360.

Humphreys, L. (1982). Inadequate data in, attractive theory out. *Journal of Educational Psychology, 74,* 424–426.

Humphreys, W. (1968). *Anomalies and scientific theories.* San Francisco: Freemen, Cooper.

Hunter, J., & Schmidt, F. (1990). *Methods of meta-analysis.* Newbury Park, CA: Sage.

Hyatt, J. (1995). The importance of pharmacokinetic/pharmacodynamic surrogate markers to outcome. Focus on antibacterial agents. *Clinical Pharmacokinetics, 28,* 143–60.

Hyde, J., & Rosenberg, B. (1976). *Half the human experience: The psychology of women.* Lexington, MA: D.C. Heath.

Hyman, H. with Cobb, W. et al. (1954). *Interviewing in social research.* Chicago: University of Chicago Press.

Hyman, H., & Sheatsley, P. (1950). The current status of American public opinion. In J. Payne (Ed.), *The teaching of contemporary affairs: Twenty-first yearbook of the National Council of Social Studies.* Washington, DC: National Council for the Social Studies.

Ifill, G. (1988, November). Voter abstention breaks 1948 record: Experts cite negative campaigning polls. *Washington Post.*

Jacob, H. (1984). *Using published data: Errors and remedies.* Beverly Hills: Sage.

Jacobson, A., Koehler, J., & Jones, B. (1987). The failure of routine assessment to detect histories of assault experienced by psychiatric patients. *Hospital & Community Psychiatry, 38,* 386–389.

James, W. (1892). *Psychology.* New York: Henry Holt & Co.

Jarman, P. (1974). The social organization of antelope in relation to their ecology. *Behaviour, 48,* 215–267.

Jones, R., Kazdin, A., & Haney, J. (1981). Social validation and training of emergency fire safety skills for potential injury prevention and life saving. *Journal of Applied Behavior Analysis, 14,* 153–164.

Jones, R., Reid, J., & Patterson, R. (1975). Naturalistic observation in clinical assessment. In P. McReynolds (Ed.), *Advances in psychological assessment* (Vol. 3). San Francisco: Jossey-Bass.

Joyce, J., Rabe, H., & Wessely, S. (1998). Reviewing the reviews: The example of chronic fatigue syndrome. *Journal of the American Medical Association, 280,* 264–266.

Kalat, J. (1980). A misuse of statistics: Reply to Rimland. *American Psychologist, 35,* 223–224.

Kamin, L. (1978). Comment on Munsinger's review of adoption studies. *Psychological Bulletin, 85,* 194–201.

Kane, E., & Macaulay, L. (1993). Interviewer gender and gender attitudes. *Public Opinion Quarterly, 57,* 1–28.

Karon, B. (1989). Psychotherapy versus medication for schizophrenia: Empirical comparisons. In S. Fisher, & R. Greenberg (Eds.), *The limits of biological treatments for psychological distress.* Hillsdale, NJ: Lawrence Erlbaum.

Karpf, D., & Levine, M. (1971). Blank-trial probes and introtacts in human discrimination learning. *Journal of Experimental Psychology, 90,* 51–55.

Kasperson, C. (1978). Scientific creativity: A relationship with information channels. *Psychological Reports, 42,* 691–694.

Kazdin, A. (1977). Artifact, bias, and complexity of assessment: The ABCs of reliability. *Journal of Applied Behavioral Analysis, 10,* 141–150.

Kazdin, A. (1978). Methodological and interpretive problems of single-case experimental designs. *Journal of Consulting and Clinical Psychology, 46,* 629–642.

Keller, E. (1985). *Reflections on gender and science.* New Haven, CT: Yale University Press.

Keren, G., & Lewis, C. (Eds.). (1993). *A handbook for data analysis in the behavioral sciences: Statistical issues.* Hillsdale, NJ: Lawrence Erlbaum.

King, A. (1994). Enhancing the self-report of alcohol consumption in the community: Two questionnaire formats. *American Journal of Public Health, 84,* 294–296.

Kinlen, L., Goldblatt, P., Fox, J., & Yudkin, J. (1984). Coffee and pancreatic cancer: Controversy in part explained. *Lancet, 1,* 282–283.

Kirsch, I., & Weixel, L. (1988). Double-blind versus deceptive administration of a placebo. *Behavioral Neuroscience, 102,* 319–323.

Koehler, J. (1993). The influence of prior beliefs on scientific judgments of evidence quality. *Organizational Behavior & Human Decision Processes, 56,* 28–55.

Kohlberg, L. (1976). Moral stages and moralization: The cognitive-developmental approach. In T. Likona (Ed.), *Moral development and behavior.* New York: Holt, Rinehart and Winston.

Kohlberg, L. (1984). *Essays on moral development. Vol. 2: The psychology of moral development: The nature and validity of moral stages.* San Francisco: Harper & Row.

Kohn, A. (1986). *False prophets.* San Francisco: Basil Blackwell.

Kolansky, H., & Moore, W. (1971). Effects of marijuana on adolescents and young adults. *Journal of the American Medical Association, 216,* 486–492.

Kolb, L. (1962). *Drug addiction: A medical problem.* Springfield, IL: Charles C. Thomas.

Kortlandt, A. (1962, May). Chimpanzees in the wild. *Scientific American,* 1–10.

Koshland, D. (1987). Fraud in science [editorial]. *Science, 235,* 141.

Koss, M. (1993). Detecting the scope of rape: A review of prevalence research methods. *Journal of Interpersonal Violence, 8,* 198–222.

Kraemer, H., & Thiemann, S. (1987). *How many subjects?* Newbury Park, CA: Sage.

Kraus, N. (1994). Scientific world's low tolerance for controversy may be what's excluding young investigators. *The Scientist, 8,* 13.

Krimsky, S., Ennis, J., & Weissman, R. (1991). Academic corporate ties in biotechnology: A quantitative study. *Science, Technology, & Human Values, 16,* 275–287.

Krimsky, S., Rothenberg, L., Stott, P., & Kyle, G. (1996). Financial interests of authors in scientific journals: A pilot study of 14 publications. *Science and Engineering Ethics, 2,* 395–410.

Krippendorff, K. (1980). *Content analysis.* Beverly Hills: Sage.

Kuhn, T. (1970). *The structure of scientific revolutions.* Chicago: University of Chicago Press.

Kunda, Z. (1987). Motivation and inference: Self-serving generation and evaluation of evidence. *Journal of Personality and Social Psychology 53,* 636–647.

Kunze, M., & Vutuc, C. (1980). Threshold of tar exposure: Analysis of male lung cancer cases and controls. In G. Gori & F. Bock (Eds.), *Banbury Report 3—A safe cigarette.* New York: Cold Spring Harbor Lab.

Kurman, P. (1977). Research: An aerial view. *Et Cetera, 34,* 265–276.

Lambert, M. (1991). Introduction to psychotherapy research. In L. Bentler & M. Crago (Eds.), *Psychotherapy research: An international review of programmatic studies.* Washington, DC: American Psychological Association.

Latane, B. (1996). Dynamic social impact. In R. Hegselmann et al. (Eds.), *Modelling and simulation in the social sciences from the philosophy of science point of view.* Berlin: Springer-Verlag.

Lau, R. (1994). An analysis of the accuracy of "trial" heat polls during the 1992 presidential election. *Public Opinion Quarterly, 58,* 2–20.

Laudan, L. (1984). *Science and values.* Berkeley: University of California Press.

Lazarsfeld, P., & Barton, A. (1951). Qualitative measurement in the social sciences. In D. Lerner & H. Lasswell (Eds.), *The policy sciences.* Palo Alto: Stanford University Press.

Leacock, S. (1916). *Further foolishness: Sketches and satires on the follies of the day.* New York: John Lane Co.

Leavitt, F. (1991). *Research methods for behavioral scientists.* Dubuque, IA: Wm. C. Brown.

Leavitt, F. (1995). *Drugs and behavior.* Thousand Oaks, CA: Sage.

Leavitt, F. (1997–1998). Resolving Hempel's raven paradox. *Philosophy Now, 19,* 31.

Leckman, A., Umland, B., & Blay, M. (1984). Alcoholism in the families of family practice outpatients. *Journal of Family Practice, 19,* 205–207.

Lederman, L. (1984, November). The value of fundamental science. *Scientific American,* 40–47.

Lee, J., & Clemons, T. (1985). Factors affecting employment decisions about older workers. *Journal of Applied Psychology, 70,* 785–788.

Leizorovicz A., Hgh, M., Chapuis, F., Samama, M., & Boissel, J. (1992). Low molecular weight heparin in prevention of perioperative thrombosis. *British Medical Journal, 305,* 913–920.

Lennane, J. (1993). "Whistleblowing": A health issue. *British Medical Journal, 307,* 667–670.

Lenneberg, E. (1962). Understanding language without ability to speak: A case study. *Journal of Abnormal and Social Psychology, 65,* 419–425.

Lessler, M., & O'Reilly, J. (1997). Mode of interview and reporting of sensitive issues: Design and implementation of audio computer assisted self-interviewing. In *The Validity of Self-Reported Drug Use: Improving the Accuracy of Survey Estimates.* NIDA Research Monograph 167, Rockville, MD: U.S. Dept. of Health & Human Services.

LeVay, S. (1991). A difference in hypothalamic structure between heterosexual and homosexual men. *Science, 253,* 1034–1037.

Levine, A. (1977). Naturalistic observation: Validity of frequency data. *Psychological Reports, 40,* 1311–1338.

Lewis-Beck, M., & Rice, T. (1992). *Forecasting elections.* Washington, DC: Congressional Quarterly Press.

Lieberman, D. (1979). Behaviorism and the mind. *American Psychologist, 34,* 319–333.

Light, R. (1984). Six evaluation issues that synthesis can resolve better than single studies. In W. Yeaton & P. Wortman (Eds.), *Issues in data synthesis.* San Francisco: Jossey-Bass.

Light, R., & Pillemer, D. (1984). *Summing up.* Cambridge, MA: Harvard University Press.

Lincoln, Y., & Guba, E. (1985). *Naturalistic inquiry.* Newbury Park, CA: Sage.

Lipman, R., Park, L., & Rickels, K. (1966). Paradoxical influence of a therapeutic side effect interpretation. *Archives of General Psychiatry, 15,* 462–474.

Little, R., & Schenker, N. (1995). Missing data. In G. Arminger, C. Clogg, & M. Sobel (Eds.), *Handbook of statistical modeling for the social and behavioral sciences.* New York: Plenum.

Livson, N. (1977, September). The physically attractive woman at age 40: Precursors in adolescent personality and adult correlates from a longitudinal study. Paper presented at the International Conference on Love and Attraction, Swansea, Wales.

Lockard, R. (1968). The albino rat: A defensible choice or a bad habit. *American Psychologist, 23,* 734–742.

Locke, E., Cartledge, N., & Koeppel, J. (1968). Motivational effects of knowledge of results: A goal-setting phenomenon? *Psychological Bulletin, 70,* 474–485.

Locke, E., & Latham, G. (1990). *A theory of goal setting and task performance.* Englewood Cliffs, NJ: Prentice Hall.

Loftus, E., & Palmer, J. (1974). Reconstruction of automobile destruction: An example of the interaction between language and memory. *Journal of Verbal Learning and Verbal Behavior, 13,* 585–589.

Lohr, J., Ingram, D., Dudley, S., Lawton, E., & Donowitz, L. (1991). Hand washing in pediatric ambulatory settings: An inconsistent practice. *American Journal of Diseases of Children, 145,* 1198–1199.

Loose, C. (1996, January 22) Antiabortion message gets a free ride on the metro system. *The Washington Post.*

Lord, C., Ross, L., & Lepper, M. (1979). Biased assimilation and attitude polarization: The effects of prior theories on subsequently considered evidence. *Journal of Personality Social Psychology, 47,* 1231–1247.

Lorenz, E. (1993). *The essence of chaos.* Seattle: University of Washington Press.

Lowe, C. (1983). Radical behaviorism and human psychology. In G. Davey (Ed.), *Animal models of human behavior.* New York: Wiley.

Lowe, I. (1998, October 24). Tell it like it is. *New Scientist.*

Lykken, D. (1968). Statistical significance in psychological research. *Psychological Bulletin, 70,* 151–159.

Lykken, D. (1981). *A tremor in the blood: Uses and abuses of the lie detector.* New York: McGraw-Hill.

MacMahon, B., Yen, S., Trichopoulos, D., Warren, K., & Nardi, G. (1981). Coffee and cancer of the pancreas. *New England Journal of Medicine, 304,* 630–633.

Mahoney, M. (1977). Publication prejudices: An experimental study of confirmatory bias in the peer review system. *Cognitive Therapy Research, 1,* 161–175.

Margraf, J. et al. (1991). How "blind" are double-blind studies? *Journal of Consulting and Clincial Psychology, 59,* 184–187.

Mark, V., & Ervin, F. (1970). *Violence and the brain.* New York: Harper & Row.

Marrie, T., Durant, H., & Sealy, E. (1987). Pneumonia—The quality of medical records data. *Medical Care, 25,* 20–24.

Marsh, H., & Ball, S. (1989). The peer review process used to evaluate manuscripts submitted to academic journals: Interjudgmental reliability. *Journal of Experimental Education, 57,* 151–169.

McClelland, D. (1967). *The achieving society.* New York: The Free Press.

McConahy, J., Hardee, B., & Batts, V. (1981). Has racism declined in America? It depends on who is asking and what is asked. *Journal of Conflict Resolution, 25,* 563–579.

McCrady, B. et al. (1986). Cost effectiveness of alcoholism treatment in partial hospital versus inpatient setting after brief inpatient treatment: 12-month outcome. *Journal of Consulting and Clinical Psycology, 54,* 708–713.

McGuigan, F. (1963). The experimenter: A neglected stimulus object. *Psychological Bulletin, 60,* 421–428.

McKellar, P. (1949). The emotion of anger in the expression of human aggressiveness. *British Journal of Psychology, 39,* 148–155.

McNemar, Q. (1960). At random: Sense and nonsense. *American Psychologist, 15,* 295–300.

Medawar, P. (1967). *The art of the soluble.* London: Methuen.

Meehl, P. (1954). *Clinical versus statistical prediction.* Minneapolis: University of Minnesota Press.

Meehl, P. (1970a). Nuisance variables and ex post facto design. In M. Radner & S. Winokur (Eds.), *Analyses of theories and methods of physics and psychology.* Minneapolis: University of Minnesota Press.

Meehl, P. (1970b). Theory-testing in psychology and physics: A methodological paradox. In D. Morrison & R. Henkel (Eds.), *The significance test controversy.* Chicago: Aldine.

Meehl, P. (1978). Theoretical risks and tabular asterisks: Sir Karl, Sir Ronald, and the slow progress of soft psychology. *Journal of Consulting and Clinical Psychology, 46,* 806–834.

Meehl, P. (1990). Why summaries of research on psychological theories are often uninterpretable. *Psychological Reports, 66,* 195–244.

Meengs, M., Giles, B., Chisholm, C., Cordell, W., & Nelson, D. (1994). Hand washing frequency in an emergency department. *Journal of Emergency Nursing, 20,* 183–188.

Melbye, M. et al. (1997). Induced abortion and the risk of breast cancer. *New England Journal of Medicine, 336,* 81.

Merton, R. (1973). The Matthew effect in science. In N. Storer (Ed.), *The sociology of science: Theoretical and empirical investigations.* Chicago: University of Chicago Press.

Miles, M., & Huberman, A. (1984). *Analyzing qualitative data: A source book for new methods.* Thousand Oaks, CA: Sage.

Millard, W. (1976). Species preferences of experimenters. *American Psychologist, 36,* 894–896.

Miller, N. (1956). Effects of drugs on motivation: The value of using a variety of measures. *Annals of the New York Academy of Science, 65,* 318–333.

Mischel, W. (1973). Toward a cognitive social learning reconceptualization of personality. *Psychological Review, 80,* 252–283.

Mischel, W. (1974). Processes in delay of gratification. In L. Berkowitz (Ed.), *Advances in experimental social psychology.* New York: Academic Press.

Mitroff, I. (1983). *The subjective side of science: A philosophical inquiry into the psychology of the Apollo moon scientists.* Seaside, CA: Intersystems Publications.

Moher, D. et al. (1996). Completeness of reporting of trials published in languages other than English: Implications for conduct and reporting of systematic reviews. *Lancet, 347,* 363–366.

Moher, D., Dulberg, C., & Wells, G. (1994). Statistical power, sample size, and their reporting in randomized controlled trials. *Journal of the American Medical Association, 272,* 122–124.

Morokoff, P. (1986). Volunteer bias in the psychophysiological study of female sexuality. *Journal of Sex Research, 22,* 35–51.

Morwitz, V., Johnson, E., & Schmittlein, D. (1993). Does measuring intent change behavior? *Journal of Consumer Research, 20,* 46–61.

Moustakas, C. (1990). *Heuristic research.* Newbury Park, CA: Sage.

Mukerjee, M. (1997). Trends in animal research. *Scientific American, 276,* 86–93.

Mulrow, C. (1987). The medical review article: State of the science. *Annals of Internal Medicine, 106,* 485–488.

Munnell, A., Browne, L., McEneaney, J., & Tootell, G. (1992, October). Mortgage lending in Boston: Interpreting HMDA Data. Federal Reserve Bank of Boston, Working Paper WP-92-7.

Munoz, R., Hollon, S., McGrath, E., Rehm, L., et al. (1994). On the AHCPR depression in primary care guidelines: Further considerations for practitioners. *American Psychologist, 49,* 42–61.

Munsinger, H. (1974). The adopted child's IQ: A critical review. *Psychological Bulletin, 82,* 623–659.

Munsinger, H. (1978). Reply to Kamin. *Psychological Bulletin, 85,* 202–206.

Murphy, S. (1990). Models of imagery in sport psychology: A review. *Journal of Mental Imagery, 14,* 153–172.

Mynatt, C., Doherty, M., & Tweney, R. (1978). Consequences of confirmation and disconfirmation in a simulated research environment. *Quarterly Journal of Experimental Psychology, 30,* 395–406.

National Cancer Institute. (1996, February 13). Fact Sheet: Risk of breast cancer associated with abortion.

National Center for Health Statistics. (1967). Interview data on chronic conditions compared with information derived from medical records. (PHS Publication No. 1000-2-23). Washington, DC: U.S. Government Printing Office.

Neisser, U. (1991). A case of misplaced nostalgia. *American Psychologist, 46,* 34–36.

Nelkin, D. (1987). *Selling science.* New York: W. H. Freeman.

Nelson, K. (1986). *Event knowledge: Structure and function in development.* Hillsdale, NJ: Erlbaum.

Nelson, T. (1996). Consciousness and metacognition. *American Psychologist, 51,* 102–116.

Neufeld, P., & Colman, N. (1990). When science takes the witness stand [see comments]. *Scientific American, 262,* 46–53.

Neuliep, J., & Crandall, R. (1990). Editorial bias against replication research. *Journal of Social Behavior and Personality, 5,* 85–90.

Neuliep, J., & Crandall, R. (1993). Reviewer bias against replication research. *Journal of Social Behavior and Personality, 8,* 21–29.

Niemi, G., Katz, R., & Newman, D. (1980). Reconstructing past partisanship: The failure of party identification recall questions. *American Journal of Political Science, 24,* 633–651.

Nietzel, M., & Bernstein, P. (1987). *Introduction to clinical psychology.* Englewood Cliffs, NJ: Prentice Hall.

Nomura, A., Stemmermann, G., & Heilbrun, L. (1981). Coffee and pancreatic cancer. *Lancet, 2,* 415.

Nunnally, J. (1975). *Introduction to statistics for psychology and education.* New York: McGraw-Hill.

Nurmohamed, M. et al. (1992). Low-molecular-weight heparin versus standard heparin in general and orthopaedic surgery: A meta-analysis. *Lancet, 40,* 152–156.

Nutrition Business Journal. (1998, Oct./Nov.). *Global Market II.* San Diego, CA.

Nylenna, M., Riis, P., & Karlsson, Y. (1994). Multiple blinded reviews of the same two manuscripts: Effects of referee characteristics and publication language. *Journal of the American Medical Association, 272,* 149–151.

Oakes, M. (1986). *Statistical inference: A commentary for the social and behavioural sciences.* New York: John Wiley.

Office of Research Integrity. (1996). *Annual report.* Rockville, MD: Department of Health and Human Services.

Office of Research Integrity. (1999). *Highlights for 1997.* Rockville, MD: Department of Health and Human Services.

O'Leary, K., Kent, R., & Kanowitz, J. (1975). Shaping data collection congruent with experimental hypotheses. *Journal of Applied Behavioral Analysis, 8,* 43–51.

Orians, G. (1969). On the evolution of mating systems in birds and mammals. *American Naturalist, 103,* 589–603.

Orne, M. (1962). On the social psychology of the psychological experiment. *American Psychologist, 17,* 776–783.

Oxman, D., & Guyatt, G. (1993). The science of reviewing research. *Annals of the New York Academy of Science, 703,* 125–131.

Pastore, N. (1949). *The nature-nurture controversy.* New York: King's Crown Press.

Patton, M. (1990). *Qualitative evaluation and research methods.* Newbury Park, CA: Sage.

Pavlov, I. (1928). *Lectures on conditioned reflexes.* New York: International.

Payer, L. (1988). *Medicine and culture.* New York: Henry Holt.

Pearson, R., Ross, M., & Dawes, R. (1992). Personal recall and the limits of retrospective questions in surveys. In J. Tanur (Ed.), *Questions about questions: Inquiries into the cognitive bases of surveys.* New York: Russell Sage Foundation.

Pedersen, D., Keithly, S., & Brady, K. (1986). Effects of an observer on conformity to handwashing norm. *Perceptual Motor Skills, 62,* 169–170.

Peters, D. & Ceci, S. (1982). Peer-review practices of psychological journals. The fate of published articles, submitted again. *Behavioral and Brain Sciences, 5,* 187–195.

Petzel, T., Johnson, J., & McKillip, J. (1973). Response bias in drug surveys. *Journal of Consulting and Clinical Psychology, 40,* 437–439.

Pflaum, S., Walberg, H., Karegianes, M., & Rasher, S. (1980). Reading instruction: A quantitative analysis. *Educational Researcher, 9,* 12–18.

Phillips, D. (1972). Deathday and birthday: An unexpected connection. In J. Tanur et al. (Eds.), *Statistics: A guide to the unknown.* San Francisco: Holden-Day.

Phillips, D. (1982). The impact of fictional television stories on U.S. adult fatalities: New evidence of the effect of mass media on violence. *American Journal of Sociology, 87,* 1340–1359.

Phillips, D. (1983). The impact of mass media violence on U.S. homicides. *American Sociological Review, 48,* 560–568.

Piliavin, I., Rodin, J., & Piliavin, J. (1970). Good samaritanism: An underground phenomenon? *Journal of Personality and Social Psychology, 13,* 289–299.

Platt, J. (1964). Strong inference. *Science, 146,* 347–353.

Pollak, R. (1997). *The creation of Dr. B: A biography of Bruno Bettelheim.* New York: Simon & Schuster.

Polya, G. (1954). *Mathematics and plausible reasoning.* Princeton, NJ: Princeton University Press.

Pope, K., & Bouhoutsos, J. (1986). *Sexual intimacy between therapists and patients*. New York: Praeger.

Popper, K. (1963). *Conjectures and refutations*. New York: Basic Books.

Popper, K. (1968). *The Logic of scientific discovery*. London: Hutchinson.

Powers, E., Goudy, W., & Keith, P. (1978). Congruence between panel and recall data in longitudinal research. *Public Opinion Quarterly, 42*, 381–389.

Presser, S., & Blair, J. (1994). Survey pretesting: Do different methods produce different results? *Sociological Methodology, 24*, 73–104.

Price, E. (1972). Domestication and early experience effects on escape conditioning in the Norway rat. *Journal of Comparative and Physiological Psychology, 79*, 51–55.

Puccio, E., McPhillips, J., Barrett, C., & Ganiats, T. (1990). Clustering of atherogenic behaviors in coffee drinkers. *American Journal of Public Health, 80*, 1310–1313.

Pyszczynski, T., Greenberg, J., & Holt, K. (1985). Maintaining consistency between self-serving beliefs and available data: A bias in information evaluation. *Personality and Social Psychology Bulletin, 11*, 179–190.

Quine, W. (1953). *From a logical point of view*. Cambridge, MA: Harvard University Press.

Rachel's Environment & Health Weekly #593 (1998, April 9). Milk, rBGH, and cancer. http://www.monitor.net/rachel/r593.html

Ramsey, F., & Schafer, D. (1997). *The statistical sleuth*. Belmont, CA: Duxbury Press.

Razran, G. (1958). Pavlov and Lamarck. *Science, 128*, 758–760.

Reese, S., Danielson, W., Shoemaker, P., Chang, T., et al. (1986). Ethnicity-of-interviewer effects among Mexican-Americans and Anglos. *Public Opinion Quarterly, 50*, 563–572.

Reines, B. (1982). *Psychology experiments on animals*. Boston, MA: New England Antivivisection Society.

Rethans, J. (1991). Does competence predict performance? Dissertation published at University of Maastricht, the Netherlands.

Richardson, A. (1984). *The experiential dimension of psychology*. Queensland, Australia: University of Queensland Press.

Richter, C. (1954). The effects of domestication and selection on the behavior of the Norway rat. *Journal of the National Cancer Institute, 15*, 727–738.

Riger, S. (1992). Epistemological debates, feminist voices: Science, social values, and the study of women. *American Psychologist, 47*, 730–740.

Riley, D., Sobell, L., Leo, G., Sobell, M., & Klajner, F. (1987). Behavioral treatment of alcohol problems: A review and a comparison of behavioral and nonbehavioral studies. In W. Cox (Ed.), *Treatment and prevention of alcohol problems: A resource manual*. Orlando, FL: Academic Press.

Rimington, J. (1981). The effect of filters on the incidence of lung cancer in cigarette smokers. *Environmental Research, 24*, 162–166.

Robins, C. (1987). On interpreting results of multiple regression procedures: A cautionary note for researchers and reviewers. *Cognitive Therapy & Research, 11*, 705–708.

Roediger, H. (1991). They read an article? A commentary on the everyday memory controversy. *American Psychologist, 46*, 37–40.

Rogers, H., & Layton, B. (1979). Two methods of predicting drug-taking. *International Journal of Addictions, 14*, 299–310.

Rootman, I., & Smart, R. (1985). A comparison of alcohol, tobacco and drug use as determined from household and school surveys. *Drug and Alcohol Dependence, 16*, 89–94.

Rosenstone, S. (1983). *Forecasting presidential elections*. New Haven, CT.: Yale University Press.

Rosenthal, M. (1985). Bibliographic retrieval for the social and behavioral scientist. *Research in Higher Education, 22*, 315–333.

Rosenthal, R. (1963). On the social psychology of the psychological experiment: The experimenter's hypothesis as unintended determinant of experimental results. *American Scientist, 51*, 268–283.

Rosenthal, R. (1966). *Experimenter effects in behavioral research*. New York: Appleton-Century-Crofts.

Rosenthal, R. (1977). Biasing effects of experimenters. *Et Cetera, 34*, 253–264.

Rosenthal, R. (1991). *Meta-analytic procedures for social research*. Newbury Park, CA: Sage.

Rosenthal, R. (1994). Interpersonal expectancy effects: A 30-year perspective. *Current Directions in Psychological Science, 3*, 176–179.

Rosenthal, R., & Gaito, J. (1963). The interpretation of levels of significance by psychological researchers. *Journal of Psychology, 55,* 33–38.

Rosenthal, R., & Jacobson, L. (1968). *Pygmalion in the classroom.* New York: Holt, Rinehart and Winston.

Rosenthal, R., & Rosnow, R. (1975). *The volunteer subject.* New York: Wiley-Interscience.

Rubin, Z. (1973). *Liking and loving: An invitation to social psychology.* New York: Holt, Rinehart & Winston.

Runkel, P. (1990). *Casting nets and testing specimens: Two grand methods of psychology.* New York: Praeger.

Sadker, M., & Sadker, D. (1985, March). Sexism in the schoolroom of the '80s. *Psychology Today,* 54–57.

Sapolsky, A. (1964). An effort at studying Rorschach content symbolism: The frog response. *Journal of Consulting Psychology, 28,* 469–472.

Sapolsky, R., & Balt, S. (1996). Reductionism and variability in data: A meta-analysis. *Perspectives in Biology & Medicine, 39,* 193–203.

Schachter, S., Silverstein, B., & Perlick, D. (1977). Studies of the interaction of psychological and pharmacological determinants of smoking. *Journal of Experimental Psychology, 106,* 3–40.

Schewe, C., & Cournoyer, N. (1976). Prepaid vs. promised monetary incentives to questionnaire response: Further evidence. *Public Opinion Quarterly, 40,* 105–107.

Schmidt, F. (1996). Statistical significance testing and cumulative knowledge in psychology: Implications for training of researchers. *Psychological Methods, 1,* 115–129.

Schmidt, F., & Hunter, J. (1996). Measurement error in psychological research: Lessons from 26 research scenarios. *Psychological Methods, 1,* 199–223.

Schrag, P. (1978). *Mind control.* New York: Pantheon.

Schulman, M., & Mekler, E. (1985). *Bringing up a moral child.* Reading, MA: Addison-Wesley.

Schulz K. (1995). Empirical evidence of bias. Dimensions of methodological quality associated with estimates of treatment effects in controlled trials. *Journal of the American Medical Association, 273,* 408–412.

Schuster, D., & Schuster, L. (1969). Study of stress and sex ratio. *Proceedings of the 77th Annual Convention of the American Psychological Association,* 223–224.

Schwarz, H. (1972). The use of subjective probability methods in estimating demand. In J. Tanur et al. (Eds.), *Statistics: A guide to the unknown.* San Francisco: Holden-Day.

Schwarz, N. (1999). Self-reports: How questions shape answers. *American Psychologist, 54,* 93–105.

Schwarz, N., & Clore, G. (1983). Mood, misattribution, and judgments of well-being: Informative and directive functions of affective states. *Journal of Personality and Social Psychology, 45,* 513–523.

Schwitzer, G. (1992). The magical medical media tour. *Journal of the American Medical Association, 267,* 1969–1971.

Scudder, S. (1874). A great teacher's method. *Every Saturday,* 369–370.

Sedlmeier, P., & Gigerenzer, G. (1989). Do studies of statistical power have an effect on the power of studies? *Psychological Bulletin, 105,* 309–316.

Selye, H. (1964). *From dream to discovery.* New York: McGraw-Hill.

Shaffer, J. (Ed.). (1992). *The role of models in nonexperimental social science: Two debates.* Washington, DC: American Educational Research Association and American Statistical Association.

Shapiro, A., & Morris, L. (1978). The placebo effect in medical and psychological therapies. In S. Garfield, & H. Bergin (Eds.), *Handbook of Psychotherapy and Behavior Change.* Hawthorne, N.Y.: Aldine de Gruyter.

Sharman, G. (1973). Adaptations of marsupial pouch young for extra-uterine existence. In C. Austin (Ed.), *The mammalian fetus in vitro.* London: Chapman & Hall.

Sharps, M., Welton, A., & Price, J. (1993). Gender and task in the determination of spatial cognitive performance. *Psychology of Women Quarterly, 17,* 71–83.

Sheldon, W. (1942). *The varieties of temperament: A psychology of constitutional differences.* New York: Harper.

Shepherd, L. (1993). *Lifting the veil.* Boston: Shambala.

Sherman, B., & Kunda, Z. (1989). *Motivated evaluation of scientific evidence.* Paper presented at the annual meeting of the American Psychological Association, Arlington.

Sherwood, J., & Nataupsky, M. (1968). Predicting the conclusions of Negro-White intelligence research from biographical characteristics of the investigator. *Journal of Personality and Social Psychology, 8,* 53–58.

Shute, V. (1994, May/June). Learners and instruction: What's good for the goose may not be good for the gander. *Psychological Science Agenda,* 8–9, 16.

Sidman, M. (1960). *Tactics of scientific research.* New York: Basic Books.

Sigall, H., & Page, R. (1971). Current stereotypes: A little fading, a little faking. *Journal of Personality and Social Psychology, 18,* 247–255.

Silverman, I., & Margulis, S. (1973). Experiment title as a source of sampling bias in commonly used "subject-pool" procedures. *Canadian Psychologist, 14,* 197–201.

Silverstein, L. (1996). Evolutionary psychology and the search for sex differences. *American Psychologist, 51,* 160–161.

Simes, R. (1986). Publication bias: The case for an international registry of clinical trials. *Journal of Clinical Oncology, 4,* 1529–1541.

Simmons, C., vom-Kolke, A., & Shimizu, H., (1986). Attitudes toward romantic love among American, German, and Japanese students. *Journal of Social Psychology, 126,* 793–799.

Simons, H. (1987). Let's hear it for science. *Nature, 328,* 677–678.

Simpson, D., & Sells, S. (1982). Effectiveness of treatment for drug abuse: An overview of the DARP research program. *Advances in Alcohol & Substance Abuse, 2,* 7–29.

Singer, J. (1975). Navigating the stream of consciousness. *American Psychologist, 30,* 727–738.

Skinner, B. (1956). A case history in scientific method. *American Psychologist, 11,* 221–233.

Smith, M., Glass, G., & Miller, T. (1980). *The benefits of psychotherapy.* Baltimore and London: The Johns Hopkins University Press.

Smith, R. (Ed.). (1997). Peer review: Reform or revolution? *British Medical Journal, 315,* 759–760.

Smith, T. (1992). Discrepancies between men and women in reporting number of sexual partners: A summary from four countries. *Social Biology, 39,* 203–211.

Sox, H., Margulies, I., & Sox, C. (1981). Psychologically mediated effects of diagnostic tests. *Annals of Internal Medicine, 95,* 680–685.

Sperry, R. (1943). Effects of 180 degree rotation of the retinal field on visuomotor coordination. *Journal of Experimental Zoology, 92,* 263–279.

Spiro, H. (1997). Clinical reflections on the placebo phenomenon. In A. Harrington (Ed.), *The placebo effect: An interdisciplinary exploration.* Cambridge, MA: Harvard University Press.

Staessen, J. et al. (1997). Antihypertensive treatment based on conventional or ambulatory blood pressure measurement: A randomized controlled trial. *Journal of the American Medical Association, 278,* 1065–1072.

Steele, C., & Aronson, J. (1995). Stereotype threat and the intellectual test performance of African Americans. *Journal of Personality and Social Psychology, 69,* 797–811.

Steingraber, S. (1997). *Living downstream: An ecologist looks at cancer and the environment.* Boston: Addison-Wesley.

Steinhauer, G. (1994). Rate of eating on simple schedules of reinforcement. *The Psychological Record, 44,* 125–148.

Stelfox, H., Chua, G., O'Rourke, K., & Detsky, A. (1998). Conflict in the debate over calcium-channel antagonists. *New England Journal of Medicine, 338,* 101–106.

Stewart, D., and Kamins, M. (1993). *Secondary research* (2nd ed.). Beverly Hills: Sage.

Stewart, W., & Feder, N. (1987). The integrity of the scientific literature. *Nature, 325,* 207–214.

Stone, C. (1939). Copulatory activity in adult male rats following castration and injections of testosterone propionate. *Endocrinology, 24,* 165–174.

Storrs, E., & Williams, R. (1968). A study of monozygous quadruplet armadillos in relation to mammalian inheritance. *Proceedings of the National Academy of Sciences, 60,* 910–914.

Stratton, G. (1897). Vision without inversion of the retinal image. *Psychological Review, 4,* 341–360.

Straus, J., & Cavanaugh, S. (1996). Placebo effects: Issues for clinical practice in psychiatry and medicine. *Psychosomatics, 37,* 315–326.

Strupp, H., & Hadley, S. (1979). Specific versus nonspecific factors in psychotherapy: A controlled study of outcome. *Archives of General Psychiatry, 10,* 1125–1136.

Stuart, A. (1984). *The ideas of sampling.* New York: Oxford University Press.

Sudman, S., & Bradburn, N. (1974). *Response effects in surveys: A review and synthesis.* Chicago: Aldine.

Sudman, S., & Bradburn, N. (1982). *Asking questions.* San Francisco: Jossey-Bass.

Sulloway, F. (1996). *Born to rebel: Birth order, family dynamics, and creative lives.* New York: Pantheon Books.

Swaab, D., & Hofman, M. (1990). An enlarged suprachiasmatic nucleus in homosexual men. *Brain Research, 537,* 141–148.

Swanson, D. (1990). Medical literature as a potential source of new knowledge. *Bulletin of the Medical Library Association, 78,* 29–37.

Swanson, D. (1991). Complementary structures in disjoint science literatures. In New York: ACM Press. *SIGIR91: Proceedings of the 14th Annual International ACM SIGIR Conference, Chicago.*

Swanson, D., & Smalheiser, N. (1997). An interactive system for finding complementary literatures: A stimulus to scientific discovery. *Artificial Intelligence, 91,* 183–203.

Swazey, J., Anderson, M., & Lewis, K. (1993). Ethical problems in academic research. *American Scientist, 81,* 542–553.

Tannen, D. (1990). *You just don't understand: Women and men in conversation.* New York: Ballantine Books.

Tanur, J. (1992). Cognitive aspects of surveys and this volume. In J. Tanur (Ed.), *Questions about questions: Inquiries into the cognitive bases of surveys.* New York: Russell Sage Foundation.

Thompson, B. (1988). Misuse of chi-square contingency-table test statistics. *Educational and Psychological Research, 8,* 39–49.

Thompson, W., & Olian, S. (1961). Some effects on offspring behavior of maternal adrenalin injection during pregnancy in three inbred mouse strains. *Psychological Reports, 8,* 87–90.

Tiefer, L. (1978). The context and consequences of contemporary sex research: A feminist perspective. In T. McGill, D. Dewsbury, & B. Sachs (Eds.), *Sex and behavior: Status and prospectus.* New York: Plenum Press.

Tinbergen, E., & Tinbergen, N. (1972). Early childhood autism: An ethological approach. *Advances in Ethology, 10,* 1–53.

Tinbergen, N. (1963). On aims and methods of ethology. *Zeitschrift fur Tierpsychologie, 20,* 410–433.

Traugott, M. (1987). The importance of persistence in respondent selection for preelection surveys. *Public Opinion Quarterly, 51,* 48–57.

Traugott, M. (1992). A generally good showing but much work needs to be done. *Public Perspective, 4,* 14–16.

Underwood, B. et al. (1977). Attention, negative affect, and altruism: An ecological validation. *Personality and Social Psychology Bulletin, 3,* 54–58.

U.S. Department of Health and Human Services. (1982). *The health consequences of smoking.* Washington, DC: U.S. Government Printing Office.

U.S. Public Health Service. (1964). *Smoking and health. Report of the advisory committee to the surgeon general of the Public Health Service.* Washington, DC: U.S. Government Printing Office.

Valenstein, E. (1980). *The psychosurgery debate: Scientific, legal, and ethical perspectives.* San Francisco: W. H. Freeman.

Veroff, J., Hatchett, S., & Douvan, E. (1992). Consequences of participating in a longitudinal study of marriage. *Public Opinion Quarterly, 56,* 315–327.

Vickers A., Goyal, N., Harland, R., & Rees, R. (1998). Do certain countries produce only positive results? A systematic review of controlled trials. *Controlled Clinical Trials, 19,* 159–166.

Vinovskis, M. (1989, November). *The use and misuse of social science analysis in federal adolescent pregnancy policy.* NIU Social Science Research Institute Distinguished Lectures, University of Michigan.

Von Frisch, K. (1950). *Bees: Their vision, chemical senses, and language.* Ithaca, N.Y.: Cornell University Press.

Voss, D., Gelman, A., & King, G. (1995). The polls—a review: Preelection survey methodology details from eight polling organizations, 1988 and 1992. *Public Opinion Quarterly, 59,* 98–132.

Wahlsten, D. (1994). The intelligence of heritability. *Canadian Psychology, 35,* 244–260.

Wakefield, J. (1992). The concept of mental disorder: On the boundary between biological facts and social values. *American Psychologist, 47,* 373–388.

Warner, K. (1977). *Possible increases in the understating of cigarette consumption.* Paper presented at the 105th annual meeting of the American Public Health Association, Washington, DC.

Warner, K., & Fulton, G. (1994). The economic implications of tobacco product sales in a nontobacco state. *Journal of the American Medical Association, 271,* 771–776.

Warner, K., Goldenhar, L., & McLaughlin, C. (1992). Cigarette advertising and magazine coverage of the hazards of smoking: A statistical analysis. *New England Journal of Medicine, 326,* 305–309.

Watson, J. (1913). Psychology as the behaviorist views it. *Psychological Review, 20,* 158–177.

Watson, J., & Rayner, R. (1920). Conditioned emotional reactions. *Journal of Experimental Psychology, 3,* 1–14.

Webb, E. et al. (1981). *Nonreactive measures in the social sciences* (2nd ed.). Boston: Houghton-Mifflin.

Weiss, B. et al. (1980). Behavioral responses to artificial food colors. *Science, 207,* 1487–1489.

Weisz, J., Weiss, B., & Donenberg, G. (1992). The lab versus the clinic: Effects of child and adolescent psychotherapy. *American Psychologist, 47,* 1578–1585.

Weller, L., & Livingston, R. (1988). Effect of color of questionnaire on emotional responses. *Journal of General Psychology, 115,* 433–440.

Wells, G., & Windschitl, P. (1999). Stimulus sampling and social psychological experimentation. *Personality and Social Psychology Bulletin, 25,* 1115–1125.

Werth, L., & Flaherty, J. (1986). A phenomenological approach to human deception. In R. Mitchell, & N. Thompson (Eds.), *Deception: Perspectives on human and nonhuman deceit.* Albany: State University of New York Press.

White, J., & Farmer, R. (1992). Research methods: How they shape views of sexual violence. *Journal of Social Issues, 48,* 45–59.

White, R. (1966). Misperception as a cause of two world wars. *Journal of Social Issues, 22,* 1–19.

Wilcox, R. (1998). How many discoveries have been lost by ignoring modern statistical methods? *American Psychologist, 53,* 300–314.

Willcox, S., Himmelstein, D., & Woolhandler, S. (1994). Inappropriate drug prescribing for the community-dwelling elderly. *Journal of the American Medical Association, 272,* 292–296.

Willems, E. (1973). Behavioral ecology and experimental analysis: Courtship is not enough. In J. Nesselroade & H. Reese (Eds.), *Life-span developmental psychology.* New York: Academic Press.

Williams, M. (1995). How useful are clinical reports concerning the consequences of therapist-patient sexual involvement? *American Journal of Psychotherapy, 49,* 237–243.

Wilson, T., De Paulo, B., Mook, D., & Klaaren, K. (1993). Scientists' evaluations of research: The biasing effects of the importance of the topic. *Psychological Science, 4,* 322–325.

Winget, C., & Kramer, M. (1979). *Dimensions of dreaming.* Gainesville: University Presses of Florida.

Wish, E., Hoffman, J., & Nemes, S. (1997). The validity of self-reports of drug use at treatment admission and at follow-up: Comparisons with urinalysis and hair assays. In *The validity of self-reported drug use: Improving the accuracy of survey estimates.* NIDA Research Monograph 167. Rockville, MD: U.S. Dept. of Health & Human Services.

Wolins, L. (1962). Responsibility for raw data. *American Psychologist, 17,* 657–658.

Women on Words and Images. (1972). *Dick and Jane as victims.* Princeton, NJ.

Woo, K. et al. (1997). Differences in the effect of cigarette smoking on endothelial function in Chinese and white adults. *Annals of Internal Medicine, 127,* 372–375.

Woodford, J. (1996, Fall). You can eat his words. *Michigan Today,* 2–3.

Woolf, P. (1988). Projection on science fraud and misconduct, Report on Workshop Number One, American Association for the Advancement of Science, page 37.

Woolfolk, R., Parrish, M., & Murphy, S. (1985). The effects of positive and negative imagery on motor skill performance. *Cognitive Therapy and Research, 9,* 335–341.

Wynne-Edwards, V. (1962). *Animal dispersion in relation to social behavior.* London: Oliver & Boyd.

Yin, R. (1994). *Case study research: Design and methods.* Thousand Oaks, CA: Sage Publications.

Yoken, C., & Berman, J. (1984). Does paying a fee for psychotherapy alter the effectiveness of treatment? *Journal of Consulting and Clinical Psychology, 52,* 254–260.

Ziman, J. (1968). *Public knowledge: The social dimension of science.* Cambridge, Eng.: Cambridge University Press.

Ziman, J. (1980). The proliferation of scientific literature: A natural process. *Science, 208,* 369–371.

Zinn, H. (1980). *A people's history of the United States.* New York: Harper & Row.

Zirkle, C. (1958). Pavlov's beliefs. *Science, 128,* 1476.

Zita, J. (1988). The premenstrual syndrome: "Dis-easing" the female cycle. *Hypatia, 3,* 188–210.

Zito, J., Safer, D., dosReis, S., & Riddle, M. (1998). Racial disparity in psychotropic medications prescribed for youths with Medicaid insurance in Maryland. *Journal of the American Academy of Child and Adolescent Psychiatry, 37,* 179–184.

Zucker, I. (1988). Seasonal affective disorders: Animal models non fingo. *Journal of Biological Rhythms, 3,* 209–223.

Zucker, I., Rusak, B., & King, R. (1976). Neural bases for circadian rhythms in rodent behavior. In A. Reisen & R. Thompson (Eds.), *Advances in psychobiology* (Vol. 3). New York: Wiley.

Zurer, P. (1993, July 12). Misconduct cases include two chemists. *Chemical and Engineering News,* 22.

Zurer, P. (1993, November 22). Survey finds researchers often encounter scientific misconduct. *Chemical and Engineering News,* 24–25.

# Name Index

# Subject Index